A BRIEF HISTORY OF PERU

CHRISTINE HUNEFELDT

University of California, San Diego

Facts On File, Inc.

A Brief History of Peru

Copyright © 2004 by Lexington Associates

Facts On File, Inc.
132 West 31st Street
New York NY 10001

Library of Congress Cataloging-in-Publication Data

Hunefeldt, Christine.
   A brief history of Peru / Christine Hunefeldt.
       p. cm.
Includes bibliographical references and index.
Contents: Ancient civilizations—The Incas : the building of an empire—Conquest and the beginnings of colonial life—Colonial Peru—Social institutions and the Bourbon reforms—Revolts and the wars for independence—The struggle for stability—The age of guano—The War of the Pacific and after—The 20th century: first decades—Depression and conflict—Dictators and reform—Agrarian reform—The last 25 years.
       ISBN 0-8160-4918-1 (hc: alk. paper)
   1. Peru—History—Juvenile literature. [1. Peru—History.] I. Title.
F3431.H86 2004
985—dc22
2003019228

Cover design by Semadar Megged
Maps by Jeremy Eagle

Printed in the United States of America

MP Hermitage 10 9 8 7 6 5 4 3 2 1

This book is printed on acid-free paper.

CONTENTS

Appendixes

LIST OF ILLUSTRATIONS

LIST OF MAPS

LIST OF TABLES

LIST OF ABBREVIATIONS

ANAPA	National Association of Parcel Holders (Asociación Nacional de Parceleros)
AP	Popular Action (Acción Popular)
APRA	Alliance for Popular Revolution in America (Alianza Popular Revolucionaria Americana)
APRA-UNO	Alliance for Popular Revolution in America–National Union of Odría Supporters (Alianza Popular Revolucionaria Americana–Union Nacional Odriísta)
CAEM	Center of High Military Studies (Centro de Altos Estudios Militares)
CAP	Agrarian production cooperative (*cooperativa agraria de producción*)
CAT	Workers' agrarian cooperative (*cooperativa agraria de trabajadores*)
CAU	Users' agrarian cooperative (*cooperativa agraria de usuarios*)
CCP	Peruvian Peasant Confederation (Confederación Campesina del Perú)
CGTP	General Confederation of Peruvian Workers (Confederación General de Trabajadores del Perú)
CNA	National Agrarian Confederation (Confederación Nacional Agraria)
CTP	Peruvian Workers' Confederation (Confederación de Trabajadores del Perú)
CUNA	United National Agrarian Congress (Congreso Unitario Nacional Agrario)
DC	Christian Democracy (Democracia Cristiana)
ETAP	Permanent agrarian workers' enterprise (*empresa de trabajadores agrarios permanentes*)
FDN	National Democratic Front (Frente Democrático Nacional)
FRADEPT	Regional Agrarian Federation of Piura and Tumbes (Federación Regional Agraria de Piura y Tumbes)
FREDEMO	Democratic Front (Frente Democrático)
IPC	International Petroleum Company

MIR	Movement of the Revolutionary Left (Movimiento de Izquierda Revolucionario)
MRTA	Tupac Amaru Revolutionary Movement (Movimiento Revolucionario Tupac Amaru)
ONA	National Agrarian Organization (Organización Nacional Agraria)
PPC	Popular Christian Party (Partido Popular Cristiano)
PSP	Peruvian Socialist Party (Partido Socialista del Perú)
PUC	Pontifical Catholic University (Pontificia Universidad Católica del Perú)
SAIS	Social interest agrarian association (*sociedad agrícola de interés social*)
SIN	National Intelligence Service (Servicio de Inteligencia Nacional)
SINAMOS	National System of Social Mobilization (Sistema Nacional de Apoyo a la Movilización Social)
SNA	National Agrarian Society (Sociedad Nacional Agraria)
UNMSM	San Marcos University (Universidad Nacional Mayor de San Marcos)

ACKNOWLEDGMENTS

Over the past few decades many publications have enriched our understanding of Peru's history, and I've used much of this research published in English and Spanish to help compile the present volume. My gratitude goes to all those colleagues from whom I have drawn—their work is immense. In particular I want to thank my Peruvian colleagues, whose work preceded mine and who were already making efforts to assemble a general history of Peru, ranging from Jorge Basadre's work of the 1980s to that of Franklin Pease and María Rostworowski on the Inca and the colonial period and to Carlos Contreras's, Marcos Cueto's, and Nelson Manrique's general republican histories of Peru. In many ways their work has been a crucial guide to this volume. Also important to the preparation of this book have been the publications of Argentinean historian Tulio Halperin-Donghi, including his history of contemporary Latin America, as well as work by Frederick B. Pike, who as early as 1967 wrote the first comprehensive general history of Peru in English, and Peter F. Klaren's history of Peru published in 2000. Without the insistence and persistence of editor Edward Purcell, the Peru project would never have become a part of the series on national histories. Special thanks to him.

INTRODUCTION

The arrival of the Spanish and Portuguese colonizers to the New World in the 15th century began a series of drastic changes in most of the territory we nowadays call Latin America. The changes were most dramatic in those areas where high civilizations, namely the Aztec, the Maya, and the Inca, had established cities, built large-scale infrastructures, and developed hierarchical societies. As the Spaniards occupied and extended their control over more and more of the Inca Empire, they introduced their way of life and their religion. The result was, and continues to be, a process that produced in modern Peru a fusion of different cultures, characterized by the emergence of new racial mixtures and an ongoing search for economic, political, and social progress.

Peru is a rich country that stretches along a section of the Pacific coast of South America and reaches eastward over the Andean mountain spine to encompass a large section of Amazon basin rain forest. It holds many natural resources, spread across one of the world's most diverse and extreme ecological landscapes, with altitudes ranging from the sea level up to 20,000 feet. To the north are the countries of Ecuador and Colombia; to the east lie Brazil and Bolivia; and directly to the south, Peru borders Chile.

The great majority of Peru's population of around 28 million people lives in the coastal zone, where to seaward the cold waters of the Humboldt current have created rich offshore fishing beds but are also subject to the severe climate disruptions caused by the notorious El Niño phenomenon. Much of today's economic activity, from farming to oil production, occurs along the coast, which historically was the source of great wealth from such resources as deposits of nitrates and bird guano, used worldwide for fertilizer.

To the east the coast gives way to the high mountains of the Andes. This region, known as the sierra, is characterized by an extraordinary landscape of towering peaks, including the Huascarán at 20,000 feet, interrupted by deep valleys and softened by areas of high plains called the altiplano, or puna. The sierra, although dotted with a few cities, is traditionally the home of much of Peru's Indian population, many of whom still live in relatively scattered communities. For many decades after the arrival of Europeans, the fabulous silver mines of the sierra

produced millions and millions of dollars worth of booty for the Spanish, and the region has continued—at a reduced level—to be the source of mineral wealth.

Moving further eastward, the extremes of the sierra give way to the gentle slopes of the *montaña* region and eventually to the rain forests

A section of the high Peruvian plains known as the altiplano (Photofrenetic/Alamy)

that mark the beginnings of the Amazon River basin, known as the *selva*. Almost 60 percent of the total area of Peru is taken up by the rain forests, and much of the region, which stretches from north to south in a broad band, is still unexplored and thinly inhabited or exploited.

To the far southeast is magnificent Lake Titicaca, the highest in the world at 12,000 feet above sea level. Peru shares the lake with Bolivia.

In addition to its physical splendors, a rich historical heritage is much in evidence in Peru, where, for example, Lima's port city of Callao was for three centuries the main Pacific port of the Spanish Empire and a center for colonial administration. Similarly the splendor and fascination of the Inca Empire are visible throughout the land, but nowhere more so than in the former Inca imperial capital of Cuzco, which holds well-preserved archaeological treasures and is a popular tourist destination. Beyond Cuzco there is the magnificent Machu Picchu, as well as other intriguing highland sites. Many archaeological remains on Peru's coast and in the Amazon basin also preserve evidence of a complex and glorious past.

This inspiring history and the availability of abundant and varied natural resources have stimulated the accomplishments of many modern Peruvians such as writers, doctors, engineers, and scientists. For example, Lima has one of the largest and most-renowned research insti-

The main square of Lima, the capital of Peru. Lima has been the political and economic center of the country since the city's founding as the City of Kings (Ciudad de los Reyes) by Francisco Pizarro in 1535. The population has increased dramatically in recent decades. (Alejandro Balaguer Photo)

tutes devoted to the study of the potato, a native plant domesticated in the Andean region. In addition, there has been sophisticated medical research over the past 100 years, and in general, Peru's medical research and teaching centers have a worldwide reputation.

These achievements are genuine; however, it is also true that Peru has one of the highest rates of social inequality measured in terms of income, standard of living, and access to resources. The nation's unemployment and underemployment rates are high, including many people who work "independently" (that is, they are self-employed) and participate in an "informal economy." Thousands of these people eke out a living on a hand-to-mouth basis, pay no taxes, and have no social security, medical care, water, or electricity. Most of these people live in the rapidly expanding *barriadas,* or shantytowns, around Lima.

The nation has also suffered from political inequities. After Peru gained independence from Spain in the early 19th century, the right to vote was restricted to a small number of literate males who owned property, and it was not until 1948 that women gained the vote, along with all males able to sign their names. By contrast, in today's Peru voting is an enforced civic obligation.

The exclusion of illiterate peasants (most of whom lived in remote provinces) from political life in Peru during most of the republican era created not only a class rift between a majority of peasants and the rest of Peru's population but also reflected the nation's ethnic-racial gap. Almost immediately after Europeans arrived in Peru there began a process of racial mixing that has continued over time. Gradually, the majority of Peruvians became—in the biological sense—mestizos, or the mixed-race descendants of both European and indigenous forebears. However, the ethnic and cultural definitions of mestizo has come to be more important in Peruvian society than the strictly genetic definition.

In modern Peru most would consider someone mestizo if he or she speaks Spanish and adheres to social and cultural patterns of behavior associated with the more Hispanic side of Peruvian life. This means that people of purely indigenous genetic background may be regarded as mestizo because of their language, behavior, and lifestyle. By the same standard someone who is of mixed genetic background but lives entirely as an indigenous person (for example, as a small farmer at a remote highland location, speaking only Quechua, the native language of most of Peru's Indian population) will likely be regarded as indigenous—a so-called cultural Indian, rather than mestizo. This cultural rather than

Alejandro Toledo, nicknamed "El Cholo" because of his Indian background, on the campaign trail during his successful run for the presidency in 2001. He made a specific and direct appeal to the Peruvians common Incan heritage, particularly of Pachacútec, the emperor who expanded and consolidated the Inca Empire. (Alejandro Balaguer Photo)

biological definition has become so widespread in Peruvian society that the government ceased many decades ago to compile demographic information on the basis of race.

When Alejandro Toledo ran for president in 2001, he called himself Peru's new Pachacútec in his public addresses. Pachacútec Inca Yupanqui (Pachacuti) was the ruler who, according to early Spanish and Indian chroniclers, expanded the empire (called Tawantinsuyu, meaning "the realm of the four quarters") and consolidated Incan predominance over many other ethnic groups around the mid-15th century. Pachacútec is regarded as the founder of Inca splendor, well-being, and success and in the minds of Peruvians is associated with times of innovative change and the inauguration of a new era. Toledo also invoked the Incan gods and sanctuaries (known as *apu*) for help in rescuing Peru from political corruption, economic crisis, and social malaise.

In doing so Toledo shocked the public. It was quite startling to hear a presidential candidate invoke an ancestral past, hoping to gain the ears and the votes of modern Peruvians in cities and rural communities. Journalists, social scientists, and competing presidential candidates criticized and even ridiculed Toledo's use of indigenous symbols and history; however, Toledo won the presidential election. The success of his rhetoric bespeaks the vitality of a collective memory anchored in the Inca past and a desire for change. Most of Peru's history—as will become clear in the following chapters—is tightly knit to Peru's large indigenous populations. The Inca people and a great variety of pre-Incan cultures are, to a certain degree, still a part of Peru's present day.

1

ANCIENT CIVILIZATIONS (10,000 B.C.–c. A.D. 1440)

What we know about the ancient peoples of America is subject to doubts and ongoing scrutiny. Most of our scant information comes from reading the archaeological record, which is by nature fragmentary and limited. These conditions hold true in the case of South America in general and Peru in particular.

The biggest questions about ancient Peruvians are basic—Who were these people? Where did they come from? How did they live?—and much speculation surrounds the process by which the American continents were occupied by humans. The intercontinental movements of populations, from Asia to North America and from North America to South America, have usually been explained in terms of theories, each based on at least a slim set of empirical evidence, but none of it is in itself complete enough to satisfy scientific scrutiny.

For example, Spanish chroniclers of the 16th and 17th centuries took it for granted that native cultures originated locally and that the early inhabitants of the continent were the descendants of a second Adam and Eve. Diffusionist theorists in the late 18th and early 19th centuries described a series of stages they believed explained how and even when America was peopled. According to these theories, cultural evolution explained the gradual geographical expansion of human populations, with the implicit assumption that people who move from one place to another had a higher cultural status and that, in consequence, the people upon whom this expansion was imposed were culturally inferior. This evolutionist view of human movements across spaces and continents assumed an unproven inferiority (measured, of course, by Western standards) and tells us little about the interaction between peoples.

More modern scientific theories concentrate less on religious explanations or invidious comparisons between cultures and rely more on puzzling out conclusions from what we do know. It is reasonable, for example, to conclude that ancient peoples came to North America across a land bridge from Asia and then spread down and across the two American continents, but almost no evidence has yet been found to show the timing and mechanisms of this great migration.

It is also reasonable to suppose that relatively early on there were sailors capable of voyaging long distances along the Pacific coasts and that there was considerable contact between various peoples as a result. The spread of common domesticated plants and common technologies, such as pot making and metallurgy, suggests the existence of trade routes over a vast territory.

The archaeological record is also clear that several pre-Columbian cultures reached similar levels of development at almost the same time. For example, the Chavín who lived in what is today Peru flourished at the same time as the Olmec of Mexico, and both cultures appear to have developed similar technologies and levels of social organization.

Andean Prehistoric Cultures			
Time Scale	Coast	Highlands	Titicaca Basin
10,000 B.C.		Guitarrero	
8000 B.C.		Pachamachay	
6000 B.C.	Paijan	Lauricocha	
4000 B.C.	Waka Prieta		Chinchoros
2000 B.C.	Salinar	Kotosh	Chinchoros
1000 B.C.	Gallinazo	Kotosh	Chiripa
500 B.C.	Paracas	Chavín	Pukara
0	Mochica	Warpa	
	Nazca		
A.D. 250	Lima	Recuay	Huaricani
A.D. 500	Pachacamac		Tiwanaku
A.D. 750	Huari	Huari	
A.D. 1000	Chancay	Killke	Chiribaya
A.D. 1250	Chimú	Wanka	
A.D. 1500	Inca	Inca	Aymara

Source: Excerpted and summarized from Moseley (1992, 22–23)

Basing their ideas on recent excavations and findings, Peruvian archaeologists have proposed a time line for the evolution of the various pre-Inca cultures, from around 10,000 B.C. to the emergence of the Inca Empire around A.D. 1500. These civilizations flourished in three main cultural regions: along the coast, in the highlands, and around the Titicaca lake basin.

The Chavín

Vestiges of human hunter-gatherer societies in America can be traced back to about 15,000 and maybe even 30,000 years ago, but the physical artifacts of such people are few, especially when measured with findings from later cultures. The picture of ancient Peru starts to be somewhat defined with the culture known today as the Chavín, which may have reached its height around 500 B.C. Peruvian and other museums hold innumerable archaeological pieces from the Chavín culture and from other important contemporary cultures, such as the Paracas. The Chavín culture is well known for its artistry and mastery in stone sculpture, and the Paracas, for its pottery and textiles. Chavín art apparently influenced many succeeding cultures, and the designs are still borrowed and reproduced in modern jewelry and textiles.

The center of Chavín culture—which may have been primarily religious rather than political—appears to have been at the site of a large temple, known now as Chavín de Huántar, located in the northern highlands of modern-day Peru. There are other, similar temple sites in the region, but the one at Chavín de Huántar is the largest and most elaborate that has survived relatively intact. The quality of the architecture and the decorative arts of the temple are impressive, and the entire complex demonstrates sophistication and a high degree of social and economic organization. The main temple is constructed and dressed with precisely cut stones, and there is evidence that the facade was decorated with intricately carved figures, which were mounted to project from the walls, depicting eagles, serpents, jaguars, and mythical monsters. The Chavín de Huántar complex, as well as other such temple sites, demonstrate clearly that the Chavín were able to draw on and focus a huge bank of human and economic resources.

The Mochica

None of the early Peruvian cultures controlled a territory as large as the Inca culture would during the 15th century, and still little is known

3

The remains of a huge Mochica pyramid built of millions of adobe bricks (© Philip Baird, www.anthroarcheart.org)

about why a procession of quite distinct civilizations came and went, or even when. There is some evidence, however, of continuity between and among cultures, and several apparently flourished at the same time.

One of the best studied pre-Incan cultures is the Mochica (also known as the Moche) of the northern coast of modern-day Peru. The Mochica culture (approximately 200 B.C. to A.D. 750 [Watanabe 1995, 193]) was paralleled in time by the Nazca culture to the south. Both societies developed highly sophisticated irrigation systems and metallurgy skills (especially with gold and copper) and had advanced levels of political and social organization. The Mochica, however, left an abundance of informative artifacts, many of which are extant and provide archaeologists with a relative wealth of material from which to obtain knowledge of their way of life.

The Mochica were apparently a warrior society that had expanded from its local base by force of arms. They were also accomplished agriculturalists who developed a productive agrarian system in the dry region along Peru's northern coast. The Mochica's main urban centers dotted an area that eventually stretched over approximately 300 miles, and they cultivated a very large area of land. Through seed selection they maximized the size and variety of crops, producing, for example, six different varieties of cotton. Other agrarian produce highly appreciated among the Mochica were *ají* (a native Peruvian chili), cassava, yams, corn, beans, *yerba mate,* pumpkins, peanuts, cherimoyas, avocados, and cucumbers. The Mochica devised irrigation systems that made the most of the arid climate along the coast, and they may have been

THE LORD OF SIPÁN

The relatively recent discovery, in 1987, of the tomb of the Lord of Sipán (Señor de Sipán), near the Peruvian city of Chiclayo, brought to light magnificent artifacts that demonstrate Mochica accomplishment and sophistication. Experts agree that this tomb, which dates from A.D. 300 to 400, is the richest royal tomb ever found in the Western world. It is often compared to the Tutankhamen finds in Egypt.

In April 1987 a team sponsored by the Bruning National Archaeological Museum began excavations in Sipán, located in the Lambayeque Valley. After working for several months, archaeologists Walter Alva Alva, Luis Chero Zurita, and Susana Meneses de Alva uncovered the funerary chambers of a person who had obviously been a very important Mochica leader. Arrayed in full ritual attire and outfitted in magnificent gold and silver decorations and objects, the remains of this Mochica leader were surrounded by eight skeletons, presumably of some of his servants, concubines, and soldiers. The Lord of Sipán himself lay in the wooden coffin in which he had been buried more than 1,700 years ago. The artifacts found with the leader led archaeologists to decipher many features of this magnificent culture that had previously been mysteries. In addition to gold and silver masks, necklaces, earrings, and other jewelry, the findings included spondylus shells from Guayaquil, which were probably used in the ancient world as trade tokens. Ritual knives and other religious objects were also present.

among the first people to exploit as fertilizer the huge deposits of bird droppings (known as guano) from coastal islands. They apparently made frequent trips to gather guano for use on their fields. They also were skilled fishermen, using reed boats and fish traps. One of their major sources of food came from domesticated animals, including ducks, turkeys, llamas, guinea pigs, monkeys, and dogs.

Some archaeologists, such as Rafael Larco in the 1940s, have gone so far as to theorize that the Mochica (unlike the later Inca) had some kind of writing in the form of markings on lima beans, but there is little direct evidence of such a system. However, anthropologists know a great deal about the daily life and economy of the Mochica because artisans developed one of the most sophisticated potteries among pre-Incan cultures. In fact, it has been possible to reconstruct much of the Mochica material culture, belief system, and social life by studying

THE NAZCA LINES

The Nazca culture flourished at approximately the same period as the Mochica, and it is best remembered today for the extraordinary linear images it produced in the dry desert of the Palpa Valley. The valley floor has a base of light-colored sand, overlaid with brown rocks. The Nazca created images of animals, such as a humming bird, a spider, a monkey, and a pelican, by carefully removing the rocks to reveal the lighter sand below. Later (perhaps as much as five centuries), the same technique was used to draw geometric forms and lines, some miles long.

The lines and the forms they create are extremely difficult to perceive from ground level and consequently were "discovered" by Paul Kosok, an anthropologist from the United States, when he flew over the valley in 1939. The lines were studied extensively by Maria Reiche, a German mathematician, who believed the lines had been laid out to serve as a calendar. Other theories hold that the lines were religious symbols or sacred roads. Today the lines are a main tourist attraction.

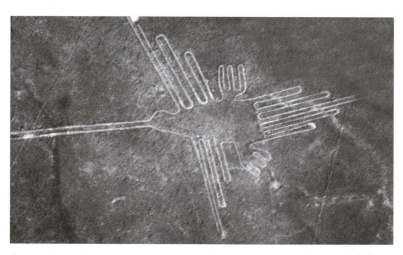

An aerial view of the hummingbird figure outlined on the desert floor of the Palpa Valley by the Nazca people. It is one of several such large-scale linear animal images. (© Philip Baird, www.anthroarcheart.org)

images from their pottery. They are most famous for their impressively realistic ceramic representations of actual people, which offer detailed information about almost all aspects of Mochica life. Archaeologist

Anne Marie Hocquenghem studied more than 500 portrait pieces of Mochica ceramic pottery and found representations of the supernatural, scenes of daily life, and images of the dead. Mochica pottery also provides ample knowledge about their views on human sexuality and social control.

Mochica religion centered on Ai Apaec, the supreme deity, who had emerged from a cave and turned into a bean, cassava root, corn, and potato on different occasions. Another important deity was the moon god Si, or Shi in Mochica, revered for its beneficial influence on fishing. The Mochica impressively engineered pyramid structures, presumed to be religious in nature, including the Pyramids of the Sun and the Moon (Huacas del Sol y la Luna) two of the largest adobe buildings in Andean America, that together measure 1,050 feet long, 480 feet wide, and 180 feet high, containing an estimated total of 140 million adobe bricks. The pyramids were uncovered by German archaeologist Max Uhle in 1899. Presumably, this impressive culture decayed because of heavy climate and ecological shifts that caused Mochica to migrate further north around A.D. 750.

The Huari

The Huari (or Wari) were an aggressive culture, flourishing between roughly A.D. 500 and 750, to some degree contemporaneous and overlapping with another culture, the Tiwanaku. The Huari dominated a territory that stretched along the Pacific coast and into the western highlands, from modern-day Cajamarca to Cuzco.

The Huari were one of the first ancient Peruvian civilizations to cast a wide political net that folded in many distinct ethnic groups, anticipating both the Tiwanaku and Inca Empires, although not nearly so grand in scale or accomplishment. The Huari are also believed to be among the first to establish walled cities built of stone rather than the traditional adobe bricks, again anticipating the Inca. The ruins of what may have been the Huari capital cover four square miles near present day Huanta, not far inland from Lima. These ruins were little known until the 1930s when they were rediscovered. Most of the buildings are made of fieldstone held together with mud mortar and faced with mud plaster.

The finest Huari art found to date is expressed in the form of painted pottery, the most significant examples of which are huge jars that feature scenes of people and religious sites. An archaeological dig near the modern Peruvian city of Ayacucho has yielded several examples of such jars. Impressive textiles with distinctive woven patterns have been found at Huari sites along the coast.

The Tiwanaku

The Tiwanaku culture dated from A.D. 300 to 1200. The main site, Tiwanaku (Tihuanaco), is located near Lake Titicaca. The modern-day Aymara-speaking Indians of the region trace their origins to the Tiwanaku. The city of Tiwanaku probably evolved from a fishing village and may have been populated by 30,000 to 60,000 at its height. A large stonework pyramid in the city, called the Akapana, was part of a religious complex that encompassed several temples.

Many smaller residential areas were built around the city. The best-known secondary sites are at Lucurmata, Paqchiri, Huancani, places that show evidence of public buildings and peasant houses. At its high point, the empire that spread out from the ceremonial city of Tiwanaku extended over southern Peru, Bolivia, northern Chile, and northwest Argentina, covering a vast and varied geography. Archaeologically, Tiwanaku is best known for its large stone sculptures representing anthropomorphic celestial beings, felines, birds, fish, and geometrical designs.

Living in a challenging environment, the Tiwanaku responded by domesticating plants that were well adapted to the climate, such as quinoa, lima beans, and potatoes, as well as the versatile highland animal the llama. The Tiwanaku ate the meat (both fresh and dried) of the llama, although fish and other lake animals were also part of their diet. They developed fabric for clothing woven from llama wool. Llamas and their smaller relations, the alpacas, were also the best beasts of burden in an arid and steep landscape with narrow dirt roads. Based on a reading of the intestines of llamas, Tiwanaku's religious leaders interpreted godly designs and intentions.

In order to increase the available land and produce higher yields, Tiwanaku farmers cultivated raised and ridged fields called *camellones*. *Huaru-huaru* is the Aymara word for this kind of farming. According to archaeologist Michael E. Moseley, the plant beds were long, narrow, and elevated, about 45 feet wide and stretching sometimes as far as 600 feet. To construct the beds, Tiwanaku farmers dug parallel ditches, throwing the excavated soil into the middle to build up a raised, flat-topped mound. The ditches served as drainage devices, and when filled with water and heated by the sun, the ditches gave frost protection to plants at night (Moseley 1992, 218–219). The city of Tiwanaku was supported by about 16,000 acres of ridged fields. Intense sun during the day and icy cold nights provided (and still provide) local people with a natural technology for dehydration and thus conservation of food. For these reasons, Tiwanaku has been called "the political quintessence of high montane adaptation and a true agropastoral state" (Moseley 1992, 228).

The Chimú

At its peak during the 14th and 15th centuries, the Chimor—Chimú Empire, or confederation—extended along 500 miles of Pacific coastland from present-day Piura to Huarmey and was the second-largest native state in South America. The area controlled by the Chimor was one of the most thickly populated, with large cities and settlements of all the Andean regions.

The capital city of Chan Chan, Chimor's main urban seat, occupied 12 to 15 square miles and may have had a population of close to 100,000 at its height of development. The city was surrounded by a high brick wall that enclosed houses, streets, temples, pyramids, and reservoirs. The stone-lined reservoirs held more than 2 million gallons of water, and the outer wall, although it has eroded over the centuries,

Gates through the massive wall surrounding the Chimú capital city of Chan Chan. The Chimú, a highly sophisticated people, were conquered and absorbed by the Inca in the 1460s. (© Philip Baird, www.anthroarcheart.org)

The huge wall protecting Chan Chan was intricately decorated with designs in relief. (© Philip Baird, www.anthroarcheart.org)

still stands 30 feet tall. The ruins of Chan Chan are located just outside the modern city of Trujillo.

Through highly sophisticated hydraulic techniques and the construction of immense stone-covered irrigation trenches, the Chimú managed to cultivate between 50 and 65 percent of the available coastal valley land. Intervalley canals not only demonstrate great labor and engineering skills but also represent sensitive claims to water and land. The Chimú built a complex system of canals to allow cultivation of fertile valley fields, although the system's northern and southern branches were never fully connected because of political divisions (Moseley 1992, 252). To expand their agricultural production, the Chimú also created low-level parcels of farmland (called *huachaques*) by removing the top layers of sand to reveal cultivatable soil. These parcels sometimes reached a depth of 35 feet, and sometimes covered areas of hundreds of square miles.

Such large public works of agricultural and hydraulic engineering required a massive use of labor, which the Chimú leaders acquired through a draft system called the *mit'a*. The invention of this economic and social device by the Chimú had far-reaching and long-lasting effects in the region. Although it was adapted over the centuries to fit changing circumstances, *mit'a* labor became a key to the expansion of the Inca Empire, which subsequently laid the foundation for the Europeanized system, *mita*, of drafting Indian laborers into Spanish-owned mines and haciendas during the colonial period. A modified form of the labor tribute system persisted in Peru until the late 19th century.

The Chimú, who were famous for their arts and crafts, organized artisans hierarchically in what resembled a guild pattern. Leaders of specific trades carried specific titles, such as "Lord of the Feathered Clothes Makers." Best known of all the Chimú's skills was goldsmithing, which reached a high level of artistry and workmanship and produced many artifacts and luxury items. Unfortunately, because of this great command of metallurgy, this pre-Inca culture has suffered drastically from artifact thieves and grave robbers. When the Inca conquered the Chimú, they took the best gold and silversmiths to Cuzco to decorate the Temple of the Sun (Coricancha) and to make luxury and ceremonial objects, many of which were subsequently lost to Spanish greed and expropriation.

In spite of fierce resistance, between 1462 and 1470 the Chimú became part of the Inca Empire. The Chimú leader Minchancaman became a vassal prince of the Inca and married the daughter of Pachacútec. Minchancaman and approximately 40,000 Chimú came under Inca rule, although Chimú traditions and practices strongly influenced Inca life, such as the custom among both the Chimú and Inca that the incoming heir to the throne could not inherit any of the wealth accumulated by his predecessor. Each new leader had to start anew to build his own temple and his own house and to acquire his own servants and his own land. This practice pressured leaders to pursue wars of expansion against neighboring ethnic groups. Consequently the Inca dismembered the Chimor, and what little was left fell prey to the first pandemics of European disease around 1500.

2

THE INCA: THE BUILDING OF AN EMPIRE (1440–1532)

The Inca, so-called after the name of their supreme hereditary ruler, were the most important of the many indigenous tribes or ethnic groups who lived in what became Peru. These people spoke the Quechua language and probably originated near Lake Titicaca but moved north at some point to the valley of Cuzco. Within a remarkably short period of time, the Inca built a huge empire, stretching from modern-day Ecuador in the north to Chile and Argentina in the south. Their political, military, economic, and engineering achievements were extraordinary, especially for a people who lacked a written language, did not know the wheel, and had limited technology. The remains of the Inca Empire still impress and amaze.

Origins

When the Inca appeared on the horizon, several other local ethnic groups occupied the southern Andes. Before the 14th century, Cuzco, which became the principal Inca city, was a minor settlement of small ethnic groups under the guidance of two chiefs, generically called Tocay Capac and Pinahua Capac. The presence of the Huari is visible, and Cuzco may have been one of the Huari's administrative centers. According to reports from early Spanish chroniclers, many different groups before the Inca had roamed the region of Cuzco looking for new places to settle. Small group leaders called *curacas* or *sinchis* were basically the heads of extended family groups known as *ayllus*. According to María Rostworowski, a well-known Peruvian historian, some names of these groups are known: the Lares, Poques, Sauariray, Antasaycs, and Guallas. These were joined somewhat later by Alcavizas, Copalimaytas, and Culumchimas.

Cuzco, originally called Acamama, was divided into four neighborhoods, termed *barrios* in Spanish and *cancha* in Quechua: the neigh-

A section of Inca-built stone wall, demonstrating the extraordinary craftsmanship of Inca masons. Walls, terraces, and public buildings were constructed of irregular blocks of stone, often weighing hundreds of pounds each, that were fitted tightly together without mortar into complex patterns. (Nature Picture Library/Alamy)

borhood of the hummingbird (*quinti cancha*), the neighborhood of the weavers (*chumbi cancha*), the neighborhood of the tobacco (*sairi cancha*), and *yarumbuy cancha*, which was probably inhabited by a mixed population of both Aymara and Quechua speakers. It was, and continues to be, very common in the Andean region to divide geographical, social, or administrative entities into halves and quarters designated as *hanan* and *hurin* (above and below) and *icho* and *allauca* (left and right). This basic division was applied not only to ancient Cuzco and other cities but to the entire Inca realm.

Why did the Inca gain such preeminence rather than some other ethnic group? Both the Lupaqa in the rich Titicaca basin and the Chanca, for instance, had successfully defeated the Quechua, though briefly. After many decades of research scholars seem to agree that the distinctive feature of the Inca people—aside from their military prowess—was their ability to negotiate politically with their neighbors. Coalition building, as much as military expansion, enabled the Inca to become the dominant power of their era. Inca expansion relied on a variety of methods: negotiation with local *curacas*, as in the case of Chincha; quick conquest, as occurred with several ethnic groups in the Chincha

13

area; and when necessary, repressing local resistance, as in the Cañete Valley and Collique. The Chimú were the most difficult rivals and largest in number, but the Inca subdued them and coopted their leaders. The political ability of the Inca people went hand in hand with the empire's ideological-religious underpinnings, Inca cosmology, and Inca social policies. U.S. scholars Geoffrey W. Conrad and Arthur A. Demarest have noted when writing of early Mexico and Peru that the imperialism of both the Aztec and the Inca was driven by ideology, mainly religion.

The pre-imperial past of the Inca is hazy. The Inca themselves told elaborate mythological stories of their founding, the development of their way of life, and their early expansion. According to this Inca tradition, the sun god sent his son, Manco Capac, and his daughter, Mama Ocllo, into the Andean world to educate the untutored and uncivilized peoples who lived there.

The legend says that Manco Capac and his sister-wife Mama Ocllo were first placed on an island in Lake Tititcaca, but they sought another home. With the aid of a golden staff called a *vara*, they found it in the valley of Cuzco, where they settled down to raise their own family, a new race of children of the sun. With the divine help of the sun god who had sent them there, they began to spread the joys of civilization among their new neighbors.

Manco Capac came to be known as the first Inca, or divine leader. He concentrated on teaching the men how to till the soil and plant seeds, and he told them to connect streams and rivers with canals that would water the fields and make them productive—a mythological explanation of the origins of the elaborate Inca agricultural system of terracing and irrigation. Meanwhile, Mama Ocllo taught the women how to spin and weave, how to make clothing, and how to cook their food. Between the couple, they instructed their new neighbors in all the arts of civilized living, and soon (according to mythology) new converts descended into the valley of Cuzco by the thousands to join the first Inca and his wife.

The story smoothes over the conflicts and difficulties that must have arisen, but it may describe accurately the system of interlocking social, political, and economic structures that came to form the basis of Inca life. The myth also explains Inca expansion: the Quechua speakers' drive to conquer, subjugate, and incorporate an ever-widening circle of neighboring peoples. According to the legend, the first Inca realized that the valley of Cuzco was not large enough for all of his new followers; Manco Capac therefore trained some of his men in the arts of war, showing them how to make and use bows and arrows, spears, and war clubs so they could convince unwilling neighbors by force. In a short time, the influence of Inca culture extended for many miles beyond the valley of Cuzco.

The Inca also had a variant founding myth, involving the legend of the Ayar brothers, which also synthesized in popular memory earlier legends about the origins of the Inca people. According to this version of the legend, four brothers—Ayar Manco, Ayar Uchu, Ayar Cachi, and Ayar Auca—came with their wives to Cuzco from Pacariqtambo (the cave of the rising sun), located in today's province of Paruro. The Ayares, together with the Mara and Tampu tribes, had migrated north in search of fertile lands, bringing their religious idols and precious seeds with them on the long trip from Paruro. However, not all of the brothers reached Cuzco. Ayar Cachi returned to the cave of the rising sun, where he was betrayed by a servant and turned into a stone. Ayar Uchu was turned into a stone on a mountain called Huanacauri, bordering Cuzco, and Ayar Auca was turned first into a bird and subsequently also to stone. Ayar Capac did finally reach the mountain of Huaynapata in Cuzco, and here his golden *vara* sank into the ground, indicating he had found a fertile new home. But before founding Cuzco, Ayar Capac had to conquer the original peoples living in Cuzco.

Such legends by nature do not reflect accurate historical events; they selectively sum up long-term processes, especially when a group in power—in this case the Inca—wants to perpetuate a certain founding myth. For example, each successive ruling Inca repeated the founding myth as part of a ritual upon his succession to the throne. The myths of the Inca Empire that involve the stories of Mama Ocllo and Manco Capac and the Ayar brothers have subsequently been interpreted and reinterpreted to make them fit historical chronological reality. (Interpretations of these myths range from psychological-anthropological interpretations to the assumption that these myths were invented by one of the chroniclers, specifically Garcilaso de la Vega, to explain the origins of the Inca Empire to the king of Spain.)

It seems safe to say the legends indicate that originally the Inca were not from Cuzco but came from Lake Titicaca. They may have been survivors of the Tiwanaku culture, and they probably were not individuals but entire *ayllus* with sophisticated knowledge of agricultural techniques. The golden *vara* could have been more than a religious symbol; it is—quite realistically—a way of detecting fertile land, especially for the cultivation of corn. Furthermore, Manco Capac and Ayar Capac of these two myths may be the same founding figure.

Inca Military Expansion

The founding myths take on a more precise historical contour in the descriptions of Inca warfare against an ethnic group known as the Chanca. The Chanca were made up of various minor ethnic groups that may have been responsible for the decay of the earlier Huari Empire. Historical sources disagree as to details of the Inca's victory over the Chanca, but there is a consensus that it served as the trigger for expansion. The Chanca may have encroached on the edges of Inca territory early in the Inca Viracocha's reign, although their actual advance on Cuzco may not have happened until Viracocha was an old man. When the ruling Inca and two of his sons fled in the face of the powerful Chanca, two other sons, Cusi Yupanqui (later renamed Pachacútec) and Roca, supported by generals and important nobles, staged a defense. They withstood the Chanca attacks on Cuzco, and according to the Inca version of the battle, at a crucial moment even the stones of the city were transformed into warriors under Pachacútec's command. These stones were collected after the attack and incorporated into shrines in the city. The defeat of the Chanca left the Inca in command of the region.

The Inca, beginning as a small ethnic group in the vicinity of Cuzco, proceeded to rapidly expand their domain. Shortly before the

BETANZOS'S CHRONICLE OF THE CHANCA WAR

A chronicle written in 1551 by Juan de Betanzos contains detailed information about the wars between the Inca and the Chanca. The chronicler had direct access to the oral tradition of the *panaca* (extended royal family) of Pachacútec through his wife, Cusimiray Ocllo, who was related to Pachacútec. Cusimaray had been the concubine of Francisco Pizarro, by whom she had a son, also named Francisco. When Pizarro died, she married the Spaniard Juan de Betanzos, fluent in Quechua and official interpreter in Cuzco. He wrote the account of the war at the request of Peru's first viceroy, Antonio de Mendoza. His account remained unpublished and a part of it was lost. Only recently was his complete chronicle rediscovered in a private library in Palma de Mallorca. According to Betanzos, final Inca victory over the Chanca was because of Prince Cusi Yupanqui, later renamed Inca Pachacútec (as he is remembered in traditional indigenous songs).

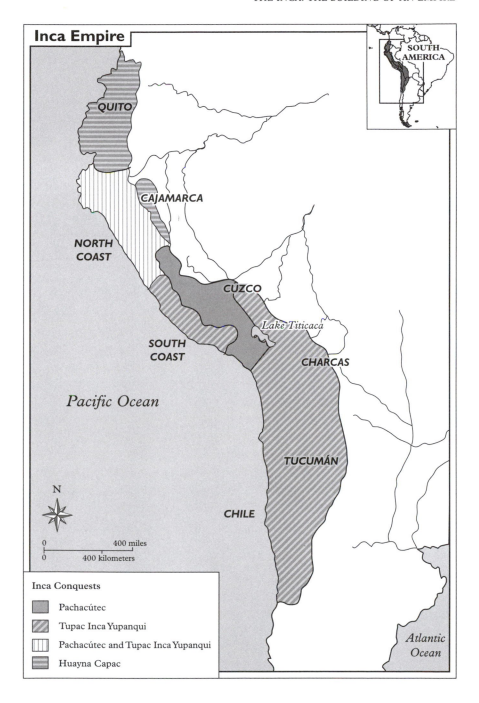

Inca Empire

SOUTH AMERICA

QUITO

CAJAMARCA

NORTH COAST

CUZCO

Lake Titicaca

SOUTH COAST

CHARCAS

Pacific Ocean

TUCUMÁN

N

CHILE

0   400 miles
0   400 kilometers

Inca Conquests

Pachacútec

Tupac Inca Yupanqui

Pachacútec and Tupac Inca Yupanqui

Huayna Capac

Atlantic Ocean

Spaniards arrived, they had gained control over an area that reached from the west side of present-day Pasto in Colombia to the Bío Bío and Maule Rivers in present-day northern Chile and in the southeast to the regions of Tucumán and Mendoza in what is now Argentina. The empire at its height covered a territory of around 3,000 miles. This expansion—as dated by archaeological findings and chroniclers' descriptions—happened in less than a century, approximately between 1440 and 1525.

The Inca had little time to consolidate their empire before the arrival of the Spanish. In the outlying areas, Inca political institutions and control were rather weak. Incan expansion began in and around Cuzco and incorporated, almost in concentric circles, more and more ethnic groups. The farther from the imperial capital of Cuzco a group was located, the less its people incorporated into the empire and settled into the empire's spheres of influence and ways of life.

Three successive Incas engaged in what has been described as "the great expansion": Pachacútec (1438–71), Tupac Inca Yupanqui (1471–93), and Huayna Capac (1493–1525). Pachacútec incorporated the Collao and highland regions of central Peru. Tupac Inca Yupanqui expanded the empire to northern Ecuador and central Chile, a stretch of 3,000 miles. Huayna Capac maintained and consolidated what his predecessors had acquired. The resulting realm of the Incas was the Tahuantinsuyo, which according to the organizational logic of the Inca Empire, was divided for administrative purposes into four *suyus,* or quarters: Chinchaysuyo (in the north), Antisuyo (east), Contisuyo (west) and Collasuyo (south).

According to three early chroniclers at the end of the 16th and the beginning of the 17th centuries—Pedro Cieza de León, Miguel Cabello de Valboa, and Pedro Sarmiento de Gamboa—the campaigns of Pachacútec and Tupac Inca Yupanqui followed this sequence: A first campaign into the Chinchaysuyo incorporated the province of the Quechua and saw an assault on the empire of Chimor and the subjugation of Tumebamba (present-day Cuenca) and Quito. The second phase of this campaign began in Quito and ran down to Huancavilca (present-day coast of Ecuador), Bracamoros, Latacunga, and Tumbes and concluded with the conquest of Chimor and its treasures in Chan Chan. A second campaign brought the Inca into the Antisuyo, located to the east and southeast of Cuzco. Here the Inca conquered less developed peoples such as the Opataris, Manosuyos, Chunchos, and Chiponahuas. Usually Inca war strategy involved careful scouting and intelligence gathering, followed by rapid incursions. Most campaigns began by taking the nearby mountain or hills and then descending to the valleys. Fray Bernabé Cobo's account of the military endeavors of the Inca slightly differs from the other three. According to Cobo (who wrote his chronicle around 1650, later than Cieza, Sarmiento, or Cabello), the Inca first conquered the Antisuyo, then ventured into the Collasuyo, followed by the Chinchaysuyo, and then again into the Collasuyo.

Soldiers for the Inca army were recruited among ethnic groups through *mit'a* assignments. Inca leaders carefully chose their soldiers from among those groups they trusted most. Those ethnic groups that had been part of the Inca Empire for a longer period of time were thus more tightly incorporated into the empire and deemed more reliable. Recruitment also took local demographics into account.

An Inca warrior, armed with a sling and protected with simple textile body armor (Vecellio's Renaissance Costume Book)

Smaller ethnic groups had lower *mit'a* assignments than larger groups. A higher concentration of population made the absence (or loss) of its males less onerous to tributary groups. Ethnic groups in the Collasuyo and Contisuyo had developed strong links to the Inca and were at the same time more densely populated regions; it was especially from these two regions, therefore, that the Inca recruited their soldiers.

Like the civil society, the army was organized in multiples of 10. Each group was under the command of its own ethnic chief; however, members of the pure Inca lineages held the highest ranks among the military leaders. The army, which at its height numbered up to 200,000 men, was divided into specialized squadrons, and each squadron carried one kind of armament (slings, bow and arrows, war axes) or played music on drums and trumpets made out of huge marine snails. During military expeditions, all soldiers from one ethnic group marched together, with those most loyal marching the closest to the Inca leader.

Gonzalo Fernández de Oviedo, a Spanish chronicler, described the sequence of arms used during a battle: First came the attack by men carrying slings and egg-sized stones, then came soldiers carrying a kind of lance; immediately behind them were soldiers with small lances. Soldiers wore special protective clothes and adornments, according to their ethnic background and their hierarchical niche in the army. Sometimes soldiers painted their faces to scare the enemy, and often they screamed and sang to show their strength, sometimes so loud that, according to the chroniclers, birds would drop dead.

Even today there is no absolute certainty about the exact boundaries of Incan dominance at the time the conquistadores arrived and even less certainty about how much or how solidly the outlying areas had been integrated into the empire. From available accounts, however, it seems that throughout the approximately 100 years of Inca expansion, there was no *pax andina*—no all-embracing social and political order imposed by a central authority. Local *curacas,* and even members of the Incan nobility in Cuzco, headed many rebellions against Inca rule, and the ruling Inca was often forced to mobilize his troops and resources against them in order to pacify them and to restore his authority. The more the Inca Empire expanded, the more difficult it became to control.

The Inca military, however, developed several strategies to maintain order and subdue unrest. One technique was to collect and store on hilltops tons of very dry wood, which could be burned as signal beacons in case of rebellion, giving authorities in Cuzco a rough idea of the location of the outbreak. Once a *chasqui* (a relay runner in the state-organized system of couriers) arrived with more detailed information in the form of the unique quipu (a knotted message string), troops were dispatched. In spite of such strategies, however, the increasing unrest in the empire was one of the main reasons why the Spaniards were able to conquer the Inca quickly and thoroughly.

Imperial Inca Organization

At its height, the Inca Empire's integrated social, political, administrative, and economic system focused on the person of the Supreme Inca, from whom all authority and power flowed, and was originally based on close family kinship to the Inca, although the system expanded greatly as military conquests brought more and more land and peoples under Inca domination. The Inca evolved a hierarchical structure by which the Inca at the top implemented his authority through 11 related royal family groups called *panacas*. Organized in part by

Pachacútec as a way to stabilize the line of succession to the throne, the *panacas* formed a royal court from which the empire's highest-ranking civil administrators, military officers, and priests were drawn. (The *panacas* also had important religious functions and had custody of the sacred mummified remains of previous ruling Incas.) This relatively small number of closely related elite Inca officials lived near the Supreme Inca in the heart of Cuzco. The great expansionist Inca Pachacútec established Cuzco as the center of the empire, building there the Coricancha (Temple of the Sun) and developing religious sites in and around the city in order to emphasize the divine origin of the ruling Inca. The most important officials were called *apus,* and each *suyu* (quarter of the empire) had an administrative head designated as the *suyuyoc apu.* In addition, Cuzco itself had four *apus,* who together with the *suyuyoc apus* formed the imperial council in Cuzco. The system stretched throughout the empire and eventually reached down to the level of individual households, which were organized into administrative units of 10. The members of the *panacas* were supported by more numerous lower-ranking nobles identifiable by their distinctive ear piercings (they were later called *orejones,* or "big ears," by the Spanish). The next in the ruling hierarchy were "Incas of privilege," also called "administrative Incas," who implemented state policy and lived on the outskirts of Cuzco.

As the empire expanded and absorbed more and more territory and population, the Inca's authority was extended widely not only by increasing the number of nobles eligible to hold office but also by co-opting the *curacas,* the leaders of local conquered ethnic groups. The result was a large bureaucratic structure organized to manage the growing empire.

Inca administrative officials assigned to the provinces included accountants who tallied tribute payments, storage houses, labor assignments, and population growth; transportation and communication specialists who oversaw the maintenance of roads, bridges, and *tambos,* and ran the imperial courier system *(chasquis);* and military administrators in charge of recruitment, training, and campaigning. The central Inca state administration also regularly sent inspectors into the provinces to report.

The empire's leaders were trained in special schools, known as *yachayhuasi* (houses of knowledge). Sons of the nobility, including the sons of *curacas* from various ethnic groups, studied at the schools over the course of four years, learning language, rhetoric, religion, mathematics, and the history of political and military strategy from their teachers.

THE INCA'S TOOLS OF ADMINISTRATION

The Inca relied on an efficient system of supply, communications, and accounting to administer the empire. Stone buildings called *tambos* were spaced every 10 to 15 miles along the empire's extensive road network. These were used by official couriers and travelers as places to rest and resupply for another day's journey. Imperial *tambos* for important travelers were larger than ordinary ones and were provisioned by laborers under the *mit'a* system. Smaller and less sturdy *tambos* were used by *chasquis,* relay runners who carried packages and messages from one place to another. In three days and nights a message sent from the coast could

The Incan quipu, a knotted string used to tally and record accounts and to transmit information among a people who had no written language (Narrative and Critical History of America)

reach the Inca in Cuzco. The systems of *tambos* and *chasquis* were the Inca's equivalent of a modern-day express courier or postal service.

Part of the empire's administrative efficiency was based on the use of the quipus, a remarkable system, probably adopted from the Chimú, that employed knotted strings to record and communicate information. The pattern of knots could carry complex messages or maintain detailed accounts. Pedro de Cieza de León, one of the most quoted chroniclers of the Inca past, commented that the accuracy and reliability of the quipus—and of skill of the *quipucamayocs* (those in charge of the quipus)—were demonstrated by their accuracy in accounting exactly for all the ransom amounts the Incas had given to the Spaniards after the arrival of the conquistador Francisco Pizarro.

Land and Labor

Land and its produce in the Inca Empire were divided three ways: one-third for the ruling Inca; one-third for Inti, the sun god; and one third for the local population. The best and most productive land went to the

Inca and to Inti. The local farmers had to work these lands on behalf of the emperor and the sun god, and they sent the harvest to Cuzco as a form of imperial tax that supported the nobility and the system of priests and temples.

The third of the land that remained for use by local farmers and herders was parceled out to individual families in units called *topos*, which comprised enough land to feed a family, although the size of individual *topos* varied according to the characteristics and productivity of the land. Couples received a *topo* when they married, and more land was added to the original *topo* as children were born to the family. The boundaries of each *topo* were designated in terms of natural features, such as trees, hills, rivers, ditches, or stones. In the highlands, families or *ayllus* (kinship groups) often possessed land in several locations, giving rise to a pattern of discontinuous fields. This form of cultivation was an adaptation to the difficult mountain environment and allowed a variety of crops to be grown at different altitudes. Seasonally, some members of an *ayllu* left their homes to work in the more distant fields, returning with their crops at the end of the harvest cycle and thus were able to provide the home community with a plentiful and varied diet. In this

Inca farming terraces built into the side of a steep slope in order to maximize available crop land. The Inca were highly skilled agriculturalists, who devised a complex but productive system of farming at varying altitudes in order to boost harvests and guard against catastrophic crop failure. (Photofrenetic/Alamy)

23

scheme, money and markets were unnecessary, and this form of cultivation reduced risk: If one crop at a certain altitude failed, communities could always fall back on crops grown at other altitudes.

Even though local groups had some leeway and strived to be self-sufficient, the Inca economy was essentially state run, and the central authorities controlled a very large share of the empire's labor force. The Inca attempted to strictly control economic production and distribution, all the way from potatoes to gold, coca, vicuñas, and spondylus shells. (*Spondylus princeps* are the red seashells that served as a trade medium and were highly valued for their use in religious rituals.)

Following the example of their Chimú predecessors, the Inca combined two systems to exploit local produce and labor: the *mit'a*, which was draft labor, and the tribute, which could be paid as labor or in kind. Laborers (*mitayos*) were drafted for public work, such as road building and repair, stone storage building construction, or military service. Tribute was also usually paid in the form of labor, thus placing a huge pool of human economic resources in the hands of the central imperial authorities.

Another source of labor recruitment rested in the *mitimaes*, large kinship groups of people from the provinces, sometimes entire ethnic groups from as far away as modern-day Ecuador, who were transferred wholesale to the Cuzco area. Not only did this practice of "importing" laborers provide a work force for the empire's capital city, but it also fulfilled another function: By transferring large groups of people, the Inca reduced the size of potentially disruptive ethnic groups, and at the same time teaching them, while in Cuzco, Inca customs. It was a way of pacifying and acculturating conquered ethnic groups. The counterpart was the practice of settling loyal ethnic groups in the territories from which *mitimaes* had been removed.

Economic Exchange and Reciprocity

At the height of the empire, the Inca tried to regulate economic exchange by applying the criteria of need and reward. For example, when a locality or settlement experienced a bad harvest, the central Inca government would provide relief from surpluses held in storage from previous years. And, when a local leader served the Inca state well, he might be rewarded with fine vicuña clothes or jewelry produced by specialists in Cuzco—and sometimes even with a concubine chosen from the *acllahuasi*, the house of religious women (*acllas*) devoted to upholding and supporting the state religion.

However, there were some forms of economic activity outside the strict control of the state. In some parts of the empire groups set up their own markets for trade and exchange. For example, local merchants used balsa rafts to trade along the Chincha coast, and they eventually also traded inland to Cuzco and as far away as parts of what is today Bolivia. When traveling north, Chincha merchants took copper with them; returning to Cuzco, they brought spondylus shells.

In a society where money and the notion of private property were unknown, social relations often regulated the economy. Many ethnic groups in the highlands did not use markets and merchants, but developed their own methods and traditions based on barter, a system sustained by the basic principle of reciprocity, which also embodied an intrinsic notion of equality. Exchange between groups was based on a shared sense of balanced giving and taking and was sustained through kinship relations involving local *ayllus*.

During the early stages, when the ruling Inca's power was still far from absolute, reciprocal exchange was vital to building the empire. The Inca had to beg *curacas* to help him expand the state's infrastructure. In return for their help, the Inca promised them concessions or future benefits. At this stage, the Inca had no choice but to show a high degree of generosity on his side of the reciprocity scheme.

The supreme Incas originally had elicited labor from Cuzco's *curacas* with booty seized from the Chanca, and Incas continued gradually to increase their power using such mechanisms and resources. Eventually, they were able to build fortresses and storage houses and to accumulate enough wealth to support further military expansion. Apparently, the only individuals or groups excluded from a reciprocity scheme were *yanas* (assigned laborers) and the *mitimaes*.

Reciprocity also operated at the level of the Incan state's relationship to local *ayllus* and ethnic groups. In this case, the chances of unbalanced exchange were high, since the state apparatus and the ruling class of high-ranking Inca nobles usually sought to tip the balance in their favor. As time went on, the Incan imperial state began regularly to substitute religious rituals for goods in offering something for exchange. Instead of returning a bag of potatoes for a bag of potatoes, the Inca state returned a prayer for a bag of potatoes, thus distorting in terms of real value the principle of reciprocal exchange.

The conquering Inca tried to use local *curacas* to administer new parts of the empire whenever possible and to pull new groups into the system of reciprocity, but the emperor also used coercion and cultural blackmail. In order to encourage compliance with imperial demands, the Inca took

INCA BRIDGES

Few societies anywhere in the world during the 15th century could boast of road and bridge network as extensive as that of the Inca. Their system covered 10,000 miles and had been knit together from roads originally built by the Chimú and Tiwanaku and extended by the Inca.

Chroniclers and European visitors in later centuries wrote detailed descriptions of the many Incan bridges, their sizes, the materials used, and the variety of their design and construction. Most bridges were built using locally available raw materials, such as twisted grass ropes, stones, and twigs.

One special kind of bridge was the *oroya,* a long double rope reaching from one side to the other with a hanging basket in which passengers sat to be pulled across. In the Lake Titicaca region, *balsas* (rafts) made out of reeds were tied together to form a bridge.

The Inca stationed groups of maintenance workers near bridges and along the roads that connected the empire. These caretakers also counted the people using the roads and bridges and thus increased the potential of the central government to control local movements.

possession of local *huacas* (tombs, mummies, representations of deities, and sacred objects) and moved them to Cuzco, where they were held hostage. The Inca threatened reprisals against the *huacas* should the conquered people attempt to rebel against Inca rule. Similarly, local *curacas* might be taken to Cuzco to learn Incan ways and to become emissaries between the conquered ethnic group and the Inca state.

Religion

Religion was a key element in the structure and the functioning of the Inca Empire. The supreme Inca's fundamental power to rule the empire rested on acceptance of the belief that he descended from the sun god Inti. The Inca was supported by a very elaborate hierarchical structure in which specialized priests served a variety of religious functions. The highest-ranking religious authority in the Inca Empire was the *villac umu,* considered the servant or slave of the Sun and a blood relative of the ruling Inca. Below the *villac umu* in the religious hierarchy were the *guacarimachic,* priests who were caretakers of holy places and objects known as the *huacas,* and the *ayatapuc,* priests who talked to the dead and prophesied the future by reading portents from the pulsating hearts and bowels of sacrificial llamas. There were also specialized diviners, called the *caviacoc* or *huatuc,* who predicted the future while intoxicated. These priests were the pillars of Inca religious rituals and the mediators between the earthly and the divine.

Women called the *mamaconas* and *acllas* were recruited from all over the empire to offer support services for the state religion. They lived in the *acllahuasi;* prepared the *chicha,* a potent corn-based liquor, for religious celebrations; and wove the Inca's fine clothes. Rituals and ceremonies for the Moon and the soil were carried out by the Inca's wife, known as the *coya,* and the women of the Cuzco nobility. However, these were not their only tasks. *Acllas* were often given, if the Inca so decided, as wives for deserving subjects as a way to satisfy the chain of reciprocity obligations.

Religion was a key element that held hierarchies and social order in place. It provided the ideological underpinnings of the empire. More worldly affairs were judged by three basic principles: *ama sua* (no stealing), *ama llulla* (no lying), and *ama quella* (no idling). Transgressions to these principles were seen as an offense to the deities and severely punished. Respecting the social order was key to appeasing the gods. In the same vein, when the Inca became sick, it was believed that something was wrong in the empire, and vice versa.

Much of the Incan economy and the exchange of produce was linked to the function of temples or sanctuaries to which people made regular pilgrimages. In recent years archaeologists have uncovered some of these impressive sites. For example, the Huaca Pariacaca, located in the central eastern cordillera, attracted many people from the coastal areas. Similarly, the temple of Pachacamac, located near the town of Pachacamac on Peru's coast, was regularly and frequently visited by people from the highlands. Pachacamac had several local smaller shrines among various ethnic groups, and there were shrines dedicated to the children and wives of the idol as well. Chroniclers also point to the existence of important *huacas* throughout Incan territory. Another such *huaca* site is Choque Ispana, located close to the Pacific Ocean (today's Huacho), which probably dates back to the Chavín period. Here, too, people from the highlands and the coast joined their prayers and probably used this sacred space to exchange goods as well.

Quite recently an astrophysicist, D. S. Dearborn, and a historian-archaeologist, Brian S. Bauer, teamed up to uncover some of the most stunning findings concerning Incan religion, especially by uncovering the connections between astronomy and the ritual, social, and political organization of the Inca Empire. Following the movements of the Sun was an important expression of imperial religion, so the team concluded that Incan astronomy was a key to understanding how the indigenous population interpreted the movements of the heavens through a native calendar. This understanding helps to explicate the social and ritual organization of the imperial capital at Cuzco by which the elites held their power.

Aside from the Sun, the Inca people and local ethnic groups also observed other stars, in which they saw night skies inhabited by animal images often associated with reproductive processes. Other natural phenomena were also observed: eclipses, thunder, lightning, meteors, and rainbows. As in other cultures, some of these phenomena inspired fears, worries, or joy. When an eclipse occurred, people began screaming and crying, and they would beat their dogs to make them howl. The appearances of several comets during the reign of the Inca Huayna Capac were interpreted as premonitions of his death, and Huayna Capac himself is said to have had dreams and visions about the annihilation of his people and his empire. The Indian narrator Juan de Santa Cruz Pachacuti recorded that when the Inca was asleep, he saw himself surrounded by large numbers of his soldiers who had been killed in previous battles. Later, Huayna Capac saw a stranger who gave him a closed box and rapidly disappeared. The box contained diseases that were to kill himself and his people.

A basic aspect of Inca religious and political life was the careful preservation of the mummies of their ancestors. Mummies were consistently a part of almost all indigenous cultures of the region, where the ultra-dry climate facilitated mummification of both humans and animals. The Inca, like many previous cultures, respected and venerated the mummified remains of their forebears, especially the royal mummies, which were lavished with attention and care by their own extended royal family groups, or *panacas*. When a new ruling Inca was enthroned there were celebrations with prayers, sacrifices, and fasting during which the mummies of the new ruler's predecessors (called *mallqui*) were brought forth by their caretakers and seated around a table where they were talked to and fed. The dead were regarded as an ongoing part of life and a part of the Incan vision of the cosmos, which was divided into three spheres, the *hanaq pacha* (the world above, the sky), the *kay pacha* (the ground and humankind, the here and now), and the *ujqu pacha* (the world beneath, the dead). All three worlds communicated through the divine Inca, and it was important to maintain the unbroken line of authority that was represented by the mummies.

THE DEATH OF HUAYNA CAPAC, ACCORDING TO THE CHRONICLER FATHER BERNABÉ COBO

Shortly after this first arrival of the Spaniards in this land [c. 1525], while the Inca was in the province of Quito, smallpox broke out among his subjects, and many of them died. Being fearful, the Inca went into seclusion to fast as was the custom in such times of hardship. . . . Then the Inca said that he would die, and later he got smallpox. While he was very sick, his servants sent two relay teams to Pachacama to ask what should be done for the health of their lord. The sorcerers, who spoke with the devil, consulted the idol, which answered that the Inca should be taken out into the sun and then he would get well. This was done, but with the opposite result, for when the Inca was put into the sun, he died at once.

His death was deeply felt by all of his vassals. Funeral rites were held for him with much weeping and solemn sacrifices; a thousand persons were killed for his burial; they were to serve him in the other life [as they believed], and its is stated that he was held in such high esteem that these people were content to die, and besides those who were designated, many others offered themselves of their own free will. This is because [according to what could be ascertained] this Inca was adored as a god in his lifetime, differently than others; and never for any of his predecessors were such ceremonies held as for him. . . . The heart of Huayna Capac was buried in Quito, and his body was taken to Cuzco. At first it was in the temple of the Sun, and later in Casana and other places. . . . (Cobo, in Hamilton 1993, 160–162).

An elaborate ritual calendar commemorated each deity and each mummy. Each year counted 12 moons and the beginning of the year was during the December solstice. Each year was divided into two halves of six months, the semester of the Inca and the semester of the Coya (the wife of the Inca), and the most important religious festivities were the Coya Raymi in September, Capac Raymi in December, and the Inti Raymi in June. In the Southern Hemisphere these months coincide with the preparation of the soil for cultivation, the planting, and harvest. The religious calendar was closely knit into the agrarian cycle.

The Santo Domingo Church in Cuzco, built by the Spanish in 1534 on top of an existing Inca sun temple and using Inca-cut stones (© Philip Baird, www.anthroarcheart.org)

Given the strong religious roots of Inca society, it is not surprising that when the Spaniards witnessed the display of mummies and what they considered to be idolatries—aside from believing, of course, in the superiority of their own god—they did everything they could to dismantle the Inca belief system. Such dismantlement involved the destruction of religious sites, the burning of mummies, and unyielding persecution, to the point that today's archaeologists and historians find it hard to trace Inca religion and rituals. The Inca belief system was closely related to nature, and by eliminating its physical and geographical references, the Spanish in a sense unanchored the visible sites of Inca religion. In many places new churches of the Christian god were literally built upon the ruins of Inca temples.

Succession to Office and the Brothers' War

Most Spanish chroniclers simply assumed that the Inca process of succession to high office followed European patterns. Today we know better. Depending on the level of succession (from the low-level *curacas* to the Inca himself), a variety of criteria functioned to define a successor. Quite frequently several criteria were at work in a single ethnic group. In the earlier stages of Inca expansion, leaders (called *sinchis*) were selected according to their military skills. The elected leader may have been the son of the chief most loved by his people. Sometimes the brother of the chief would be chosen before the son came to power. In some cases the most able man was chosen even if he was not related to the chief. The successor may have been chosen after the chief died, but sometimes the new leader was put in place while the chief was still in command in order to benefit from the old chief's experience and to improve the new chief's governing skills. Local succession patterns may have been in place, but on occasion, the Inca himself would impose a successor. In some places female and male descendants could claim to succeed their fathers or mothers. Only persons with experience and merit and, when available, close to the Inca were eligible, and every appointment needed the supreme Inca's final approval.

As the Inca Empire reached consolidation, stricter rules applied to succession. Rulers were interested in better defining the qualifications of a successor and the mechanisms through which a new Inca could take power. Only by doing so could the supreme Inca prevent the continued and prolonged fights for succession resulting from the multiple and varied sets of possibilities. Many criteria meant many candidates, and many candidates meant political uncertainty. This was one of the reasons why the death of an Inca was kept secret until it was clear who would succeed him.

The predominant rule of succession among the Inca was to designate the son of the supreme ruler's "sister." This "sister" was not necessarily his blood sister but could also be his half sister, cousin, or any woman from his lineage. Thus, succession followed a matrilineal logic, and *panacas* and women in these royal clans were key to understanding political life in the city. What we know about the brothers Huáscar and Atahualpa, the last two independent Incas who died in the wake of the Spanish conquest, helps to illustrate patterns of succession to high office.

While in the north attempting to subdue a rebellion by a non-Incan ethnic group, the ruling Inca, Huayna Capac, died from disease in 1525. He was apparently the victim of a European illness that spread as an epidemic among the native population, even before the Europeans themselves appeared. (Deadly, unknown germs were the first messengers of Spanish presence in northern coastal Peru.) One of the Inca's sons, Atahualpa, had been with him in the north when the ruler died; a second son, Huáscar, was in Cuzco. Unfortunately, when Huayna Capac died, the line of succession had not been clarified. Subsequently there were many misunderstandings between the two half brothers, made worse by political conflicts among vested interests in the Cuzco

MACHU PICCHU

Located about 50 miles from Cuzco, Machu Picchu is the best known of all Incan historic sites in Peru and one of the most famous archaeological sites in all of South America. It had largely receded from outside notice until the summer of 1911, when Hiram Bingham III, a history professor at Yale University in the United States, was led to the site by Indian guides. His subsequent writings about the magnificent buildings and location popularized the place as a "lost city," although Bingham's ideas about it have proved to be in error.

Bingham thought variously that Machu Picchu was the original center of Inca civilization, the last stronghold of a 16th-century supreme Inca who had resisted the Spanish conquerors, or perhaps an exotic residence for ritual Inca virgins. Modern researchers have concluded that the story is probably less romantic than any of Bingham's explanations. Based on studies of artifacts, skeletal remains, and written records, the current opinion holds that Machu Picchu was a personal vacation estate of Inca Pachacútec, and that it probably never had a large population and was likely all but abandoned after the Inca's death.

Whatever the exact nature of its historic role in Inca times, the complex was a marvel of engineering, which included extensive reforming of the landscape as well as the more obvious examples of superb Inca stonemasonry and architecture. Today Machu Picchu is a popular tourist destination, and thousands each year trek along the Inca Trail to reach the city or take packaged tours to experience the awe-inspiring beauty of the site.

Machu Picchu, about 50 miles from Cuzco in the Andes (Photofrenetic/Alamy)

panacas and the generals who aligned with one or the other of the brothers. The result was a year-long war that divided and completely unsettled the empire. The Inca political and administrative system relied on specific orders and directives from the supreme ruler, but during the so-called Brothers' War, no one knew who the supreme Inca was. There were several battles between huge armies, and with the last of these military clashes, Huáscar was in prison. The victor, Atahualpa, carried out cruel revenge against Huáscar's *panaca* in Cuzco.

Huáscar's mother was Raura Ocllo, a sister of Huayna Capac in Tupac Yupanqui's *panaca,* the Capac Ayllu. As her son, Huáscar was considered to belong to this extended royal family. On Atahualpa's orders, all members belonging to the Capac Ayllu, including male and female servants, were killed, and their belongings were confiscated. The mummy of their ancestor, Inca Tupac Yupanqui, was burned. Among the Inca, the burning of the mummy of an ancestor was considered the worst punishment anyone could suffer. Atahualpa's actions underline that Inca lines of descent were not traced through patrilineal kinship ties, as in Europe and elsewhere, but were matrilineal, that is through the *ayllu* or *panaca* of the Inca's mother. Descent from the paternal side did not establish a kingship tie. Had Atahualpa considered himself a descendant of Tupac Yupanqui, he would not have taken revenge against Huáscar by dishonoring the mummy of his paternal grandfather.

3

CONQUEST AND THE BEGINNINGS OF COLONIAL LIFE (1532–1568)

In 1532 a small group of Spanish soldiers and adventurers led by a tough commander named Francisco Pizarro invaded the Inca Empire, and in a stroke that combined daring and luck, the men captured Atahualpa, who had just seized power from his brother after a destructive civil war. After wringing a fortune in gold and silver from the Inca ruler, Pizarro executed him and moved on almost unmolested by the Inca people to take Cuzco. The empire collapsed, and the Spaniards seized political and economic control of Peru. Failing to take advantage of subsequent quarrels and civil war among the Spaniards, who were bent on grabbing as much personal treasure and land for themselves as they could, the Inca aristocracy fell into disarray, and attempts at resistance failed. Within a few years the far-off Spanish Crown had asserted its authority and established an administration to run what was to become a colonial empire.

Pizarro's Conquest

Francisco Pizarro, the illegitimate son of a minor Spanish nobleman, was born in the city of Trujillo in Extremadura circa 1478. He began a career as a soldier at a very young age in Spain's wars in Italy. He came to the Americas in 1509 with the expedition of Alonso de Ojeda, and he was a member of Vasco Nuñez de Balboa's expedition to the Pacific in 1513. Eventually Pizarro became captain, alderman, and then mayor of Panama City. He heard rumors about a rich civilization to the south and made plans with his friend Diego de Almagro (he also consulted priest Hernando de Luque) to investigate the kingdom referred to as "Biru," a name later modified to "Peru."

Pizarro left Panama in September 1524 on his first exploratory voyage south, but instead of treasure he found hardship for his men, many of whom died from starvation or were killed by natives. A second trip followed in 1526, and Pizarro discovered evidence of a rich kingdom, although he returned with little to show for his effort. His third expedition left Panama on January 20, 1531, with 180 men and 37 horses.

The Spanish conquistador Francisco Pizarro (Pageant of America)

This time Pizarro landed on the coast and established a base, spending the following months gathering intelligence about the empire of the Inca. He doubtless learned about the war between Huáscar and Atahualpa and may have surmised the time was ripe for him to strike. In November 1532 Pizarro and his small group of men left Tumbes on the coast and began a difficult march into the highlands, aiming for Cajamarca. In the meantime Atahualpa had received messages from *curacas* on the northern coast about the arrival of white bearded men coming from the sea on floating houses and riding huge animals. This news came as no surprise since the first reports of the Spanish presence had reached the Inca Huayna Capac during his campaigns in the north almost a decade earlier. Instead of confronting the Spaniards or opposing their advance, Atahualpa, surrounded by an army of tens of thousands, decided to wait for them to arrive at his camp. On their way from Tumbes to Cajamarca, the Spaniards met no resistance, and in fact, messengers brought them gifts of the alcoholic drink *chicha*, llamas, and food from the Inca. The Spaniards in return sent back silk shirts and glass trinkets.

Pizarro and his men arrived at Cajamarca to find it almost deserted, so they took possession of the town. Atahualpa's huge army was camped nearby, and Pizarro sent an invitation to the Inca to meet in Cajamarca. On November 16, 1532, Atahualpa entered the town with hundreds of retainers but few guards. Most of the Spanish soldiers, many armed with the firearms of the day as well as their fine Toledo-made swords, were hidden in ambush. Pizarro sent a priest, Fray Vicente de Valverde, forward to harangue Atahualpa about Christianity.

When the priest offered Atahualpa a Bible, the Inca either dropped it or threw it aside. Perceiving this as blasphemy from a heretic, the Spaniards unleashed a ferocious attack on the Incas, killing hundreds of them while suffering not a single loss. Moreover, the supreme Inca himself was captured. At the end of the day, despite fears the massed Inca army would attack in revenge for the capture of their ruler, Pizarro was in control.

The Inca's army, as it turned out, was paralyzed with no one at the top to give orders. The Spaniards were left unmolested, and as they gained confidence, they began to exploit the situation. Pizarro demanded a ransom from Atahualpa, who responded by issuing orders for an entire room to be filled with gold for the Spaniards and two more with silver. The treasure carts rolled in from the corners of the empire, until by spring 1533, a ransom calculated at 1.5 million pesos was in Pizarro's hands. For his part, Pizarro reneged on his promise to spare

---

THE DEATH OF ATAHUALPA, ACCORDING TO THE CHRONICLER PEDRO CIEZA DE LEÓN

When Atahualpa learned of the cruel sentence, he lamented to God Almighty how those who had seized him had failed to keep their word. He could not find a way to escape. If he believed that he could do it with more gold, he would have given them another house, even four more. He said many pitiful things: that those who were listening to him should have mercy because of his youth; he asked why they were killing him, even though he had given them so much and not caused them any harm or injury. He complained about Pizarro, and with reason.

At about seven in the evening they removed him from where he was held. They took him to where the execution would take place; Friar Vicente, Juan de Porras, Captain Salcedo, and some others went with him. On the way he kept repeating: "Why are they killing me? Why am I being killed? What have I done, and my children and my wives?" and other similar words. Friar Vicente was admonishing him to become a Christian and abandon his beliefs. [Atahualpa] asked to be baptized, and the friar did it. And then they strangled him, and to fulfill the sentence they burned some of his hair with pieces of straw, which was another foolishness.

Atahualpa, and after condemning the Inca on trumped-up conspiracy charges, he executed the supreme ruler on July 16. The Inca, who had ordered the death of his imprisoned brother Huáscar from his own prison cell, chose a last-minute conversion to Catholicism to avoid death by burning at the stake, a fate that would have made the preservation of his mummy impossible. He died by garroting. Atahualpa was solemnly buried in the church the next day, but shortly afterward his corpse disappeared, probably destroyed by the Spaniards to prevent his followers from using a royal mummy as a rallying point for resistance, or taken by his followers to rescue their Inca and bring him safely to the *hanaq pacha*.

When the Spanish king, Charles V, heard about the execution, he was deeply upset. Pizarro had killed a monarch, and no vassal could ever kill a king (even if he was a foreigner and a heretic) without seriously disturbing the monarchical order itself.

Some of the Indians say that before they killed him, Atahualpa exclaimed that they should await him in Quito, that they would see him again in the form of a snake (Cieza de León, Cook and Cook 1998, 256–257).

A modern-day view of Cajamarca, where Francisco Pizarro captured in 1532 and executed in 1533 the Inca Atahualpa, effectively bringing the sprawling Inca Empire under the control of the Spanish Crown and gaining a fortune in ransom for himself and his men (Harryhausen/Alamy)

Civil Conflict and Inca Resistance

Even before the death of Atahualpa, the Spaniards began to quarrel among themselves. Over the course of the following several years, the early conquistadores and settlers fought so vigorously among themselves that the period might accurately be labeled one of civil war.

The basic conflict was between Francisco Pizarro—backed by his three brothers, Hernando, Juan, and Gonzalo—and Pizarro's former ally Diego de Almagro. Almagro and his men had arrived at Cajamarca too late to take part in the ambush and capture of the Inca, and therefore Pizarro refused to give them much of a share in the fabulous ransom. This was only the beginning of the bad blood between them. Pizarro took political control of Peru. He ruled from his new city of Lima, established on the coast, and, more important, he handed out land grants, called *encomiendas,* to himself, his brothers, and his followers with a liberal hand. Almagro and his party failed to receive what they felt was their due. After an expedition to Chile failed to produce riches, a disappointed Almagro occupied Cuzco and took two of the Pizarro brothers captive.

There were a series of disagreements and temporary settlements over the next several years, but since these were violent times and these men were soldiers, the conflict eventually worked itself out through violence. In April 1538, at Las Salinas, near Cuzco, Pizarro's army defeated Almagro's outnumbered men in a brief battle. Almagro was captured, and on orders of Hernando Pizarro, he was beheaded in the main square of Cuzco. (Hernando was tried and imprisoned for this execution when he returned soon thereafter to Spain.)

Three years after Almagro's defeat and death, a group of his supporters led by Almagro's mestizo son, also named Diego de Almagro, assassinated Francisco Pizarro in his home in Lima. The Almagro faction then claimed control of the colonial government, but their triumph was short lived. The king appointed a new royal governor, Cristóbal Vaca de Castro, in an attempt to bring order to the unruly colony. Vaca de Castro assembled an army, defeated and captured the younger Almagro in 1542 at the battle of Chufas, and executed him afterward.

Meanwhile, the hopes of the Incas to return to power had been dashed several times. When Huáscar and Atahualpa died, the potential leadership was thrown into disarray. Pizarro understood the need to restore order and therefore named a puppet Inca, Tupac Huallpa, a son of Huayna Capac. Tupac was poisoned only a few months later and was replaced by Manco Inca II, another son of Huayna Capac, brother of Huáscar. Manco Inca had initially sought an alliance with the Spaniards in his struggle against the followers of Atahualpa, but he soon came to

INCA COOPERATION

During the period of disruption following the execution of Atahualpa, some members of the Cuzco Inca nobility tried to bargain with the Spaniards. Paullu Inca, for example, the younger brother of Huáscar, Atahualpa, and Manco Inca, first sided with Diego de Almagro. Later he allied himself to Cristóbal Vaca de Castro and took the Christian name of Cristóbal Paullu Inca. Soon afterward, Paullu Inca moved on to court Gonzalo Pizarro, while at the same time secretly helping Pedro La Gasca to mobilize against Gonzalo. In 1545 Spanish king Charles V extended a form of recognition to Paullu by granting him a coat of arms.

Paullu Inca's history demonstrated the willingness of some of the Inca elites to cooperate with the Spaniards, including participation in Spanish civil strife. Without Indian help the conquistadores would not have been able to subdue the empire, and without siding with Spaniards the Indian nobility would not have had an opportunity to rescue some of their privileges, such as obtaining larger tracts of land, collecting tributes, or wearing better clothes.

understand that the Spaniards did not intend to become his allies and was virtually a prisoner in his own palace. He bribed Hernando Pizarro with several massive gold statues, and on April 18, 1536, Manco Inca was freed and made his escape to the Urubamba Valley. From there, he organized an army to fight the Spaniards.

Four times between 1536 and 1537, Manco Inca's troops laid siege to Cuzco, hoping to dislodge the Spaniards; however, several other ethnic groups, wishing to free themselves from Inca dominion, aided the Spaniards. Apparently, the *curacas* of these ethnic groups little suspected the miseries they would face shortly afterward.

Not the least of the difficulties was the displacement the Spaniards inflicted on much of the indigenous population. From the early days of their control, the Spanish needed labor to create the wealth they so craved. As a consequence the Spaniards insisted on moving and reorganizing ethnic groups. The largest groups, which may have numbered several units called *guarangas,* each of which had 1,000 households, were often subdivided into smaller units, called *pachacas,* of 100 households each. The smaller units were then assigned to work where the Spaniards felt the sharpest needs for labor. The organization into thousands and hundreds was an Inca custom and thus preserved some sense of the traditional past, but in spite of these organizational efforts, disarray and demographic decline prevailed.

Manco Inca's rebellion was nearly successful, but ultimately he could not dislodge the Spanish from Cuzco or their new capital at Lima, and his campaigns slowly faded away. By 1539 Manco Inca had retreated to the east of Cuzco and established his headquarters in Vilcabamba (modern-day Espíritu Pampa). For five more years Manco Inca contested Spanish power with sporadic attacks but avoided direct and large-scale confrontations. In the end he was murdered by followers of the Almagro faction who hoped to prove themselves to the newly appointed Spanish authorities. After stabbing Manco to death in front of his son, the murderers were killed by Manco's followers.

Native Chroniclers

Despite the dramatic, destructive impact of the Spanish conquest, aspects of Inca society survived: sometimes in the original version, sometimes in transmuted forms, and sometimes hidden from Spanish view. A great deal of information has come down to us through the works of native chroniclers, who made efforts to record what seemed to the casual observer to be passing away or hidden. While the conquistadores and their successors filled their pockets with Inca gold and silver, a few of the descendants of the Inca learned to use paper and pens as tools to preserve some of their own culture.

Among those Inca who learned to read and write Spanish, at least six became chroniclers, who wrote about the Inca past and the impact of the Spanish conquest. Most also eventually made recommendations to the king for better governance of the colonies. Five such chroniclers are known to us by name: Garcilaso de la Vega, Felipe Guamán Poma de Ayala, Juan de Santa Cruz Pachacuti, Yamqui Salcamaygua, and Diego del Castro Titu Cusi Yupanqui—plus the anonymous author of the Huarochiri chronicle. They wrote the initial colonial history.

Perhaps the best known of this group is Guamán Poma de Ayala, an Indian chronicler from Huamanga, who wrote a 1,000-page letter to the king of Spain suggesting a radical change of royal Spanish policies. Guamán Poma de Ayala based his ideas on his knowledge of the Inca past and on his own observations, having witnessed the dire consequences of Spanish presence among his people at the beginning of the 16th century. He advanced arguments to the king to restore the land to the indigenous people, to keep non-Indians out of native settlements, to reinstate and honor traditional privileges of local Indian authorities, and to remedy personal and collective grievances. In short, he invited the king to reassess and revise the colonial enterprise by taking Indians' rights into consideration.

Guamán Poma de Ayala buttressed his request by demonstrating that Andeans were not historically or culturally inferior to Europeans. To the contrary, he argued that lower-status Spaniards had had no right to kill an Inca. He also attempted to dismantle the religious argument for conquest by stating it was not a "just" war against heretics for the sake of Christian beliefs because the apostle Saint Bartholomew had visited Peru before the Spaniards; thus, Indians had heard about the "real" Christian god and were not pagans. He also argued that the king's interests would be better served if the indigenous people regained lost venues, because most Spanish emissaries were corrupt and unprepared to serve the king well. Guamán Poma de Ayala was not entirely Inca-friendly, and he did not want to return to Inca hegemony, but he reinterpreted the Inca past to make sense of a dismal present and, more important, to advocate a change in colonial policies.

It is not known if the king read Guamán Poma de Ayala's long letter, or if he read it, how he understood it. Much of what followed throughout the colonial period was, however, far removed from Guamán Poma de Ayala's wishes and interpretations; in fact, those who survived the dramatic decline in numbers of the indigenous population were subdued ever more firmly to Spanish interests. Indigenous struggle for recognition and autonomy disintegrated but did not disappear. It took time, however, before the Spanish Crown recognized that only by upholding indigenous rights and access to land would it be able to continue exacting tribute and labor from its vassals. And the only way of upholding indigenous rights was by restraining the power and the greed of the Spanish population in its colonies. In a way it was self-interest that proved Guamán Poma de Ayala right in the long run.

Spanish Colonialism

In contrast to limited sources of knowledge about the Inca Empire, the Spanish colonial period from the 16th to the early 19th centuries was well documented by the Spanish colonial bureaucracy. Historical documentation of specific subjects throughout the colonial period abounds, especially for the initial stages of colonial domination in the 16th century and for the second half of the 18th century up to the wars of independence from Spain in 1825. Research on the colonial period is also marked by regional bias because of Peru's uneven regional development. Researchers, for example, know more about Peru's southern highlands in and around Cuzco than about the northern coast, and the same is true in the case of Lima versus other, minor cities in the country.

When Pizarro founded his new capital city of Lima on the coast in 1535, he deliberately pushed Cuzco, the former seat of the Inca Empire, into the political background. Initially Pizarro had declared Xauxa (present-day Jauja, located in the central Peruvian highlands) as the capital city of the Viceroyalty of Peru; however, by 1535 the axis of power connected Lima, and its port city of Callao, to the port of Seville in Spain.

Hundreds of other towns and cities were founded in Peru during the 16th century, although they were spread out over a vast agrarian landscape. By 1580 there were 225 populated cities within the Spanish domain; by 1630 there were 331. U.S. historians Louise Hoberman and Susan M. Socolow have concluded that the Hispanic culture imported to the New World was essentially and "profoundly" urban (1986, 3, 5).

When the Spanish conquistadores reached the shores of Peru, they were experienced in dealing with cultures and environments different from their own. Spaniards had dealt with Arab culture for more than seven centuries on the Iberian Peninsula, expelling the Arabs from Iberia only just as the New World was discovered. Conquistador Hernán Cortés's encounter with the Aztec Empire provided a backdrop to Pizarro's conquest of the Inca. In the wake of Spanish experiences with the Aztec, much enticing information had reached the royal palace in Madrid and the ears of Charles V. America had ceased to be regarded as a collection of uninteresting islands and had become the focus of adventure and possible fortune for the Spanish Crown as well as for individual Spaniards.

The men who came to Peru with Francisco Pizarro were of varied backgrounds and status: Some were career soldiers, but others were artisans or merchants. All of them claimed to be "old Christians," "unstained" by Judaic or Muslim blood. All of them knew how to handle arms. None of the first expeditions included women, but every expedition had a priest and a scribe to bring native pagans under the Christian god and to duly record the adventures and deeds of the group.

Conquistadores were imbued by an ideology of "blood purity," a mindset directly related to their centuries-long experiences with Jews and Muslims at home. The Spaniards extended their attitudes to the Indians of Peru, deeming them inferior and impure heretics and thereby justifying conquest, enslavement, and even murder without remorse. Indian women were expropriated to meet the demands of Spanish male sexual needs and became the mothers of a mixed-blood population, the mestizos.

The Spanish conquest and religious enterprise was blessed by the Roman Catholic Church. Pope Alexander VI entrusted America to the Catholic king of Castile. The Treaty of Tordesillas (1494) sealed this political-religious pact. Sword and Bible were the powerful instruments of conquest. Thus, from the Spanish viewpoint the destruction of the Inca culture and Andean sacred places blessed the perpetrators doubly: They were doing something important to spread the belief in the "real" god, and they also got to reap plunder.

The *Encomienda*

A key factor in the settlement of the Spanish colonies was the *encomienda,* a grant of land by the king to loyal subjects, principally the early conquistadores, that carried with it the assigned labor of Indians. The combination of land and workforce made the *encomienda* a potent source of wealth and power. The more Indians an *encomendero* received, the richer he was. He collected tribute payments from the Indians, and in return for the land grant, the *encomendero* had two obligations to the Crown: to turn the Indians on the *encomienda* into good Catholics and to protect them. As long as the *encomendero* fulfilled these duties, he was allowed a free hand to use Indian labor and to demand payments for himself from the Indians.

From the point of view of the Spanish Crown, *encomiendas* provided a way to account for and control the king's new Indian vassals, to funnel tribute to the Crown, and to limit the indiscriminate appropriation of laborers by individual Spaniards. It was a way to protect the indigenous populations and also a way to prevent any single individual from accumulating too much power and wealth, which could lead to the feudalization of the colonies and eventually to the separation of the colonies from Spain. For the same reasons, the Spanish Crown granted *encomiendas* only temporarily, initially for the duration of the lifetimes of the *encomendero* and two heirs, later only to the *encomendero* and one heir.

Pizarro granted the first *encomiendas* to his followers after reserving the best sites for himself. Typically his foot soldiers received approximately 3.5 acres, and his horsemen received approximately 17.5 acres, along with their respective allotments of Indian laborers. Pizarro was interested, of course, in revenues; however, in his reports to the Council of the Indies in Spain, the governing body of the colonies, he also expressed his hope of avoiding the annihilation of Indians and the theft of all their property by putting them under the tutelage of an *encomendero*. In 1540 he ordered a first inspection (*visita*) of the various *encomiendas* in order to establish the tribute amounts owed to the Crown from each and to reinforce the idea that the ultimate beneficiary of the conquest was the *encomenderos'* king. Pizarro's initial settlement initiatives were contested, and conflict over his division of the land and Indians was part of what led to the civil war. In it

ENCOMENDERO LUCAS MARTÍNEZ VEGAZO

Lucas Martínez Vegazo was born in the city of Trujillo, in Extremadura, Spain, in 1511 or 1512. Little is known about his childhood. He learned to read and write at a time when Vasco Núñez de Balboa and others where discovering new lands, and he grew up listening to the stories told by these first discoverers, most of them from his hometown. He also witnessed the return of Francisco Pizarro to Trujillo as a rich man. At age 19, Martínez left Spain and traveled to Panama and then to Peru under the command of Pizarro. As a foot soldier, Martínez received one of the smallest portions of gold or silver that Pizarro distributed to his men from the Inca Atahualpa's ransom. Martínez was given 3,330 gold pesos and 135 silver coins from the treasure.

Martínez invested about 80 percent of his gold in a horse, which transformed him from a foot soldier into a cavalry man, a promotion that would guarantee him larger shares of future gold and silver distributions. Martínez also participated in the sack of the Pachacamac temple as one of 14 horsemen, or *caballeros,* joining Hernando Pizarro.

After traveling throughout the Inca territory, Martínez reached Cuzco in 1533 and participated in the Spanish takeover of the city and partook of the distribution of urban lots *(solares)* to all Spaniards. In a distribution of wealth in Cuzco, Martínez received 2,000 gold pesos, silver coins valued at 1,517 pesos, and fine clothes valued at 2 million pesos. In 1535 he added an *encomienda* to his wealth with Indians from Carumas under his command. In only five years the poor youngster from Trujillo had become a *caballero,* a citizen of Cuzco, and an *encomendero.*

In the following years he served with Hernando de Soto and Juan and Gonzalo Pizarro and was involved in several military expeditions to defeat the last remnants of Inca resistance. He continued accumulating more lands and Indians on his *encomienda.* By 1540 Martínez controlled a total of 9,730 Indian children, women, and men in Tarapaca, Carumas, Arica, Pica, Ilo, and Arequipa, of whom 1,208 were tribute payers, from whom he obtained all kinds of crops, animals, labor, and clothes (Based on Trelles 1982).

some of the principal *encomenderos* died during battles and skirmishes and others, including Pizarro himself, were assassinated.

In spite of their important political role, *encomiendas* in the Viceroyalty of Peru never numbered more than 500, and by 1555 only about 5 percent of approximately 8,000 Spaniards living in the viceroyalty were *encomenderos* with assigned Indians (Burkholder and Johnson 2002, 118). By the time civil strife in the viceroyalty abated, around 1569, the early *encomenderos* had lost much of their power and were gradually replaced by a new emerging group of Spanish bureaucrats, the *corregidores*. Toward the end of the 16th century, *encomiendas* subsisted only on the fringes of Spain's colonial dominions.

Colonial Administration and Organization

A viceroy, appointed as the representative of the king, was the most important Spanish official in the colonies, and the overarching unit of Spanish colonial administration was the viceroyalty. For most of its reign in the New World, Spain divided its American colonies into three viceroyalties: New Spain (Mexico), Peru, and New Granada (Panama, Colombia, Ecuador, and, temporarily, Venezuela). As affairs in the colonies grew more complex and trade shifted to the Atlantic coast, a fourth viceroyalty, Río de la Plata, was split off from the Viceroyalty of Peru in 1776.

Each viceroyalty was in turn divided into *audiencias* (the term referred not only to a territory within the larger viceroyalty but also to a high court that exercised considerable executive functions). Until 1739, the Viceroyalty of Peru covered a huge part of Spanish South America and included eight *audiencias:* Panama, Lima, Santa Fe de Bogotá, Charcas, Quito, Santiago de Chile, Buenos Aires, and Cuzco. When the Viceroyalty of New Granada was created in 1739, however, the *audiencias* of Santa Fe de Bogotá, Panama, and Quito fell under its jurisdiction. Then in 1776, when the Viceroyalty of Río de la Plata was established, the *audiencias* of Charcas, Buenos Aires, and Santiago de Chile became part of it.

Audiencias were subdivided into *gobernaciones* (town councils), and the administrative head in each *gobernación* was called the *gobernador*. The Audiencia of Lima, founded in 1542, had five *gobernaciones* (in Huarochiri, Tarma, Huancavelica, El Callao, and Cuzco). Under the *gobernadores* were the *corregidores*, then the *tenientes de gobernador* (governor's assistants) and *alcaldes mayores* (mayors), and at the bottom were the *gobernador de indios* (governor of the Indians), the alderman of the *cabildo de españoles* (municipality of Spaniards), and the alderman of the *cabildo de indios* (municipality of Indians). The *cabildos* were key to

Spanish Viceroyalties in South America, 1776

Caribbean Sea

NEW GRANADA

PERU

Pacific Ocean

RÍO DE LA PLATA

Captaincy General of Chile

Atlantic Ocean

N

0   400 miles
0   400 kilometers

The Viceroyalties

Viceroyalty of New Granada, including Captaincy General of Venezuela

Viceroyalty of Peru

Viceroyalty of Río de la Plata

Spanish settlement in the colonies. At the outset the *cabildos* administered town affairs, including local justice. The elected aldermen in the *cabildos* distributed land among Spanish settlers and provided guidance and eventually money to build and maintain public works. They also supervised local markets, police, weights, prices, and ceremonies, such as holidays and religious processions.

From Spain, the Crown administered affairs in the Americas and made colonial policy through the powerful Council of the Indies (Consejo de Indias). Beneath the council were several administrative bodies that dealt with specific areas. For example, the administration of state finances for the colonies fell to a powerful Spanish merchant guild, the Casa de Contratación, which was controlled by important Spanish merchants engaged in the Atlantic and Pacific trade. The guild was directly responsible to the Council of the Indies. Another powerful financial institution, the Commission of Audits (Tribunal de Cuentas), was also directly responsible to the Council of the Indies.

By around 1610 the colonial administrative structure in Spain had developed even more specialized entities to deal with the increasingly more complex affairs of the colonies. Departments of justice, civil administration, military affairs, and finances all had their own administrative structures and worked independent of the Council of the Indies. The Board of Finance (Junta de Hacienda) and the Commission of Audits, both entities dealing with the financial administration of the colonies, were also responsible to the viceroys, the captains-general (military governors found in some places), and the *gobernadores*. Some financial matters were also dealt with by local royal banks (*cajas reales*) controlled by the provincial *gobernadores*.

The New Laws

This bureaucratic structure, which was impressive by contemporary standards, was geared toward reinforcing Spanish presence in its colonies. Such control, however, was never fully accomplished in spite of administrative sophistication. From the very beginning, the problems the Spanish Crown would face over and over again were apparent: The geographical distance from the center of power in Spain made the colonies more independent than the Spanish Crown would have liked. An inherent autonomy had dangerous separatist tendencies that increased or diminished according to the loyalty of bureaucrats sent out from Spain, and loyalty often depended on the salary a bureaucrat received.

Although initially the *corregidores*, who numbered around 80 in the Peruvian viceroyalty toward the end of the 16th century, fulfilled the role envisioned for them by the Crown, they soon became a threat to the Crown's interests in the colonies. Around 1557 under Philip II, the Crown went bankrupt and to raise money began selling offices in the American colonies. The subsequent decline in professionalism in the administrative ranks meant less efficiency and more corruption, and it gave American-born Spaniards, or Creoles, the chance to acquire power. *Limeños*, as residents of Lima were known, began purchasing offices in the city council in 1561. By 1575 Lima-born whites held more offices than their peninsular-born counterparts. The only control the Crown retained was limiting the tenure of positions and mandating that offices were not to be sold in perpetuity.

Philippus II. Caroli V. filius, Hispaniarum, Indiarum, Neapolis, Siciliæ, Hierosolymæ, etc. rex catholicus. Mediolani, Brabantiæ, Geldriæ, etc. dux. Flandriæ, Hollandiæ, Hannoniæ, etc. comes. Aetatis suæ 59. 1516

King Philip II, who began selling the office of corregidor *in colonial Peru to the highest bidders after Spain went bankrupt in the 1550s* (Library of Congress)

Under this system local officials known as *corregidores* were no longer state-appointed bureaucrats but powerful local agents who had received loans from the merchants in the Casa de Contratación in Seville to buy their positions. To repay their loans *corregidores* forced the sale of goods at exorbitant prices on the indigenous population. The Indians suffered extortion and punishment under these circumstances. Those Indians not living on an *encomienda* or under the jurisdiction of a *corregimiento,* the land under the *corregidor's* command, had to pay their tributes directly to the king through the royal bank. Due to the population decline, corruption, neglect, and the ongoing civil strife, tributes often went unpaid.

The Council of the Indies dealt with this situation by promulgating the so-called New Laws (Leyes Nuevas). The New Laws were a collection of royal decrees meant to reform the *encomienda* system and, more important, to limit the growing power of the *encomenderos.* The man put in charge of implementing this more rigorous set of laws was Peru's first viceroy, Blasco Núñez Vela, with the help of Peru's first archbishop, Jerónimo de Loayza.

Both appointees arrived in Peru in March 1544, well after the news about the provisions of the New Laws had reached the colonies. Núñez Vela received a hostile reception when he officially proclaimed the laws in the cities of Piura and Trujillo. Protests grew the closer he came to Lima, and when he finally reached the capital, the *audiencia* members rebelled against his authority, deposed him, and sent him back on his way to Spain under guard. Núñez Vela, however, escaped his captors and assembled an armed force to reassert his authority in Lima. He never made it. He died near Quito in a battle against one of the Pizarro brothers.

In 1546 Pedro de La Gasca (1485–1567?) was sent from Spain to try again to implement the new legislation. La Gasca may have been one of the first Spanish representatives to the colonies who was appointed for merit. He had been born near Ávila in 1493 and was of humble origins. He attended the University of Alcalá de Henares and the University in Salamanca. In 1537 he became a vicar to the archbishop of Toledo and eventually became a minister of the Inquisition and a *visitador* (inspector) of the kingdom of Valencia. The Council of the Indies selected him, rather than a military man, to bring peace efforts to the trouble-ridden Peruvian viceroyalty.

La Gasca carried new orders, new appointments, and new goals in his luggage. He had been appointed president of Lima's *audiencia,* and as such, he was to become a powerful arbiter of ongoing disputes. Additionally, he was to interrogate and judge past and present state officials; he could pardon or punish transgressions, initiate new conquests, and renew or cancel existing *encomiendas*. His power was almost unlimited, all the more so because he was allowed to use royal income to pay for any expenses he considered necessary and engage in businesses on behalf of the Crown.

While on his way to Peru, La Gasca heard about the death of Núñez Vela. He returned to Panama and began to organize his takeover of the Peruvian viceroyalty. He wrote numerous letters to Peruvian *encomenderos* and made sure each one of them also received the letter signed by Charles V disapproving the *encomenderos'* separatist stances. He garnered support through his diplomatic efforts, but warfare could not be avoided. Within a year of La Gasca's arrival, the new viceroy defeated Gonzalo Pizarro in 1548 at a small battle at Jaquijaguana near Cuzco. Twenty people were killed, and Gonzalo Pizarro and his main associates were captured and executed. Disloyal *encomenderos* lost their properties, and La Gasca—aided by the archbishop of Lima, Jerónimo de Loayza—redistributed land and Indians to those who had proven loyal to the king. Due to the tremendous opposition, the New Laws were not fully implemented until the beginning of Viceroy Francisco de Toledo y Figueroa's reign (1569–81).

The makeover of the tribute system went hand in hand with an interesting debate on who or what Indians were, how they should be treated, and what their obligations would be. Some denied that Indians (and blacks) had souls, were thus unredeemable for eternal salvation, and thereby available as slaves. Others advocated treating Indians fairly as human beings; without the voluntary submission of the indigenous population to the Crown, they argued, Spain would never be able to exercise real power, and the king would be considered a despot rather than a benevolent father. The practical consequence of the second position was the abolition of the *encomienda* system. The main spokesman for this position was the friar Bartolomé de Las Casas, who debated the issues before the Council of the Indies. As a result of these discussions, Indians were declared to have redeemable souls and to be potentially loyal, thus protected vassals of the king.

Amid civil strife, ideological debates, and the gradual disappearance of the *encomiendas*, the silver mines of Potosí in modern-day Bolivia were "discovered" in 1545 (the Indians had long known of their existence). The rapidly increasing profits from silver mining and substantial reforms went hand in glove.

4

COLONIAL PERU (1568–1700)

While serious problems remained for the long term, by 1569, when Francisco Toledo y Figueroa became viceroy, the colonial system had begun to settle into a pattern that provided some measure of stability. The indigenous population, whose numbers went into a drastic decline soon after the conquest, was manipulated and exploited for the benefit of the Spanish colonists in Peru and of the Spanish Crown. The backbone of the colonial economy came to be the mining of silver after the discovery of one of the world's richest silver sites at Potosí, but agriculture and to a lesser degree manufacturing were also important economic endeavors.

The Viceroy and the *Reducciones*

The first attempts by the Spanish Crown to govern Peru through a viceroy had failed to bring stability and order to the colony. Núñez Vela was killed by rebels before he could claim his office, and the second viceroy, the elderly Antonio de Mendoza (who had been viceroy of Mexico for 15 years), died after a year in office. The third viceroy, Andrés Hurtado de Mendoza, marqués de Cañete, was replaced after only two years, a period during which he attempted to quell unrest among the settlers with large-scale executions and deportations. His successor, Diego López de Zúñiga, conde de Nieva, was perhaps the most unfortunate choice of all. He had a taste for ostentation and dissipation, and he was found one night lying mortally wounded in the gutter outside the home of his mistress, presumably the victim of an outraged husband.

However, the selection of Francisco de Toledo y Figueroa as fifth viceroy of Peru proved to be fortuitous and ended the string of failures. Toledo was born in Oropesa, Spain, in 1515. At age 19 he became one of the soldier-monks of the Order of Alcántara and fought in the religious wars in Europe. He was closely attached to Charles V, and he transferred his service to Philip II when the new king ascended to the throne. Like his royal master, Toledo was intensely religious, but he was also an able administrator.

When he came to the Peruvian viceroyalty in 1569, Toledo faced great challenges. The state coffers were empty because few revenues had been collected since 1552, pirates were approaching the extended coasts of the viceroyalty, and two indigenous groups were in revolt—the Araucanians to the south and the Incas in Vilcabamba.

Perhaps most ominous were the accounts he heard from everywhere in the viceroyalty of a rapidly decreasing indigenous population. It was clear that demographic disaster had hit the native population, although modern scholars widely disagree as to its dimensions. Estimates of the preconquest population of the Andes region range widely from 3 million to 30 million people (or more). Estimating a population of around 9 million people in 1520, Noble D. Cook, a U.S. historian and demographer, states in *Demographic Collapse: Indian Peru, 1520–1620* (1981) that the population in the viceroyalty had plummeted to 1.3 million natives a half century later and decayed still further to 600,000 by 1630. Peru's indigenous population reached its lowest after the 1718–20 epidemics. Such astronomical death tolls were the result of the devastation and disruption caused by military defeat, complicated by its psychological effects and accelerated by the spread of European diseases to which the Indians had no immunity. Epidemics continued well into the 19th century. In Peru it was not until 1800 that the population showed signs of an upward curve, reaching a total of approximately 700,000 people at the turn of the century.

Viceroy Toledo disembarked at Paita on the northern Peruvian coast in September 1569 and decided to continue his trip to Lima by land. This trip was symbolic of his grand reform plan to personally visit all of his new dominion. Others before him had undertaken a similar task of evaluating the human and natural resources of the colony, but their energy and will had failed. Toledo enlisted the help of 60 specially appointed *visitadores* (inspectors) to travel and study the 14 provinces into which the Viceroyalty of Peru was initially divided (Lima, Trujillo, Guayaquil and Puerto Viejo, Zamora, Loja and León, Quito and Cuenca, Chachapoyas and Moyobamba, Huánuco, Huamanga and Cuzco, Arequipa, Chucuito, La Paz, La Plata, and Potosí). Among these *visitadores* were some of the most brilliant thinkers of their time, mostly priests and lawyers, including Juan de Matienzo, Cristóbal de Molina, Damián de la Bandera, and Cristóbal de Albornoz. The main goals of these visits were to regulate the tribute amounts Indians were to pay, to manage the *encomenderos* and others who had mistreated or abused Indians, and to assess the demographic disaster as tribute exactions had to be lowered according to the reduced number of Indians in each settlement.

A major result of the study was a new policy to relocate and concentrate the dispersed Indian population into *pueblos* (villages), where they could be better controlled, counted, exploited for labor, and cared for. These new villages were called *reducciones*. The idea was not new. A royal official named Lope García de Castro had previously proposed the relocation of Indians in connection with the establishment of the *corregimientos*. In the province of Huarochiri, for example, more than 100 small settlements had been converted to 17 *reducciones*, each holding between 1,000 and 1,700 people.

The establishment of *reducciones* often meant that different ethnic groups had to adapt their lifestyles and their lives together in the same village under an increasingly strong colonial state presence. The *reducciones*, for example, partially dismantled the dispersed settlement pattern of the Incas that was meant to ensure a varied diet with produce from different ecological niches for local communities. As such, *reducciones* increased the risks of a bad harvest and disrupted peasant self-sufficiency and long-established customs.

Reducciones were administered by local agents called *corregidores*, and each *reducción* within a *corregimiento* had a *curaca* or cacique (native chief) as representative and leader. These agents became the hinges of a dual society with Spaniards on one side and Indians on the other, or, as the sections were called then, the *república de españoles* and the *república de indios*.

The relocation of the indigenous populations was key to organizing tribute collection and, perhaps more important, to exploiting Indian labor through the *mita*. Mit'a was originally a labor draft system used in the Chimor kingdom and by the Inca. The Spaniards, however, reintroduced the Europeanized, state-organized *mita* especially for the newly discovered silver mines in Potosí (in present-day Bolivia).

A total of 13 provinces in the vicinity of the mines were subjected to *mita* obligations. Every year in these provinces one-seventh of the adult males subject to paying tribute had to labor in the mines (between the ages of 18–50). Indians dreaded labor in the unsafe and unhealthy mines and often escaped the *reducciones* to return to their former homes. As more and more peasants fled to their earlier communities and some disappeared outright, never to be accounted for again, the *mita* provinces soon lost most of their population. Empty *mita* provinces were then repopulated by the forced resettlement of another indigenous population. These incoming Indians often did not own land but worked for other peasant families. With no land, their tribute payments were lower. Having no access to land also meant, at least in principle, that they could not be recruited for *mita* obligations.

Indian resistance and high mobility led to labor shortage in the mines, a continued problem for mine owners and the colonial state alike. Mechanisms were invented to retain *mita* laborers or to hire more expensive salaried laborers. To retain laborers, mine owners advanced money to workers, making sure that *mitayos* would not be able to repay the accumulated debt. As a consequence workers were forced to stay in the mines, and many were never able to return to their homes. For this reason, over the course of time, *mitayos* brought their families with them to the mines. Children and women ended up working in the mines to supplement the meager income.

The Indian *reducciones* soon subsidized the extraction of ore. Slowly the composition of the labor force in the mines changed from a predominantly *mita* labor force to an increasing number of salaried and more specialized workers. Nonetheless, working conditions in the mines did not improve. Hundreds of *mitayos* died from accidents in the mine tunnels, and silicosis, a lung disease produced by ore dust, greatly lowered life expectancy among mine workers.

The Agrarian Landscape

In spite of the depopulation of vast areas of the Peruvian viceroyalty, much of the local agrarian economy survived the immediate impact of conquest. Moreover, the early *encomiendas* assigned to Spanish conquistadores greatly relied on what was already in place, especially the indigenous ways of organizing space and exchange. However, there were also some salient changes. The redistributive role played by the Inca state disappeared. Cuzco was replaced by Lima and Potosí; *mitimaes* (indigenous groups displaced for labor) returned to their communities of origin; and labor-intensive farming tracts were abandoned, thus reducing the total of usable agrarian land. The land formerly assigned to the Inca or the Sun now reverted to the Spanish Crown. The Spanish Crown in turn, reallocated those portions of land either to a new *encomendero* or, eventually, to any Spaniard capable of paying for it. In addition to laboring their own fields, Indians now had to work on the land of the *encomendero* instead of the land of the Inca or the Sun.

THE *ENCOMENDEROS'* BOUNTY

According to the regulations imposed around 1549, an *encomendero* or *encomendera* (there were some women, usually inheriting widows, who had *encomiendas*) could request from every 1,000 Indians under his or her control the following items and services over the course of a year.

Tributes/payments in kind:

- 200 pesos in gold or silver
- 1,400 cotton robes
- 8 tablecloths
- 80 handkerchiefs
- 60 pounds of cotton thread
- 50 baskets of chilies
- 3 loads of potatoes at each harvest
- 1,200 chickens
- 100 eggs
- 24 pounds of fresh fish each Friday and holiday
- 60 ounces of salted fish
- 30 loads of salt
- 25 pigs
- 600 loads of carob
- wood and wood products

Personal services:

- The planting of 25 *fanegas'* worth of grains, 10 of wheat, and two of beans on communal lands (a *fanega* was equal to one and a half bushels)
- 60 Indians delivered by the *curaca* to plant and harvest 10 *fanegas* of wheat and corn on the land of the *encomendero*
- 15 Indians for domestic service
- 14 Indians to take care of cattle
- Indians for all transportation

The allocation of land to private Spanish owners through a mechanism called the *composición de tierras* initiated the development of the haciendas (farming estates) and some haciendas also developed out of the *encomienda* system.

An Indian's official tribute obligations as imposed by the colonial government involved the delivery of a large share of local produce and

The llama was, and continues to be, a central symbol of the Andes. Much of the agriculture of the region in the 16th century depended on the animal for food, fiber, and transportation. (Photofrenetic/Alamy)

free labor, but the list of items an *encomendero* was legally allowed to receive was accepted only grudgingly by *encomenderos* because it limited their exploitation of Indian labor and wealth. Since government control over *encomenderos* was still weak by the mid-16th century, *encomenderos* probably obtained higher revenues than those suggested by the official regulations. Similarly haciendas were organized along much the same lines. Instead of paying for labor used to cultivate the hacienda lands, hacendados insisted that laborers had to pay in kind and labor for their use of hacienda lands.

Three distinct phases are recognizable in the evolution of the relationship among *encomiendas,* Indian tributes, and state policies. Each phase reshaped the agrarian landscape.

The first phase, from 1532 to 1548, saw the most intense period of civil strife among *encomenderos* and the feuding and warfare between Almagro's and Pizarro's followers. During this first period there still was no regulated taxation, and locally most of the preexisting patterns of production, exchange, and consumption prevailed. Spanish settlers adapted the practices of tribute and *mita* implemented by the Inca state to obtain labor and produce from Indians but altered the top of the

CONCENTRATION OF THE TRIBUTE-PAYING POPULATION

The Indian population that owed tribute was densely concentrated. In 1570, for example, only 5.8 percent of all highland encomiendas were in Huamanga. But in this one province was 47 percent of the total highland population, and there 55 percent of all cloth was produced; 29 percent of all wheat, 29 percent of all corn, and 33 percent of all potatoes were grown; and 58 percent of all chickens and 70 percent of all sheep and llamas were raised (Urrutia 1985, 31, 36).

political ladder: the supreme Inca was replaced by the Spanish king, and the elite Incan *orejones,* by the Spanish *encomenderos.*

In the second phase, from 1549 to 1570, the first regulatory decrees reached the colonies, and official tax regulations were implemented. The lists of exactions varied according to local conditions and were mainly paid in kind. Money was still a scarce commodity in the colonial internal market. Slowly at first, and more rapidly with the growth of mining production in Potosí, a tribute in money emerged.

The third phase, from 1570 to around 1630, witnessed the uniformity of tribute payments in money and a state-organized *mita* system. Gradually, under Viceroy Toledo the Spanish Crown gained control over the colonies and diminished the tremendous power of the *encomenderos.*

Although the *mita* labor system empowered *encomenderos* who were in charge of organizing this labor draft, it was also a system that in the long run hampered the *encomenderos'* ability to obtain Indian labor, especially for their own fields. Every Spaniard in the colonies, *encomendero* or not, could, in principle, petition *mita* labor. This included especially hacienda owners and *obrajes* (textile workshop) owners. The higher the number of Spaniards requesting *mita* labor, the less labor was available for the *encomenderos* and, eventually, the mines, the economic endeavor the Spanish Crown was most interested in. A higher demand for labor and a rapidly decreasing population made labor more valuable than land itself. Without labor, *encomenderos* saw their revenues dissipate as they were left with less agrarian produce to sell in nearby cities and in the mines. As a result, and particularly in Peru's coastal cities, food prices increased, especially food prices for products consumed by the Spanish. Wheat, for instance, cost six reales per *fanega* (a measure equivalent to about one and a half bushels) in 1558; in 1593 it cost six pesos, or eight times as much. On average (depending on the actual silver content of the coins used) one peso was equivalent to eight reales. For the sake of comparison the average tribute amount paid by Indians amounted to four reales per semester.

Encomenderos responded by specializing their production and adding cattle and sheep to their commercial ventures. To do this they needed more land, in particular pasture land, which they gradually obtained through the *composición de tierras;* by purchases from caciques; through rental agreements turned into ownership, often through legal trickery and dishonesty; and by the violent seizure of lands belonging to communities and peasant families. Seemingly all this happened without much Indian protest, in large measure because there were few Indians left to protest.

As a part of royal policies meant to limit the power of *encomenderos,* around 1540 the Spanish Crown not only appointed *corregidores* but also actively sought to incorporate non-*encomenderos* into the local *cabildos* (municipalities) and sell smaller tracts of land to Spanish newcomers. Gradually, some *encomiendas* were split into smaller estates, introducing a more dispersed land tenure pattern with more people (especially Spaniards) owning more land. Labor for the growing number of agrarian enterprises came through competition for Indian *mita* labor and, increasingly, through the rapidly expanding slave trade. Money to acquire landed property came from Spain's rich merchants and the Catholic Church.

With the power of the *encomenderos* diminished and the *corregidores* in place to guard the Crown's interests, the colonial scheme seemed to be finally in place. In reality this was far from true. Continued warfare in Europe emptied royal coffers, and in order to produce income, the Spanish Crown resorted to selling bureaucratic offices, among them the office of *corregidor.* Earlier provisions forbidding *corregidores* to own land within their jurisdictions were ignored. They bought land or obtained it through illegal means, used Indian labor as much as possible, and in general wrung the system for all the profits they could. Some *oidores* (judges for the courts of the *audiencias*) overlooked or even participated in contraband transactions, and administrative corruption down to the level of the *cabildo* scribes became more evident after 1633, when more bureaucratic positions, especially in the state's accounting and treasury offices, became available to the highest bidder in spite of stern resistance from the Council of the Indies. Depending on the position, bids ranged from 2,500 pesos to up to 20,000 pesos, roughly the value of five to 50 slaves.

A *CORREGIDOR'S* ACCOUNTING

Following were the tradeoffs for a *corregidor* in the province of Chancay on Peru's northern coast around the mid-18th century.

Manuel de Elcorrobarrutia paid 16,000 pesos for his appointment, plus an additional 4,000 pesos for fees and taxes. Paying an assistant and an agent and a lawyer in Lima required yet another 7,000 pesos. He estimated his personal living expenses at 15,000 pesos. Gratuities to officials in Lima, entertainment for the viceroy when he visited Chancay, and expenses for the audit and *residencia* (audit after tenure) cost 9,000 pesos. Interest on this total was 8,700 pesos. To distribute through reparto (forced sale of goods to Indian peasants) 1,900 mules, the *corregidor* anticipated paying 67,004 pesos. This amount purchased the mules and paid for their feed and distribution, tax, salary for collection agents, and interest. But he expected to receive only 80,000 pesos from selling the mules and thus had to sell 46,724 pesos' worth of other items to cover his investment. With only 1,125 able-bodied adult males in the province in 1754, each household had to contribute an average of 112 pesos for this *corregidor* to break even after his tenure. And, these were payments Indian peasants had to contribute aside from the tribute and the *mita* owed to the colonial state (Burkholder and Johnson 2001, 88).

In many parts of Peru mules and donkeys provided the principal means of transportation for both people and goods. This watercolor from the 19th century shows a seller of grass fodder. (Library of Congress)

Most bidders were Criollos, or Creoles (American-born whites of Spanish descent), rather than Spaniards born in Iberia (*peninsulares*), despite the rise in the number of Spanish people coming to the colonies, especially between 1550 and 1650 (Mörner 1976, 766–767). This immigration itself spurred the demand for office as a means of fast enrichment and enhanced social standing. Toward the end of the 17th century one could buy a place on an *audiencia,* the high court. By 1700 the office of viceroy in Mexico was for sale, too. This general trend led to a closer alliance between Criollos and bureaucrats and also opened the doors for Criollos to reach high office. It was also the beginning of an emerging regionalism and era of rifts between the central power and regional interests that would later lead to the continent's fragmentation into many nation-states as a result of the wars of independence.

Silver Mining, *Mita*, and Economic Changes

In 1545 what turned out to be nearly an entire mountain of silver (Cerro Rico) was discovered at Potosí, then part of the Viceroyalty of Peru and now in modern-day Bolivia. The fabulous mines of Potosí created an incredible stream of wealth that flowed from the mountain to Lima and eventually to Spain. Silver worth hundreds of millions of pesos was removed from deep tunnels and galleries, refined, and converted to coins in Potosí's Mint (Casa de la Moneda). The cost, however, was high on the Indian *mitayos* who provided the labor for the mines.

Almost as important as the silver mines at Potosí was the mercury mine at Huancavelica, discovered in 1563. Mercury was crucial to the processing of silver ore, and before mercury from Huancavelica became available, it had been necessary to import mercury at great cost from Europe and haul it over the Andes. The proximity of the silver and mer-

Annual Silver Exports from Callao, 1600–1780	
Year	Amount in Pesos
1600	2,444,376
1610	1,640,625
1620	573,453
1650	2,720,000
1675	1,837,155
1708	300,000
1739	586,043
1780	400,000

Note: The sharp fluctuations in value were owing to political conditions, fluctuations in the production and availability of mercury, costs of maintaining the colonies, level of smuggling, the diminution of the population in Potosí, and the decreasing availability of rich ores.
Source: Fisher (1977, 29–30)

cury mines in Peru, however, amplified the potential for exploitation of the colony's mineral wealth.

The several silver mines in and around Potosí were privately owned, often by merchants who had acquired the mines when previous mine owners failed to repay loans. The principal resource needed to work these mines was labor. To achieve production and export goals, the mine owners needed labor from approximately 13,500 *mitayos*. *Mitayos,* most often with their entire families, were sent out by *corregidores* and *encomenderos* from the provinces closest to Potosí. The amount of laborers provided by each province could not exceed one-seventh of the male adult tributary population between 18 and 50 years of age. *Mitayos* were required to stay for only one year in the mines. Once Indians had fulfilled their *mita* duty, they were not legally required to become *mitayos* again until seven years had elapsed. Mine owners were required to pay for the transport costs of the *mitayos* from their home community to the mine. In exchange for their labor, *mitayos* were to receive a salary. This salary, however, was fixed at a lower level than the current salaries for free labor and often was only a minimal salary equal to the tribute payment. According to British historian Peter Bakewell, the nominal daily salary for a *mitayo* was 2.75 reales, whereas a mine owner could receive 8 reales (one peso) if he resold the labor of a *mitayo* to another mine owner, a hacendado, or an *obraje* (textile factory)

Preconquest Indian laborers work a surface mine with hand tools and crude equipment. When the Spanish dispossessed the Indians and took over the mines, they slowly introduced more sophisticated methods and specialization, especially in the lucrative silver mines at Potosí. The labor, however, was supplied by Indians fulfilling their mita *obligations. (Art Today)*

owner (1984, 101, 125). Thus, the earnings obtained from owing a mine could be based on reselling Indian labor as well as extracting silver.

Although the daily hours of labor were supposedly regulated, few mine owners obeyed the law. Most tried to lower *mitayos'* salary as much as they could. Working conditions were insecure, unhealthy, and, in general, devastating. Every *mitayo* who possibly could tried to evade *mita* labor in the mines or moved to provinces where *mita* labor in the mines was not yet imposed. Often Indians turned to haciendas where a Spanish hacendado (himself interested in keeping the labor) could provide some protection against the mining *mita*. Some Indians hired other Indians to replace them, often by paying a full salary to their surrogates.

Initially 81,000 Indians lived in the *mitayo* provinces, but by 1633, this number had dropped to 40,115. In 1662 the number was down to 16,000 in 1662; in 1683 it was at 10,633. In response, Spanish mine owners, with the colonial state's endorsement, began looking for new *mitayos* in other provinces, thus expanding the geographic area from which *mitayos* were recruited, ever more removed from the mining sites. This pushed Indians to seek new places to live and generated large numbers of uprooted peasant families. Some settled on haciendas, others in existing peasant communities to become tributaries without land. In the early 1680s the total Indian population of Upper Peru (modern Bolivia) was half its size of 1570, and half the population in the 16 *mita* provinces were *yanaconas* (sharecroppers) or *forasteros* (landless peasants who had migrated from other communities) who paid tribute at a lower rate. This situation alarmed colonial authorities and the Council of the Indies because more Indians without land also meant less revenues to the state, both from tribute payments and from silver production.

The colonial state recognized that this situation needed to change and, after 1659, attempted to enforce new regulations. In 1670 Viceroy Pedro Fernández de Castro, conde de Lemos even proposed to replace *mita* labor with free labor. However, any proposed change encountered strong resistance from mine owners, and it was not until 1718 that the Council of the Indies—after failing to apply any previous regulations—reassessed the issue. Members of the council argued that mining in New Spain was very successful without the *mita*. In consultation with officials in Lima and Charcas (the seat of colonial government for Bolivia at the time), the council signed a decree in 1719 that in writing abolished the *mita* in the mines. But this decree was never applied in Potosí. It was not until 1812—in the wake of liberal reform in Spain—that *mita* was actually abolished. Indians continued to provide "free services" of various kinds for many decades after this.

The *mita* for the mercury mines in Huancavelica followed a similar historical pattern but on a small scale. At the peak of the mines' production, 620 Indian *mitayos* labored in Huancavelica. Toward the end of the 18th century the number declined to only 165. Unlike the silver mines in the Peruvian viceroyalty, the mercury mines of Almadén in Spain were a state monopoly from very early on, around 1555. A similar pattern was put in place when the mercury mines in Huancavelica were discovered. Only the transport of mercury to Potosí was allowed to be taken over by private individuals, who were restricted to a certain amount of mercury. Private entrepreneurs were allowed to extract the mercury but were forced to sell the mercury to the state. The state would then allocate mercury to individual silver mines and also organized the export of excess mercury. This state control was a way to keep mercury prices low, assure a market to producers, and, most important, regulate silver production.

The most efficient control on silver production, however, was the mint in Potosí. Without minting, silver could not circulate in the colonies or elsewhere. The image of the king on circulating coins was also an endorsement of the silver content of the coins and thus a trustworthy medium of exchange. By controlling the minting process the state not only knew how much silver was produced in the privately owned silver mines but also cashed in one-fifth of the minted coins as a tax (called the *quinto real,* or royal fifth) imposed and paid at the mint. For many decades this tax—together with the Indian tribute—was the major source of income for the Spanish Crown.

Besides the *mita* in the mines (mainly Potosí and Huancavelica, but also in smaller mines in Puno and Oruro), *mitayos* were also allocated to other Spanish enterprises: road construction, textile workshops, haciendas, urban water and sewage projects, and ditch cleaning. This distribution of *mita* labor was often mediated by mine owners, who "resold" mita labor to people willing to pay up to 365 pesos a year. With around 40 reallocated Indians, mine owners could obtain an income that was equivalent to the annual salary of a high bureaucrat within the colonial state, basically without doing a thing. These reallocated Indians were called *indios de faltriquera.*

Aside from labor the mines and the people working in the mines needed a minimum survival infrastructure: mules, horses, water, clothes, food, and housing. Located at an altitude of approximately 15,000 feet, Potosí could not provide for itself; consequently, these needs had to be provided for through imports from other regions in the colonies and from Spain. Mules and horses were brought in from

ORGANIZATION OF THE MINES

Historian Peter Bakewell has described the specialization and diversification of labor in the mines at Potosí that slowly developed in colonial South America. When the Spanish took over the mines, they adopted the unsophisticated methods and crude technology of the native miners. During these early days the only specialists were probably the *guayradores,* who ran windblown furnaces, and the operators of the ore-crushing machine called a *quimbalete.* Otherwise, there was little apparent distinction made between workers who cut the ore from the facings and those who carried it to the surface. Native miners to whom the Spanish owners leased portions of the mines were known as *indios varas,* and they served as supervisors of the ordinary native workers, most of whom were presumably *yanaconas.* The miners probably replaced their native tools with European iron picks and bars early on, but not until the second part of the 16th century were more efficient methods of mining and extraction put in place and native miners trained for specialized roles. The use of mercury in the refining process led to higher levels of labor specialization in the mines and the replacement of the *guayradores.* An additional consequence of this technological change was that Indian mine workers lost the technical control of silver production (Bakewell 1984, 137–138).

Tucumán and Piura; water had to be channeled to the mining sites, and ditches had to be built; clothes came from the *obrajes* in Quito and Cuzco; food came from various haciendas and peasant communities; wheat reached Potosí from Cochabamba. Mining production, in fact, activated a wide circuit of internal commerce with a clear regional specialization. As more regions were drawn into the mining circuit, they became new sites of a lively commercial exchange. When many people in Quito worked to produce cloth for Potosí, other local people provided the goods needed in these textile workshops. Often the emergence and continued growth of haciendas, plantations, and *obrajes* occurred in the wake of the expansion of mining production and urban growth.

Producing Textiles in the Colonies

Even though the Spanish Crown never encouraged textile or any other manufacturing industry in the colonies, textiles were produced there.

Although not as important in terms of state revenues as mining, textile workshops *(obrajes)* were an important part of the economy and had long-term significance.

Major numbers of salaried workers—Indians, blacks, mestizos, and even Spaniards—worked in the *obrajes* side-by-side with *mitayos. Obraje*

MINING CYCLES

Acccording to Argentine historian Carlos S. Assadourian, mining in Potosí underwent several cycles between 1540 and 1650. Mining cycles greatly influenced other sectors of the colonial economy and the ways in which remote regions interacted with one another.

During the first cycle, from 1540 to 1570, mines were dispersed and privately owned, and ore was extracted using Indian technology *(huayra)*. Food for the miners and other needs were provided by *encomenderos,* based on an in-kind tribute.

A second cycle occurred between 1570 and 1580, when the Spanish colonial government created a monopoly on the purchase and distribution of mercury, which was essential to refining the silver ore by the newer amalgamation process. The need for food and other services expanded during this period, and these essentials were provided by haciendas. The increased demand prompted more haciendas to specialize in producing for the mines, and that in turn helped reshape land tenure, as more land came into the hands of Spanish landholders. *Encomenderos* received tribute in money, often directly from the mine owners, and Indians were regrouped in *reducciones* (large, consolidated villages) under 83 *corregidores*. More and more *mitayos* became salaried laborers on a stable basis. As a result of these developments a new regional division of labor stimulated the consumption of imported merchandise, and Lima lost some of its hegemony. Mines remained dispersed and privately owned, but the sources of capital expanded to accommodate the increasingly costly investments in mining.

During a third cycle, from 1580 to 1650, no new technologies were introduced, despite the diminishing silver content of the ore. The number of *mitayos* fell from 13,500 to approximately 4,000, and the reduced demand for food and other needs led to a decay of haciendas tied to mining production but allowed the survival of haciendas whose markets were in the growing urban centers. Revenues to the colonial government declined also (Assadourian 1982, 18–55).

owners did not hesitate to use conscript labor if needed. In principle Indians were barred from wearing Spanish clothes, but the Spanish Crown had to allow for some local textile production in order to clothe the native population. The government, however, did not want textiles produced in the colonies to compete with imports from Spain. Colonial textile production fluctuated sharply, therefore, but saw amazing peaks during times of crisis in Europe and when the sea routes were temporarily blocked. Sharp drops of textile production followed Crown-decreed shutdowns of the *obrajes* to suppress competition: As the colonies became more self-sufficient, less money entered the Spanish economy and the royal coffers.

Economic and political fluctuations affected the large *obrajes,* especially those that produced high-quality cloth. The first decades of the 17th century were a particularly difficult time period for *obrajes* because of more stringent government control in the form of *visitas* (inspections), legal disputes among *obraje* owners, and labor shortages. Mining was still at a peak, and most laborers were used in mining production. Later, during most of the 18th century, in spite of prevailing restrictions, *obrajes* expanded under Bourbon crown rule and even received a large injection of church-owned capital, followed by an increase in productivity and quality. As a consequence, internal regional commerce expanded and labor conditions improved.

Quito and Cuzco were major textile producers from around 1550 onward. *Obrajes* with more than 1,000 workers produced cloth that was exported to the Atlantic coast port of La Plata. Textile production used Andean technologies to transform cotton and, increasingly, sheep wool. Whenever the textile production declined it also affected sheep and cotton producers, who lost an important market for their products. Whenever textile production expanded, herds and cotton fields multiplied. Puno's economy, for example, depended on the export of its wool to the Cuzco *obrajes* and followed their ups and downs very closely.

Large *obrajes* coexisted with smaller textile workshops, the so-called *obrajillos. Obrajillos* were generally operated by peasant families and peasant communities and as such were much less subject to state control or economic policies. Nevertheless, it was the produce from *obrajillos* that reached Potosí, clothed *mitayos,* and was part of the revenues received by *corregidores* through the forced sale of goods—in this case, coarse cloth.

When Spain changed its international economic policies to adopt free trade in 1778, it was a huge blow to the large *obrajes* in Peru. Cuzco's production of textiles dropped from 3 million *varas* (a linear measurement of 33 inches) in 1770 to only 700,000 at the beginning of the 19th century. The decree opened the door to competition from overseas, mainly British manufactures, and from the region, such as *obrajes* in La Paz, La Plata, and Córdoba. While most large *obrajes* had to shut down, the smaller *obrajillos* survived unchanged.

The economic influence of textile production was perhaps even wider than that of the mines. In contrast to mining, which was basically the extraction and export of raw materials with little added value beyond the smelting and minting processes, the textile industry required more skill, from producing the raw materials to spinning, weaving, coloring, and tailoring. It involved a wide array of specialized artisans and thus created labor opportunities for the increasing number of mestizos. Overall it encouraged a diversification of the social-occupational structure and an incipient salaried labor force. When this process was truncated by metropolitan rulings, the colonial internal market was hampered.

Maritime Power and the Organization of Colonial Trade

Spanish merchants and the Spanish Crown were interested in maintaining tight control over maritime commerce. Commercial centralization—in other words, a monopoly—was the strategy the Crown used to control the flow of goods from Spain to the colonies and back. After mining, commerce was the most profitable economic endeavor during colonial times and the main link between the colony and the motherland and between the merchant guilds in Seville, Lima, and Mexico City. In spite of high revenues (or because of them), Spain's monopolistic control of trade was riddled with problems and contradictions that gradually led to its demise and to its replacement by free trade toward the end of the 18th century. Before this happened, however, a rich array of commercial activities developed that created what sociologist Immanuel Wallerstein has called the first "world economy."

The Casa de Contratación, the Sevillian merchant guild, was established in 1503, before the Council of the Indies even existed. When silver became a crucial part of the equation, the Crown saw the need to tighten its control not only on commerce but also on the Seville-based merchants. Hence the Crown made the Casa de Contratación an agency of the state to implement the state's control on commerce: It granted licenses to engage in trade, regulated the amounts of goods exported, accounted for revenues, and collected trade taxes.

Commercial monopoly was organized through the "fleet system," which reached its final form around 1560. Twice a year, the Spanish fleet—after 1537 accompanied by warships guarding against pirate attacks—left Seville loaded with goods for the colonies. One fleet docked at the ports of Portobello (Panama) and Cartagena (Colombia). From Portobello the merchandise was carried by mules, horses, and Indian porters across the isthmus of Panama and then reloaded on ships on the western side to reach the ports on the Pacific coast of South America. From Cartagena the merchandise reached its southern destinations, Bogotá and Quito, by land.

The second fleet anchored in Veracruz (Mexico), and the merchandise continued its way to Puerto Rico, Santo Domingo, and Cuba. Commercial transactions took place in the ports of arrival. Merchants from all over the colonial territory participated in the annual markets (ferias), and it was also during these markets that the silver money destined for Spain was handed over to purchase the arriving goods. Both fleets rejoined in Havana to return to Seville.

CALIOV DE LIMA

The Callao harbor in the 16th century was the main seaport for Lima, from which ships shuttled silver and merchandise to and from Portobello, in Panama, as part of the Spanish fleet system. The wealth of the Peruvian mines and income from the Indian tribute flowed to Spain, and manufactured goods flowed back to the colonies. (Narrative and Critical History of America)

As the trade cycle reached a peak, Lima became a lively place, especially between April and June. During this time Lima was filled with new merchandise from all over the world. The fleet then returned to Panama, loaded with the money from Lima's merchants and the tributes paid by the indigenous population. According to chronicler Bernabé Cobo, 6 million ducados in silver bars, coins (reales), and *tejos* (disks) of gold left Lima every year until the beginning of the 17th century.

The fleet system was meant to protect the silver shipments from the colonies to Spain and enforce the Crown's monopoly. It consisted of, in essence, a basic exchange of controlled goods: Spain would provide manufactured items and food, and the colonies were to pay with silver and some tropical products (hides, sugar, tobacco, and cochineal). The ships were to be Spanish, and the benefits would increase fiscal revenues and fill the pockets of Castilian merchants.

Several historical processes explain the decay of the fleet system and with it the collapse of Spain's monopoly on world trade. Spain proved to be increasingly incapable of satisfying colonial demands, which were ever better met by local production—of textiles, for example, as well as traditionally Spanish goods such as wine, olive oil, and wheat—and by smuggling—especially of manufactured goods from England and France. Spain had to spend more and more money to protect its fleet and port fortifications in the colonies. In spite of such efforts smuggling increased, and along with the diversification of production inside the colonies, it diminished the importance of Spain as a supplier. The problem was temporarily alleviated when toward the end of the 16th century and the beginning of the 17th century, the Netherlands was added to the kingdom of Charles V, filling the ships of the Spanish fleet with more manufactured goods from northern Europe (mainly England). Spain itself soon became a re-exporter of goods manufactured elsewhere and a net exporter of silver, especially to England, to maintain its balance of trade. In 1567 the Netherlands became involved in great political turmoil, a turn of events that strengthened the hand of British merchants and Queen Elizabeth's piratical "sea dogs." Costs to protect the fleet skyrocketed. Still, the amount of merchandise kept growing, from 17,000 tons in 1540 to 32,000 in 1585.

Crisis Ensues: The 17th Century

Spain was less prosperous in the 17th century than it had been previously, because many of the basic premises of the fleet system had changed. The supply of silver had diminished, especially after 1630, and Lima-based merchants were no longer as dependent on products coming from Spain because local intracolonial production had diversified and increased. The defeat of the Spanish Armada by the English in 1588 was a devastating blow to Spain's monopoly. Thereafter, the number of foreign ships in the fleet system kept increasing. Between 1579 and 1587 foreign ships accounted for 5.9 percent of all ships leaving Seville; between 1588 and 1592 this percentage had increased to 21.3 percent. By 1630 one-third of the fleet consisted of non-Spanish ships. Toward the end of the 17th century, the majority of merchants within the mercantile elite in Seville were foreigners who had become "Spanish" through naturalization. In dire fiscal straits, the Spanish Crown not only took to the selling of the "privilege" of participating in the fleet, and thereby in colonial trade, but also increased taxes.

Between 1585 and 1630, the *avería*, an export tax, was increased from 1.7 to 6.0 percent on the reported value of the merchandise. The *almojarifazgo,* a tariff on exported and imported goods, was as high as 15.5 percent for products leaving Spain and 17.5 percent for products coming into Spain. To evade burdensome taxes Spanish merchants underdeclared the value of their shipments. Increasingly, foreign ships met the fleet in the open ocean, where they transferred their loads to fleet ships, thus escaping the watchful eye of the Casa de Contratación employees. Instability was further fueled by the outright confiscation of private silver shipments to Spain in 1620, 1629, 1635–38, and 1649, eroding confidence in the system. The consequences were the disintegration of the nation's tax system and bankruptcy. The Thirty Years War and the long war in the Netherlands had consumed the Potosí silver. At this point the fleet system was an international venture rather than an enforced Spanish monopoly. The total volume of exchange, both in terms of number of ships and amount of tons, had diminished by more than 50 percent between the end of the 16th and the end of the 17th centuries.

In the meantime port cities on the South American continent other than Lima were gaining momentum. Between 1615 and 1700 Buenos Aires grew from 1,000 inhabitants to 7,000 and flourished following a surge of smuggling. As a consequence more money from Potosí went to the eastern shores of the continent—to the detriment of Lima—and to Portuguese, Dutch, and British merchants—to the detriment of Peru's and Spain's merchants.

Inflation compounded these problems. Around 1640 the minting house in Potosí and the local Spanish officials decided to replace some of the silver contained in the silver peso with copper, thus tacitly diminishing the coin's real value. The "strong peso" (*peso fuerte*) became the "weak peso" (*peso feble*) and it did not take long for the alarm signals to reach European merchants.

Natural disaster also struck. In 1687 Lima was devastated by a series of earthquakes. Even the viceroy, Melchor Navarro y Rocafull, duque de la Palata, had to move to a tent on the Plaza de Armas, Lima's central plaza, for two months. Lima's archbishop estimated the damage at 150 million pesos. Devastation also reached the coastal valleys, where irrigation systems were destroyed, and the fields subsequently languished through many years of drought. Wheat had to be imported from Chile to prevent Lima inhabitants from starving. Another similarly devastating earthquake happened on October 28, 1746. Lima and Callao were completely destroyed, 10,000 people were killed, and only 25 houses remained (Hardoy 1951, 227, based on Bromley and Barbagelata, 1945).

By the end of the 17th century there were many signs that the economy of colonial Peru was in a state of decline, resulting primarily from the continuing drop in silver production and the disappearance of Spain's trade monopoly. Economic woes, coupled with the effects of natural disasters, pointed toward a similar decline in political life. Moreover, a change in the ruling dynasty in Spain transferred power to the Bourbon family, which tried—unsuccessfully—to reform the colonial system.

5

COLONIAL INSTITUTIONS AND THE BOURBON REFORMS (1700–1780)

A s the Spanish colonial enterprise took root and began to mature, a series of institutions developed that came to characterize life in the colony. Lima, for example, grew into a cosmopolitan center of Hispanic and Peruvian culture during the 17th and 18th centuries, and it became a place where *peruanos* of racially and ethnically mixed backgrounds encountered one another amid a bustling urban life. Among the most important colonial institutions based in Lima was the Roman Catholic Church, which in its various forms enjoyed wide powers and deep influence throughout Peru from the very beginning of the Spanish conquest. The church controlled many aspects of Peruvian society, although when it became a political or economic threat, the government made clear there were limits. After the Spanish Crown passed from the House of Hapsburg to the French Bourbons at the beginning of the 18th century, the new dynasty made vigorous attempts to reform the administration of the colony and bring it more closely into the orbit of the mother country but with only partial success. Stresses appeared that would lead to serious fissures.

The City, the Church, and the Orders

Lima, originally called the City of the Kings (Ciudad de los Reyes), was founded as the capital city of the Viceroyalty of Peru by Francisco Pizarro on January 18, 1535, when he solemnly declared his intention to establish a city there on the coast for the service of God and the king. That same day, Pizarro distributed city lots to his men, following the traditional grid plan common in Spain. Lima became a showcase of imperial power—the administrative, ceremonial, economic, political, and social center of a dominion that, at least during the first century of Spanish presence, controlled a geographical space larger than the Inca Empire.

Almost all important colonial institutions including the viceroy, the *audiencia,* the *cabildo,* the archbishopric, and the Inquisition were centered in Lima. By contemporary standards Lima was a cosmopolitan city with people from many different continents. According to the 1614 census, Lima counted more than 20,000 people and its black population from different regions in Africa (and their mixed-blood descendants) accounted for more than 50 percent of this. A total of 1,720 clergy members were counted in this same census.

Impressive ceremonies enhanced the image of the city. No fewer than 150 days a year were Sundays or holidays. Some festivities could last several months, such as to mark the birth of a new heir to the Spanish Crown. Typically the viceroy presided over a military parade marching toward the cathedral. There the archbishop held a solemn mass, a Te Deum. People then were in the streets celebrating, drinking, listening to band music, and wearing their best attire. All guilds participated, and so did slaves and freedmen and -women. At night there were more parades, with the participation of the cavalry and presided over by the *alcalde* (mayor) and the *oídores* (municipal judges). Celebrations reached a peak with fireworks and bullfights. Many holidays and festivities were religious and served to teach and reinforce Catholic ideas and principles.

Aside from churches, monasteries, and convents, one of the main instruments of power of the Catholic Church was the Inquisition, an

URBAN CATHOLICISM

Lima was the center of the Roman Catholic Church in Peru, and it attracted hundreds of priests, nuns, and monks. The Franciscan friar Buenaventura de Salinas y Córdoba, writing in 1630, claimed there were at least 400 parish priests in the city, not counting those in the port of Callao and the immediate surrounding countryside. He also recorded the presence of 1,366 nuns, served by 899 female slaves (known as *donadas*). The Augustinian Convent of the Incarnation alone occupied an entire city block and housed 450 nuns, 50 novices, and 276 slaves. There were similar numbers of friars from the Dominican, Franciscan, Mercedarian, and Jesuit orders, many of the latter serving as teachers in the city's schools (Salinas y Córdoba 1646, in Tibesar 1953).

institution whose existence long preceded Spain's conquest of the Americas. The Holy Inquisition was established in 1233 by Pope Gregory IX, and in 1238 in Spain by the Aragonese Crown, and was controlled by the Dominican order, which deferred to Rome for final decisions. The Spanish Inquisition was put in place in 1478 by King Ferdinand and Queen Isabella to suppress clandestine Jewish and Muslim worship, in addition to cults, magic, witchcraft, and sodomy.

According to Peruvian 19th-century essayist, Ricardo Palma, the Inquisition in Lima sentenced 44 people to death by burning at the stake (1983, 199–325). The main victims of persecution were Jewish merchants from Portugal, who apparently were condemned more on the grounds of their economic power and the subsequent envy of rivals than on real religious transgressions. Indians escaped the grip of the Inquisition because they were deemed "minors" who rather than burned should be converted and their traditional idols destroyed.

From the very beginnings of its colonial presence, the church's main goal was the conversion to Catholicism of the native Indians, though this evangelical commitment weakened somewhat after the 1570s. In this endeavor the church undertook the spiritual conquest of the new dominions. It was not an easy conquest; the Indians clung to their ancestral beliefs, and the indigenous populations spoke different languages and were dispersed in wide settlement patterns. Many Indians came to practice a syncretic form of religion that blended elements of their traditional beliefs and practices with selected parts of Catholicism. This produced a multilayered belief system and a great variety of combined rituals.

Several religious orders, whose members were organized outside the usual hierarchy of the church, were present at the very beginning of Pizarro's adventures in Peru. Franciscans and Mercedarians arrived prior to Atahualpa's execution, and Augustinians first stepped on Peruvian soil in 1551. In Peru—unlike Mexico—efforts at conversion of the Indians were hampered by the civil war between the early conquerors. It was the mid-16th century before the Catholic Church in Peru launched a massive campaign against traditional indigenous beliefs. *Huacas* (sacred shrines) and reverence of ancestors (that is, mummies) were banned, and the shrines and mummies themselves were destroyed by the Spaniards. In response an apocalyptic movement known as Taqui Onkoy appeared in the central Andes in 1560 and lasted until about 1570. Religious leaders of the Taqui Onkoy movement asked Indians to return to their *huacas*. The *huacas* were angry, they said, because Indians had neglected them; because they felt angry and abandoned, the *huacas* had in revenge caused epidemics to kill

A Peruvian Creole woman consults a Roman Catholic animero, *a priest who solicited charity for souls caught in purgatory.* (Library of Congress)

thousands of Indians. This was how indigenous religious leaders interpreted population decline.

In the early 17th century, however, in Jesuit historian Antonine Tibesar's interpretation, the church became an important social and economic player in the colonies; it had more American-born than peninsular priests and identified itself with the needs of colonial society. The ultimate control over church activities, nevertheless, remained with the Crown. The Crown maintained control over tithe collection (a 10 percent tax levied on agricultural production and livestock belonging to non-Indians) to feed the priests and nuns, and it also decided on church activities, buildings, and nominations, all the way to the archbishop. The Crown's right to make ecclesiastical appointments was called the royal *patronato.*

Throughout the colonial period tense relationships existed between the secular clergy, who were members of separate orders, such as the Jesuits or the Franciscans, and the regular clergy, who answered to the usual church hierarchy, headed by bishops and archbishops. Frequently, the Crown had to intervene to separate their spheres of responsibility in the colonies. Sometimes mutual antagonisms led to physical confrontations and the plunder of churches. In the long run the regular clergy in the orders were kept on the fringes of the colonial territory, preferably doing mission work among tribes in the Amazon basin.

The period's tensest moment of state-church relationships came with the expulsion of the Jesuit order by the Spanish Crown in 1767. Underlying this decision to oust the Jesuits were longstanding tensions between Rome and the European states. In Spain the king held the *patronato* right to appoint high ecclesiastical authorities, yet the Jesuits, since their founding as an order by Ignatius Loyola (1491–1586), pledged obedience to the pope. (Pope Paul III approved the order's statutes in 1540.) The Jesuits stood at the crossroads between two powers, the state and the church, and their ejection from the Spanish colonies had much to do with their questioning of the king's absolute power.

In Peru Jesuits had a long-standing history of rebellion against state direction and orders. The first eight members of the Jesuit order arrived in Lima during Francisco Toledo's viceroyalty. Toledo wanted them to take care of Indians living in Lima, in a district called Cercado. The Jesuits resisted and instead founded a school that soon came to compete with the University of San Marcos, founded in 1551 by royal decree. The viceroy allowed the Jesuit school, San Pablo, to keep its doors open, but only San Marcos could grant academic degrees. However, the Jesuits' educational prestige grew, and many Jesuits became the cultural and political leaders throughout the colonies. In their library at San Pablo in Lima, one could find books on how to build houses, construct water fountains, pave streets, plant vegetables, or raise cattle, as well as books on commerce, navigation, astronomy, and the French language. The Jesuits were a modernizing element in an otherwise very conservative society. The composition of their library also reflected the order's interests. They were owners of large-scale, very successful rural enterprises, often using Indian and even slave labor. The value of their properties in Peru, mainly their 97 haciendas, has been estimated at 5,700,000 pesos, and they owned 5,224 slaves (Macera 1966, in Klarén 2000, 103). Jesuit property reverted to the Spanish Crown after the expulsion.

There were schisms throughout the ecclesiastical hierarchies that were pervasive and often loudly outspoken. Aside from the rifts between regular and secular clergy and the antagonisms between Spanish-born and American-born priests, all parties involved competed for Indian labor and land. The Catholic Church became a major property owner of both landed estates and urban property and the main source of loans, for which the church lenders obtained a 7 percent interest in the 16th century. Priests also participated actively in market production and commerce. Other income for the church came from private donations, bequests, and the dowries that women were required to pay to enter a convent.

In Lima many women sought to enter convents. During the 17th century, the 13 convents in Lima housed more than 20 percent of the women living in the city. Of these some were nuns of the black veil (that is, fully voting members in the convent), and others were nuns of the white veil (their servants and maids, or *legas* and *donadas*), who were often Indians, mestizas, and slave women (Millones 1995, 177).

Slaves and Slavery

Of a total of about 9.5 million people forcibly brought from Africa to the Americas between 1500 and 1800, about 17 percent, or more than 1.6 million, were brought to the Spanish colonies. The total number of slaves brought to Peru is difficult to determine, but the first African slaves accompanied Pizarro on his earliest ventures into Inca territory. Many conquistadores spent their first gold and silver booty to buy slaves, in part to give themselves status as property owners.

Slaves played an important role in colonial Peru as laborers in all kinds of enterprises, but they were especially vital during the earliest years as agricultural workers on haciendas and plantations. Black slaves produced most of the crops to feed the growing cities, especially after the decline of the indigenous population due to disease and war reduced the available supply of Indian workers.

Slaves also made up a large percentage of the urban workforce. In Lima and other coastal cities they became valued house servants and manual laborers, and a crucial class of skilled urban artisans was largely made up of slaves. They filled many occupations, from concubine to sailor, in a society where white masters viewed manual labor as demeaning. Over the course of the colonial period black slaves and their descendants (often of mixed race) changed from being mere property that conferred status on the owners to an essential part of Spanish-American colonial society.

The slaves were tenacious in holding on to at least parts of their African heritage, despite repeated and vigorous attempts by white slave owners to eradicate what they perceived as threatening aspects of slave culture. The music, dance, and religious practices of the slaves showed remarkable cultural persistence. Religious brotherhoods, known as *cofradías,* were formed to promulgate Christianity among the slave population, but they often served to promote and preserve distinctive African slave culture, especially when neighborhood *cofradías* were made up of slaves from the same African tribe. For example, the religious brotherhoods encouraged the development of various dance forms (some of which persist today) such as the *zamacueca* and its better-known derivative the *marinera.*

Urban slaves also filled distinctive roles as healers parallel to white doctors. Black slave sorcerers and faith healers found many adherents, but black barbers were also important, even to white society. Barbers were the only practitioners who could administer medicinal bloodletting, which was thought to be the cure for many maladies and diseases, and blacks had almost a monopoly on the trade.

Slavery was an ingrained part of Peru's social and economic structure well into the 19th century. In spite of growing pressure from international antislavery forces, especially Great Britain, Peru kept importing slaves—mostly from other parts of the American continent—until the beginning of the 19th century. The Spanish colonial financial administration fostered the trade by eliminating the import duty on slaves in 1796. Peruvian slave traders lobbied Spanish officials in Madrid for even more lenient treatment, claiming that at least 1,500 new slaves were needed each year. As a result almost 66,000 slaves were brought to Peru between 1790 and 1802, increasing the slave population in this short period by approximately 25 percent.

Despite the vitality of the slave trade and the high demand for slaves, the institution of slavery in colonial Peru was undermined by the slaves themselves, who were able to take advantage of official Spanish domestic policy on slaves. In 1789 the Spanish Crown promulgated a code for white colonial slave owners that enjoined them to treat their slaves as "human beings" and to provide adequate food, clothes, housing, medical care, rest days, and religious instruction for their slaves. Many slaves in the cities used this code to petition through the colonial legal system against ill treatment by their masters. They claimed that they were mistreated and that their masters had failed to provide sound Christian examples of behavior, especially in the case of sexual abuse of slaves.

Even more effectively, many slaves learned to manipulate the hiring-out system that was typical of slavery in the cities. Because urban slaves were valued artisans, their masters profited by hiring out their services to

Black slaves and increasing numbers of free blacks (the latter primarily in the cities) fostered and maintained a lively culture, including dance forms originating in Africa. (Library of Congress)

others in the community. Slaves were allowed to find their own paying jobs, and after returning a stipulated "salary" called a *jornal* to their owners, they were allowed to keep a portion for themselves. They used this money to fund their lawsuits against mistreatment and, even more important, to gradually purchase their freedom. They made installment payments to their owners over time, thereby incrementally reducing their purchase price. The accounts were recorded on handwritten documents called *conques,* and with each recorded installment, the slave moved closer to freedom. In some cases dissatisfied slaves bargained themselves to new masters, based on the reduced purchase price they themselves had paid for. The spread of such strategies among the urban slave population gradually but persistently undermined the institution of slavery, making the slaves themselves the agents of their own freedom.

The institution of slavery outlived the Spanish colonial administration, despite some efforts to the contrary. When General José de San Martín arrived in Peru and took control of the government in Lima, he promised freedom to black slaves and their descendants who enlisted in the armies fighting for independence. Simón Bolívar assumed the role of liberator of Peru in 1823 after San Martín had withdrawn. Peruvian slaves may have expected to see soon the end of slavery, but Bolívar shared with San Martín a fear of free blacks, fostered by the bloody example of the successful slave rebellion of 1804 in Haiti. His government only reiterated the terms of the Spanish colonial code of 1789.

Slavery continued in independent Peru for three more decades, albeit with reduced numbers of slaves. Around 1825 slaves accounted for about 3.8 percent of the total population of Peru, or 50,000 of 1.3 million, and there were also approximately 40,000 free blacks, including mixed-race descendants of former slaves. By 1845 only 20,000 slaves were counted, including pockets of black slavery in rural areas (where a black population persists to this day). The decrease in numbers was due in part to the social and economic chaos of the period of independence and the years immediately following, when many Spanish owners fled the country, but in general, the growth in the free black population was due to the efforts of slaves themselves as they gradually purchased their own freedom. Slavery was officially abolished in republican Peru in 1854.

Increasingly Complex Race Relations

The attempt by the Spanish Crown immediately after the conquest to establish separate "republics" for Indians and for Spaniards faded in the face of ethnic, racial, and social reality. The scarcity of Spanish women and the availability of Indian women led to the rapid growth of a mixed-blood population, the mestizos. Pregnancies had more far-reaching consequences in Peruvian history than battles; Lima, for example, witnessed rising illegitimacy rates during the colonial era in spite of the fact that some Spanish fathers recognized their mestizo offspring and in some cases even sent them to study in Spain. Such was

By the early 19th century, when slavery was in theory abolished in Peru, there were tens of thousands of black slaves and free blacks living in the country. This young woman's occupation was listed as "incense burner," which would have made her one of the many black service workers and skilled artisans who kept Peruvian cities running. (Library of Congress)

the case of chronicler Garcilaso de la Vega. More often than not, biologically mestizo descendants became cultural Indians when growing up with their indigenous mothers. After black slaves were added to the mix, most prominently through expanded slave trade in the 17th and 18th centuries, there formed a complex socioracial pyramid and a visible defeat of the notion of "purity of blood" that formed part of the ideological climate at the time of the Spanish conquest.

In the wake of racial mixing, different groups of people produced distinctive and enduring popular cultures. From very early on, black slaves and their drums and dances in the city streets drew notice and severe regulations from Lima's city council, but without much success. Indians in the highlands sang and developed their own musical instruments; best known and still widespread today are the Andean pan flutes (the *quena* and *zampoña*), a sort of small guitar (the *charango*), and a native harp. Elites and intellectuals at the same time, founded free-standing theaters and in some of their writings exalted and encouraged a growing national pride. Lima's Corral de Comedias theater opened its doors in 1604, and the reconstructed (after the 1746 earthquake) Coliseo de Comedias was quite popular. Two pieces of writing had an especially long-lasting and decisive impact; they were *La Araucana* (1569), an epic poem by Alonso de Ercilla, and *Comentarios reales de los Incas* (1609), a chronicle by mestizo Garcilaso de la Vega. Priests also had an impact on nonreligious cultural life by translating Christian texts into native languages, which helped preserve native languages.

Race mixing occurred most prominently in the cities of the viceroyalty, and most notably in the capital city, Lima, in spite of what seemed to be rigid racial segregation. Lima had concentrated indigenous and black (slave and free) sections; the European and Creole elites lived in and around the central plaza. Segregation, however, did not prevent people from interacting. Many Indians and blacks worked as house servants or service providers for the white elite. As such they were deeply enmeshed in city life. The genetic mixing of races tended to dissolve physical boundaries and by the late 18th century was beyond reversal, in spite of insistent attempts to restore racial purity. The baroque multiplication of complex names for racial combinations was soon replaced by a broader distinction between "respectable folk" (*gente decente*) and the populace (*plebe*). A flood of immigrants to the city, most coming from the immediate rural hinterlands of the city, further changed the faces of the crowd toward the end of the colonial period.

People interacted on various occasions and in different settings. Large social gatherings were an opportunity to disseminate information before newspapers came into being by the late 18th century. During holidays, everyone in the city could watch the viceroy and the archbishop in their carriages hauled by six mules. (Six mules carried the highest social standing and prestige. Lesser nobles or merchants only had four or fewer mules, and black water-carriers used one mule.) The *pulperías* were noisy, popular bars owned by women where men would

A young woman of mixed race sat for this photographic portrait around the mid-19th century, when Peru (especially the city of Lima) was a "panorama" of mixed racial inhabitants, blending white European, indigenous South American, and black African genes in various patterns. (Library of Congress)

drink and gamble. Overall, the city was, according to U.S. historians Louise Hoberman and Susan N. Socolow, "the place where local elites—landowners, merchants, bureaucrats—came into contact with artisans, street vendors, beggars, and vagrants; where Spaniards and Portuguese were confronted by Indians, blacks and the panorama of mixed races" (1986, 10). As such it was a microcosm of the larger society.

Marriage and the Role of Women

The urban social elites in colonial Peru, like elites elsewhere, sought to increase their status and wealth, and their success often depended on diversifying their holdings and investments, finding advantageous placement of their children, and last but not least, creating beneficial marriage alliances. Put differently, they wanted patriarchal control over all economic operations of the extended family, including marriage.

Marriage for elite women in colonial Peru was, according to historian Luis Martin, an institution not of romantic love but rather one that functioned as an instrument by which families, the church, the state, the schools, and even the religious orders and guilds sought to achieve their economic, political, and social goals through controlling the conditions for young women's marriage and choice of partners (1983, 104). Some of the formal aspects of marriage were within the exclusive realm of the church. The civil aspects, such as inheritance issues and dowries, were dealt with by the state through its judiciary. Especially toward the end of the 18th century, the viceroy himself would intrude into the marriage plans of even petty employees; receiving a state-funded pension, for example, often depended on getting official approval of the right marriage choice (Chandler 1991, 38, 47).

The allocation of a dowry was parents' key economic instrument to influence their daughters' choice of partner. Dowries were introduced to Spain by the Romans and had been part of the laws of Castile two centuries before Europeans reached America. The dowry laws were reaffirmed in the Leyes de Toro issued by the Castilian parliament in 1505, revised during the reign of Philip II (1527–98), and finally found their way into the Novísima Recopilación, the 1805 codification of all the laws of Spain. The institution of the dowry led to arranged marriages, and marriage without a dowry was socially and legally unacceptable. By controlling their daughters' marriage choice, colonial elites were able to expand their social and economic networks, extending in some cases from Lima to Panama, Charcas, and Chile (Burkholder 1990, 11). A banker in Spain could even be enticed to marry the daughter of a wealthy merchant in Lima by the offer of a bountiful dowry.

The dowry, however, was also meant to allow husbands "to sustain the burdens of matrimony," and as such a dowry also symbolized a woman's standing within marriage. She was not meant to be a servant, but the husband nevertheless administered the dowry, and only in case of death, divorce (meaning in colonial times a temporal physical separation of the spouses with church approval, not the cancellation of the marital bond, which was considered to be a sacrament), or annulment would the dowry and the income derived from investing it return to the wife or her legal heirs. The existence of the dowry made marriage a social and public endeavor.

Love and romantic attachment were often formed instead in the beds of mistresses and concubines. Marital litigation and divorce rates were high in Lima, as were illicit sexual relations. Some contemporary observers described this as a social disease: The many men and women with unlawful sexual partners often lived in imitation of a legal marriage, yet in the local view the problem was the concubine, not the male lover. Furthermore, concubines often were *casta* (a generic term used to describe mixed-black people), black, or Indian women, so condemnation of concubines was tinged with racism. The moral double standard underlying these perceptions was laid open in a widely followed discussion in Lima's most prominent newspaper in 1791, when the editors attempted to shed some light on the nature of love and its relationship to marriage and concubinage. This discussion showed women with a heightened sense of dignity and rights, whereas "Don Juanism" was portrayed as demeaning for men and women.

When women in colonial Peru decided to leave their husbands and the safe harbor of their homes, they had to resort to church mediation and often had to stay under the guidance of a nun in an institution called a *beaterio,* a shelter originally created to house repentant prostitutes and concubines on their path to reform. In spite of a repressive moral context and threatening institutions, many women in Lima sought divorce, which in colonial times meant a temporal separation of the spouses in the hopes of future reconciliation. Such marital disruptions demonstrate the weakness of church influence on intimate relationships in spite of the church's institutional strength. For many racially mixed women, illegal relationships could become a mechanism of upward social mobility. By engaging in relationships with whiter men they incurred social scorn but stood to gain—eventually—some of the assets of their lovers.

In the course of time, perceptions and representations of women changed: "As Spain's American colonies were transformed from frontier settlements into imperial viceroyalties, and later into centers of revolutionary activity, female types and their characteristics changed. The courageous female warrior was replaced by the beautiful courtly lady as the feminine ideal, and from the opposite perspective, increased racial discrimination and the growth of crime and vice in the cities adversely affected the descriptions of women" (Johnson 1983, 185–186).

The Bourbon Reforms

When the last Spanish king of the Hapsburg family line died insane and without an heir, a long struggle ensued between European powers over who would succeed him. In 1701 Philip V, a member of the French Bourbon family, took the Spanish throne. When the Bourbons replaced the Hapsburgs, a new French-influenced, and perhaps more enlightened, era began in the relationship between Spain and its colonies. Conflict in Europe continued, however, with the British, the Dutch, and the Austrians fighting the new Spanish-French family alliance for continental hegemony. These wars lasted until 1713 and ended badly for Spain, which was forced to make many concessions, including control of its colonial trade monopoly. Great Britain was the major beneficiary, gaining, for example, access to the highly profitable slave trade that had initially been in the hands of the Portuguese by papal concession. Aside from the French Enlightenment, it was Britain's rapidly growing eco-

---

JUAN Y ULLOA, A CONTEMPORARY OBSERVER, COMMENTS ON THE CORRUPT SYSTEM

Corregidores use many tricks to enrich themselves by taking much away from the Indians. It all starts with the tribute Indians have to pay. The way they go about it shows much rigor, little justice and no sense of charity or fear of God. Bringing in the Indian tribute is known to be one of the most rewarding facets of their tenure. Would they proceed with honesty, no harm would be done to the Indians and the king's interest. However, their greed and selfishness accounts for disastrous results. After they undergo the final visita, after having bribed the visitador, all their past abuses are forgotten, and Indians with no belongings and much anger are left behind (Juan y Ulloa in Millones 1995, 240–241; translated by Christine Hunefeldt).

nomic power that triggered what came to be called the Bourbon Reforms. The main purpose of these reforms was to regain economic and political control over the colonies. The reforms began in Spain with the advent of the Bourbons to power, and they reached the colonies piecemeal over a long period.

The Bourbons intended to invigorate the Spanish economy and to promote colonization projects and Spanish immigration to the colonies. The enlightened state, thus, was to become the instrument of reform, working through bureaucrats who would be loyal to their source of power. The policy worked in Spain, according to David Brading, who maintains that the Spanish monarchy moved ahead of contemporary practice in France (where the selling of the office of tax farmer continued until the French Revolution) by relying on a salaried bureaucracy. As a result, public revenues rose from 5 million pesos in 1700 to about 18 million in 1750. By the last decades of the 18th century, Spanish revenues reached an average of 36 million pesos. These figures help explain Spain's revival (1988, 118).

The Bourbon reforms also changed the political life in the colonies and were one of the triggering elements leading to the wars of independence in the early 19th century. In the wake of the Bourbon Reforms, especially under Charles III (1759–88), there were many fiscal and administrative changes, but economic reforms were much less successful, particularly the ones pertaining to international trade. The Bourbons were never able to curtail British contraband simply because Spanish goods were expensive and in short supply, whereas British manufactured goods had become much cheaper as a result of a burgeoning industrial revolution. By 1759 British contraband was valued at approximately 6 million pesos a year. A new war against Britain in 1761 brought more disaster for Spain and expanded Great Britain's commercial privileges further, gradually leading to the recognition of what was already tacitly in place: free trade. By 1778 free trade was extended to other European nations. New Spain (Mexico) and Venezuela remained the only strongholds of Spanish trade monopoly, at least until 1789. Shortly afterward the Spanish Crown lowered import taxes and in general tried to suppress everything that made Spanish products more expensive in order to achieve a higher level of competitiveness.

The opening of markets and the resulting competition actually stimulated Spanish trade exchange with the colonies. Between 1778 and 1788 Spain's commerce with the colonies increased by 700 percent. At the end of the 17th century, only 15 percent of the goods sent to the colonies were Spanish; by 1798 this percentage had grown to

50 percent, an increase that reflected an important growth of Spanish industry, especially industry based on cotton and iron.

In the colonies free trade had dramatic effects: Merchants could no longer create artificial scarcity to increase prices. Prices dropped, earnings from merchant activities decreased, and consumers had access to a greater variety of products when they needed them (instead of waiting for the uncertain arrival of the fleet from Seville). New merchants, including Indian *curacas,* who were well informed about local conditions, emerged on the scene as new social and economic actors. Indians were no longer subject to sales imposed by *corregidores* and other merchants.

The overall result was a dramatic change in how commerce and investments were organized and in the locations of the main trading centers. After 1778 exports from the colonies saw unprecedented heights, especially on the Atlantic side. Until then, for example, Buenos Aires exported 150,000 hides annually; by 1783 the count of hides was up to 1.4 million. In contrast to such success, the textile industry and its large *obrajes* stopped production when faced with much cheaper British manufactures. Increased commercial agriculture for the world market led to a new regional specialization on an international scale and, at the end, to a new and enduring division of labor: cocoa in Caracas; sugar in Cuba and Brazil; coffee in Colombia; rice, cotton, and sugar in Peru. It was during this period that Latin America, in general, based economic growth on the export of raw materials, a situation that lasted well into the 20th century.

An interesting outcome of the decaying fleet system was that in spite of the large amounts of money the Spanish Crown spent on warfare, more money produced in the colonies actually remained in the colonies, providing necessary cash to a traditionally cash-poor economy. More circulating money also meant more market and investment opportunities. Lima's treasury expenses demonstrated these changes. Around 1600, half of Lima's treasury budget went to Spain. Toward the mid-18th century the Crown still obtained about 20 percent of revenues (corresponding to the *quinto real*), but the remaining 80 percent was used to defend the viceroyalty and its various dependencies and to pay for administrative expenses (employee salaries and pensions and the purchase of mercury) (Fisher 1977, 28–33). Although some of this money was later remitted in the form of private money to Spain, colonials—because of the absence of produce coming from Spain—increasingly invested in colonial enterprises and engaged in trade ventures. As a consequence the number of haciendas and (for a few years) *obrajes* increased, as did the number of Peruvian merchants, the so-called *peruleros,* Creoles who independent of their Spanish counterparts engaged in purchasing goods in Spain and other European countries to sell in the colonies, including the Philippines. Some historians read these indicators as a reversal of colonial dependency: Spain was becoming increasingly dependent on its colonies.

Administrative changes—especially important for Lima—involved the creation of the new Viceroyalty of Río de La Plata in 1776, confirming the growing importance of Buenos Aires in the previous century, and the establishment in 1782 of *intendencias* (intendancies) in replacement of the *corregimientos.* Both measures were implemented under the strict surveillance of *visitadores* from Spain. The *intendencias* were larger jurisdictions than the *corregimientos* ever had been. *Intendentes,* the appointed heads of the *intendencias,* also had more power than a *corregidor,* and they had direct access to Spanish high authorities, aside from military, financial, economic, and judicial jurisdictions.

Antonio de Areche, the minister who had already introduced and implemented the intendant system in New Spain, was appointed to carry out the reforms in the Peruvian viceroyalty. He arrived in Lima in 1777 as the *visitador general* of Peru, Chile, and Río de la Plata. With him came a new viceroy, Manuel de Guirior, marqués de Guirior. Until the end of his mandate in 1780, Guirior was in constant conflict over hierarchy and jurisdiction with *visitadores,* in large measure because the administrative jurisdictions between the viceroy and the *intendentes* and *visitadores* were not clearly demarcated. When the conflicts reached a peak, Areche managed to have the viceroy removed and replaced by another, Agustín de Jáuregui y Aldecoa, who in turn ousted Areche, replacing him with Jorge de Escobedo, an *oidor* from the Audiencia of Charcas.

Amid bureaucratic squabbles and in spite of them, the *visitadores* implemented many of the planned reforms. The internal customs tax (*alcabala*) was increased in 1772 from 2 to 4 percent, and again in 1776 from 4 to 6 percent. A product traditionally exempted from the *alcabala,* coca, was included in the list of products subject to customs taxes, as was *aguardiente,* a native sugarcane brandy, with a 12.5 percent tax. Customhouses were established throughout the region in Cochabamba (1774), La Paz (1776), Buenos Aires (1778), and Arequipa (1780). Artisans and peasants who had been exempt from tribute or taxes, such as those without land were now included in the list of tributaries. Artisans had to pay 4 percent on their transactions, whereas landless Indian peasants had to pay half the tribute of peasants with land.

These measures encountered resistance from many social groups in the form of judicial protests and proceedings, *pasquines* (mostly handwritten letters or poems that appeared overnight on doors and in public places), and even open revolt (in La Paz and Arequipa). Smaller merchants from mixed racial backgrounds saw their businesses suffer, especially those that had catered to the needs of those at the silver mines. With the creation of the Viceroyalty of Río de la Plata, Potosí became part of the new viceroyalty and many of the former muleteer routes leading to Potosí from the Peruvian side were no longer active.

The Spanish Crown knew the reforms would be met with resistance. Even before *visitador general* Areche arrived in Lima, Manuel de Amat, viceroy from 1761 to 1776, had established armed forces totaling more than 96,000 men, including infantry, cavalry, and dragoons. However, most of these were militias—that is, improvised groups called upon when needed, and not a standing, well-trained army. Mostly they were ill equipped and ill trained. During the 16th and 17th centuries militias had been recruited predominantly among Europeans; in the 18th century, more Creoles, blacks, and mixed-race descendants of blacks participated. These militias were deemed less trustworthy because of their racial composition; nevertheless, the viceroy's efforts in organizing military forces (a total of approximately 35,000 men) signaled his expectation of unrest.

In the higher colonial administration, many Creoles were replaced by peninsular-born Spaniards. The resentment of Creoles against Spain consequently grew because of their exclusion from political office. Spaniards were labeled in denigrating terms, such as *chapetones* or *gachupines* (similar to "carpetbaggers"). The Spanish, in turn, considered the American-born whites inferior due to poor upbringing, poor education, and—as was then argued—the deleterious effects of the climate of Peru on the native born. Creoles responded with a heightened "Creole nationalism" by which Lima, and even Potosí, became examples of glory and beauty (Millones 1995, 204). Lima was compared to Seville and also became, in poems and newspaper articles, the New Jerusalem. These debates involved the white population, not Indians or blacks. Nevertheless, they created—albeit for different reasons—a sense of a common cause.

Although the establishment of the intendant system was a first step to diminishing the role and the power of the *corregidores,* the collection of tributes still gave *corregidores* the power to extort Indians and to cheat the Crown. The power of *corregidores* resided in the control of Indian labor, and with this tool in hand they could impose many other demands. One of the most profitable of these endeavors was the forced sale of merchandise (the *repartos*). By this system the *corregidores* forced

Indians to buy merchandise from them, often items, such as pink silk stockings, for which Indians had no need and usually at exorbitant over-market prices.

The new intendant system barely addressed such long-standing misuse of power. The corruption in the system, in tandem with the implementation of the Bourbon reforms, laid the ground for Indian rebellion, especially the Tupac Amaru II uprising. This coincidence in time and place made the leader of the biggest colonial Indian rebellion firmly believe that by acting as a leader against *corregidores,* he was merely carrying out what the king had decided. Soon, however, he would come to be painfully aware of how far removed he was from royal intentions.

6

REVOLTS AND THE WARS
FOR INDEPENDENCE
(1780–1826)

Throughout much of the 18th century, colonial Peru was racked with violent uprisings and revolts among the Indian population, often led by able and charismatic leaders. Although they may have won concessions in the short run, few of these revolts were ultimately successful, and they were put down by military repression. By the first decades of the 19th century, however, unrest in the colony, and indeed in all the Spanish colonies in South America, had spread to the Creole and mestizo classes. Independence movements sprang up across the continent, and armies commanded by the Río de la Plata general José de San Martín and Simón Bolívar from Caracas eventually reached Peru. Between them these men threw off Spanish control and set Peru on a new course as an independent nation, albeit not without great strife and struggle.

Inca and Indian Revolts in the 18th Century

There were many Indian rebellions throughout the 18th century, ranging from local skirmishes to larger and longer-lasting uprisings and one very big revolt. Two insurrections were particularly representative of a growing unrest among Indians in the colonies: Juan Santos Atahualpa's revolt from the Amazon basin and Tupac Amaru II's rebellion.

Juan Santos Atahualpa

When Manco Capac II (Manco Inca), the last rebellious Inca of the 16th century, was defeated in Cuzco, he fled to Vilcabamba in the Peruvian Amazon basin, a region that remained an isolated refuge for decades despite occasional Spanish expeditions looking for illusory hoards of gold. In fact, the Amazon *selva* (rain forest) was a place with few material rewards. Franciscan missionaries were some of the few Spaniards to settle in the region, known as the Gran Pajonal. It became a part of the Intendancy of Tarma in the wake of the Bourbon reforms, and the indigenous people living there in a series of *pueblos* still had to pay tribute to the king and the church. In general the Amazon was a frontier of conflict with the native populations, generically called *chunchos* by highland Indian peasants.

In 1742 Juan Santos Atahualpa, a Christianized Indian originally from Cuzco, took over the *pueblo* of Huanta with his followers, then proceeded down the Jauja River to foment rebellion among other *pueblos* and the missions. Juan Santos Atahualpa proclaimed himself the new Inca, who would liberate all Indians from the Spanish yoke. Indians from the *pueblos* and missions soon came to greet him and acclaim him as their redeemer.

When news of Atahualpa's uprising reached the Spanish colonial government in Lima, the viceroy quickly organized a military expedition against the proclaimed Inca. The Spanish forces, however, proved to be unequal to the task. They were ill equipped to fight jungle warfare against sporadic, hit-and-run attacks from Indians. Two successive viceroys—José Antonio de Mendoza Caamaño y Sotomayor, marqués de Villagarcía (1736–45), and José Antonio Manso de Velasco, conde de Superunda (1745–61)—tried to defeat Atahualpa, but the government eventually became convinced that to pursue more fighting in the *selva* was a lost cause and that the most that could be achieved was to limit the spread of the rebellion. The missions were abandoned, and Atahualpa turned the Gran Pajonal into an independent region, far from European influence and control. It remained as such for more than 100 years. Eventually reports of Atahualpa faded, just as Tupac Amaru II emerged.

Tupac Amaru II

José Gabriel Condorcanqui was born in Surinama, near Cuzco, on March 9, 1738, and went to the Jesuit school of San Francisco de Borja for *curacas* (local ethnic leaders) in Cuzco. He claimed to be descended from Tupac Amaru. After his schooling he returned to his family home in Surinama and married the mestiza Micaela Bastidas in 1760. Condorcanqui became a wealthy *curaca* governing a jurisdiction that included the towns of Tungasuca, Pampamarca, and Surinama. He had inherited 450 mules from his parents, which indicates that he and his

TUPAC AMARU

According to historian John H. Rowe, José Gabriel Condorcanqui was greatly influenced by his stay in Lima in 1777, when he lived in the city while defending himself in a lawsuit against a rival who also claimed descendancy from Tupac Amaru. New ideas from the Enlightenment in Europe were then circulating among the city's intellectuals. In addition the impact of the revolt of the North American colonies against Great Britain was fresh and significant. Despite the efforts of the Peruvian colonial government to suppress books and discussion of these matters, Condorcanqui probably was exposed to these ideas and events when he visited San Marcos University and spoke to his *limeño* acquaintances. His wife later said that this was a visit that opened his eyes.

Perhaps even more important influences were the contemporary ideas of a neo-Incan revival and Incan nationalism that were also circulating at the time. These ideas were circulating throughout the Andes during the latter decades of the 18th century, when the descendants of the Incan elites were making conscious efforts to rediscover and reclaim their indigenous traditions, which included a "nostalgic" (in Rowe's characterization) affirmation of the glorious imperial Inca past (Rowe 1976, summarized in Klarén 2000, 116).

family were in the transportation business. As a *curaca* he was exposed to the double pressures of the *corregidor* on one side and the requests from his constituent Indians on the other.

Condorcanqui led a revolt that eventually put Spanish colonial domination in jeopardy, though it began as an attempt to end the corruption of the *corregidores*. It started in 1780 in the small town of Tinta, near Cuzco, where a corrupt and venal *corregidor,* Antonio Juan de Arriaga y Gurbista, had for years abused the Indians under his jurisdiction and extorted large sums from them. Condorcanqui seized the *corregidor,* threw him in jail, and six days later hanged him publicly in the plaza of Tungasuca. During the execution a *pregonero* (town crier) playing the drums announced that from there on the *alcabala* (internal tariff), customs, and *mita* in Potosí were abolished.

While confusing news of the uprising reached Cuzco and Lima, Condorcanqui, who took the name Tupac Amaru II, began to organize a rebellion with Tungasuca as his headquarters. Cuzco's inhabitants decided to send troops to Tinta under the leadership of Fernando Cabrera, the *corregidor* of Quispicanchis (another Cuzco province). Cabrera was defeated by Tupac Amaru's troops at Sangarara, and the rebels killed hundreds of royalists, including Cabrera, who died under the rubble of the local church where he had taken refuge.

As the rebellion expanded Condorcanqui's cousin, Diego Cristóbal Tupac Amaru, joined the leadership of the rebel army, as did Tomasa Titu Condemayta, the woman *curaca* of Acos, in Quispicanchis. Not all *curacas* in and around Cuzco supported Condorcanqui, however, and some actually joined the royal army. Most notable of all was Mateo García Pumacahua, the *curaca* of Chinchero, who would himself lead an armed rebellion against royal troops 30 years later (in 1814–15).

As word spread of Tupac Amaru II's rebellion, there were outbreaks of violence throughout the highlands. Indians rose up and attacked the *corregidores*, burned hated colonial institutions such as *obrajes* and churches, and killed anyone who was not an Indian. Tupac Amaru II himself tried in vain to include Creoles and mestizos and even slaves in his rebellion, but as the situation grew more violent and more non-Indians suffered, the Creole and mestizo population turned on the Indian leader and his forces. Creoles might have agreed that *corregidor* Arriaga was a

A modern view of Cuzco, which in 1781 was captured by the rebellious forces of José Gabriel Condorcanqui, known as Tupac Amaru II, and became the center of his revolt against the colonial Spanish government. (Photofrenetic/Alamy)

corrupt state employee deserving to be put to death, they were less inclined to relinquish their properties or their Indian workers. It has been estimated that 100,000 people, around 10 percent of the viceroyalty's population, died in the uprising. Tupac Amaru II was defeated after attempting to lay siege to Cuzco and captured in April 1781.

Soon after his capture, Tupac Amaru II was publicly executed. He was torn apart by horses after he had been forced to witness the torture and death of his children and wife. His dismembered body was displayed at several locations in and around Cuzco as an example to would-be rebels. In spite of Condorcanqui's defeat and horrendous death, rebellion had spread to the highlands in Oruro and Tupiza. Under the commander Tupac Catari (Julián Apaza), Indian troops continued to attack colonial figures and institutions. The repercussions of this upheaval reached Ayacucho in the south of modern-day Peru, and even into modern-day northern Chile.

The Wars of Independence

Peru had for more than 300 years been the center of Spanish colonial domination in South America, and Lima in particular had strong, long-standing links with Madrid. Lima's elites were tied through economic, political, and even kinship interests to their counterparts in Madrid. Moreover, the Tupac Amaru II rebellion had shown many Creoles how shaky their hold on the colony was and how much they needed Spain to legitimize and support their social and economic preeminence. Peru took much longer than other Spanish colonies to embrace the independence movement, and it remained for years a bastion of Spain in the midst of other colonies that had proclaimed their freedom. Yet as Madrid tried to reinstate its control on colonial territory after the Tupac Amaru II uprising, the Spanish government succeeded only in further alienating Peruvians. Increased taxes, the reorganization of the administrative boundaries of the viceroyalty (via the new intendant system), and the replacement of Creole high-state administrators with Spaniards were issues that triggered the movement toward independence.

Long-term structural conditions also explain what has been called the "colonial crisis." Although in the 16th century silver and labor were abundant in the Peruvian viceroyalty by the 18th century both were scarce. The population decline (reaching its low point around 1720) affected all other economic endeavors in the colony, and Spain's ability to finance and wage wars in Europe in defense of its hegemony declined accordingly. In need of ever more money, the Spanish Crown increased the pressures on the diminishing Peruvian indigenous population. As a result the Peruvian viceroyalty witnessed increasing rural unrest in the decades leading up to independence.

Historian Scarlett O'Phelan cites more than 150 uprisings during the 18th century. Growing unrest was closely knit into the resurgence of what has been labeled an "Andean renaissance," or varieties of Inca nationalism. This ideological revival was based on a reinterpretation of preconquest history that envisioned and celebrated a benevolent Inca ruler and the existence of an ideal society, the Tahuantinsuyo. The mounting discontent had converged in the Tupac Amaru II rebellion, which in turn

The entrance to the Church of San Francisco in Lima, built in an 18th-century baroque style that reflected the period of Bourbon rule in Spain. (Photofrenetic/Alamy)

set off continued distrust of everything indigenous by all non-Indians. In the long run, this wariness hampered common political and military efforts for independence, and to a large degree it explains why Peruvian Creole leaders were inclined to wage a political revolution without a social revolution (Manrique 1995, 37).

Peruvian intellectuals and politicians were also influenced by what was happening in other parts of the world. The generation of thinkers associated with the journal *Mercurio peruano* between 1790 and 1796 carefully watched and commented on worldwide issues. Both the successful war for independence against Britain by the North American colonies and the French Revolution put ideas such as the right of self-governance, popular sovereignty, the merits of nationalism, and the desire to do things differently (and inherently better) in the minds of many Peruvians. However, these Peruvians did not necessarily see separation from Spain as the solution. Rather, they envisioned a more moderate relationship in which the voices from the colonies could and would be heard in Madrid. The most prominent figures among these politicians and intellectuals were lawyers Manuel Lorenzo Vidaurre and José Baquíjano y Carrillo, the priest Mariano José de Arce, and the doctor Hipólito Unánue. One member of the group, Vicente Morales Duárez, in 1810 became a representative from the colonies in the Cortes de Cádiz, the assembly of elected representatives that replaced Ferdinand VII after his deposition by Napoléon Bonaparte in 1808.

Events in Europe played a crucial role in nudging Peru (and other Spanish colonies in South America) toward independence. Spain was thrown into chaos and turmoil when it was occupied by Napoléon Bonaparte's troops in 1808 and King Ferdinand VII was deposed. At least temporarily, Spain was an occupied territory and had almost no control over its colonies. The situation became even more confused in 1810 when a national assembly, known as the Cortes de Cádiz, was called in the king's absence, with Morales Duárez as its president. This assembly drew up a new, quite liberal constitution that would affect both Spain and the colonies. When this new constitution reached Peru in 1812, it produced much discussion, unrest, and even open rebellion. The new proposed form of government was to be a constitutional monarchy, and the constitution abolished the Indian tribute and the *mita* and required that elections take place. Depending on the population size, the varied colonial dependencies were instructed to hold elections to nominate local bureaucrats and representatives (all the way from *cabildos* to *audiencias*) and to send representatives to Spain. It was the first time in colonial history that the colonies' voices would be heard in an open public forum in Spain.

Fernando de Abascal, the viceroy in Lima, refused to implement this liberal constitution, an action that led to several upheavals throughout Peru between 1812 and 1814. A Cuzco rebellion, co-led by the *curaca* Mateo Pumacahua, embraced most of the southern Andes and covered an area closely coincident with the region affected by the Tupac Amaru II rebellion. By 1814, however, King Ferdinand was back on the Spanish throne, and the rebellions in Peru were successfully suppressed through military actions and their leaders publicly executed. Four years later, in 1818, Viceroy Joaquín de la Pezuela was able to report to Spain that in Peru few dared to discuss self-government or talk about a Peruvian nation, whereas a strong support for Spain had been demonstrated in very material ways. It has been calculated that between 1777 and 1814, Lima's merchant guild (the Tribunal del Consulado), donated more than 5 million pesos to the Spanish Crown toward the payment of Spain's wars in Europe. Over the following years, until it went bankrupt, the guild continued to loan and donate money to support the Spanish colonial government's armed struggle against the invading patriotic armies and to help suppress local uprisings (Manrique 1995, 62).

Outside forces now came into play and began to shape the direction of the independence movement in Peru. The Spanish colonies to the south (modern-day Argentina and Chile) had been liberated and declared independent after successful military campaigns led by the Argentine general José de San Martín, a veteran of the Spanish army who had proved brilliant in organizing a disciplined army, composed mostly of black slaves, mulattoes, and mestizos. In 1816, San Martín had defeated a royalist Spanish army in Argentina, then crossed the Andes into Chile and defeated the Spanish forces there in a series of battles the following year. San Martín's goals, however, encompassed more than gaining independence for Argentina and Chile. He understood that as long as Spanish authorities retained control of Lima and the rest of Peru, the newly won freedoms of the regions to the south would be in peril. He recruited and trained a new 4,500-man army of Argentines, Chileans, and expatriate Peruvians and he assembled a naval squadron, commanded by the British admiral Lord Cochrane. In August 1820, San Martín embarked on an invasion of Peru.

The patriot army landed at Pisco and then marched north and surrounded Lima, the center of Spanish royalist power, while Lord Cochrane blockaded the harbor at Callao. San Martín had hoped the presence of his forces would stimulate an independence movement among the Creole elite of Lima, but there was no organized response from the limeños and only scattered support for the independence movement from individuals.

San Martín was in a strong military position, but the Spanish viceroy Joaquín de la Pezuela was still in command of a huge army and had control of Lima. Moreover, earlier in 1820 the government in Spain had promulgated a new, more liberal constitution that granted equal civil status to Spanish subjects living in the colonies. In the eyes of the royalists in Lima, this obviated the need for Peruvian separation and weakened the patriot argument for independence. The situation was at a stalemate, which prompted Pezuela to open negotiations with San Martín, but in January 1821 Spanish general José de La Serna deposed the viceroy and took control of the royalist government and army. La Serna and San Martín had served together in Europe as officers in the Spanish army fighting the French. They now entered into discussions about the future of Peru, and for a short while appeared to reach an

FEMALE CAMP FOLLOWERS

Flora Tristán (1803–44) was born to a Peruvian father and a Parisian mother. A prominent pre-Marxist socialist, she fought for workers' and women's rights in France during the late 1830s and early 1840s. Following is her description of the camp followers of South America, *rabonas* as she calls them, which she recorded during a visit.

In Peru each soldier takes with him as many women as he likes: some have as many as four. They form a considerable troop, preceding the army by several hours so that they have time to set up camp, obtain food and cook it. To see the female avant-garde set out gives one an immediate idea of what these poor women have to suffer and the dangerous life they lead. The rabonas are armed; they load onto mules their cooking-pots, tents and all the rest of the baggage, they drag after them a horde of children of all ages, they whip their mules into a gallop and run along side behind them, they climb high mountains, they swim across rivers, carrying one or even two children on their backs. When they arrive at their destination, they choose the best site for the camp, then they unload the mules, erect the tents, feed the children and put them to bed, light the fires and start cooking. If they chance to be near an inhabited place, they go off in a detachment to get supplies; they descend on the village like famished beasts and demand food for the army. When it is given with a good grace they do no harm, but when they are refused they fight like lionesses and their fierce courage overcomes all resistance. Then they sack the village, carry their loot back to the camp and divide it among themselves.

These women, who provide for all the needs of the soldier, who wash and mend his clothes, receive no pay and their only reward is the freedom to rob with impunity. They are of Indian race, speak the native language, and do not know a single word of Spanish. The rabonas are not married, they belong to nobody and are there for anybody who wants them. . . . The rabonas adore the sun but do not observe any religious practices (Hahner 1998, 26).

agreement to establish a constitutional monarchy, basing their ideas on the political theories of 18th-century Enlightenment political philosopher, Charles Montesquieu, who had believed only geographically small and socially homogenous nations could function well as democracies. From this point of view, Peru's sprawling, diverse topography and the acute racial, social, and economic divisions among the population made it an unlikely candidate for any form of government except monarchy.

The discussion, nonetheless eventually came to nothing, and La Serna withdrew from Lima in order to consolidate the royalist forces. He seized the silver mines in the highlands and established headquarters in the old Incan imperial capital of Cuzco. Meanwhile, San Martín occupied Lima. Despite a noticeable lack of enthusiasm for the cause of independence on the part of the Creole elite, San Martín took a bold step and declared Peruvian independence from Spain in a solemn ceremony in Lima's central plaza on July 28, 1821. To this day, July 28 is celebrated as the Peruvian independence day, the equivalent of the Fourth of July in the United States. Proclamations alone, however, do not win wars, and Peru faced three more years of armed conflict before definitively achieving independence.

San Martín discovered that he had little choice but to assume political control of Lima himself as provisional governor, as the Creole leaders he had counted on for support were slow to step forward and take responsibility. In fact, many native-born Spaniards, as well as Peruvian-born Creoles, fled Peru in the face of the dislocations caused by the war for independence, and those who remained feared for their property and lives if the large slave and Indian population of the city should be infected with the idea of liberty and rise up against them. The Creole elite of Lima also viewed San Martín's army of black and mixed-race soldiers with fear and suspicion. Nonetheless, San Martín hoped to establish order and quell the fears of the white population by taking power.

His official decrees did little to win over the Creoles to the cause of independence, however, especially after he mandated the liberation of slaves born after July 28, 1821, a move that would eventually lead to the full abolition of slavery. San Martín also abolished the Indian tribute and the requirement that the Indian population render personal services to whites, and he cancelled commercial monopolies. All of these decrees struck at the heart of Creole security and power, and they resulted in unsettling the political situation rather than achieving stability. The *limeños* distrusted San Martín and were pushed further into opposition when they found themselves subjected to harsh state and police control, and when food became scarce after viceregal troops surrounded the city.

While San Martín and his army controlled northern Peru and the central coast, Viceroy La Serna controlled the central and southern highlands. With the military situation at a stalemate San Martín petitioned in July 1822 the help of Bolívar, the "Liberator" of Granada (Venezuela and Colombia). The generals met in Guayaquil. The exact nature of their conversations remains a mystery; however, from

Simón Bolívar, the Liberator (Art Today)

what little is known, Bolívar offered to send only 800 men to support San Martín's efforts even after San Martín offered to submit to Bolívar's command. Disappointed, San Martín returned to Lima only to find that his ministers had been deposed for their anti-Spanish policies and attitudes. Many Peruvian Creoles in Lima resented San Martín's monarchical aspirations and even feared he would crown himself king. San Martín, however, was completely disillusioned and renounced power. Shortly afterward, he left the American continent, never to return.

The newly inaugurated congress that had been called by San Martín before his departure drew up Peru's first republican constitution in 1823 and chose José de la Riva Agüero as the nation's first president. After the promulgation of the new constitution, Riva Agüero launched new military campaigns against the viceregal troops in the highlands only to be defeated in battles at Moquegua and Torata. Empowered by its victories, the viceregal army regained control of Lima and Callao. At this point congress members decided to call once more upon Bolívar to save the independence movement.

When Bolívar arrived in Peru, he encountered political chaos, dissension, and lack of resources, and most serious of all, there was no army in place. The so-called Army of the South, the only force made up of Peruvian soldiers, had been defeated and subsequently disbanded. By 1823, only a few hundred soldiers remained of the army's original 5,000. San Martín's Chilean troops had returned to Chile, and the Argentine troops from Río de la Plata were mutinous for the lack of pay The patriots' naval squadron, commanded by Thomas, Lord Cochrane, had left Callao after not being paid, taking with it the last penny of the national treasury. The only organized troops in place were Colombians under General Antonio José de Sucre. Given the disarray, congress transferred all powers to Bolívar over the objections of President Riva Agüero, who fled Lima and set up a parallel government in the city of

BOLÍVAR AND SUCRE

Late 19th-century U.S. historian Clements R. Markham described Simón Bolívar, the Liberator, and General Antonio José de Sucre 70 years after they intervened in Peru's struggle for independence.

> Bolívar entered Quito on the 16th of June, annexed Guayaquil and obtained leave from the obsequious congress of Colombia to proceed to Peru. His age was then forty.
>
> Bolívar was a little man, only five feet, four inches in height. His face was long, with hollow cheeks and livid brown complexion, eyes sunk deep in the head, body thin and meager. A large moustache and whiskers covered part of his face. He was passionately fond of dancing and lolling in a Spanish hammock. His character was made up of vanity, ambition, profound dissimulation and a thirst for absolute power. He had read little and was a bombastic writer. He never smoked. His voice was loud and harsh, and he indulged in fits of passion and personal abuse, his temper being fiery and capricious. His manners were generally good, but not prepossessing.
>
> Antonio José de Sucre, Bolívar's second in command, was born in Cumana, in Venezuela, on the 13th of June, 1793. . . . Entering the army in 1811, he served with credit under Miranda, and afterward under Piar [both Colombian presidents]. From 1814 to 1817 he was on the staff of the Colombian army, and he afterwards commanded a division sent to assist the province of Guayaquil. His great military achievement, before his arrival in Peru, was the victory of Pichincha.
>
> For two years and a half the destinies of Peru were placed under the absolute control of these two men, Bolívar and Sucre (Markham 1892, 269–270).

Trujillo. Soon afterward, Lima's congress discovered that Riva Agüero had opened conversations with Viceroy La Serna to oust Bolívar. Riva Agüero was officially exiled. His replacement, José Bernardo de Tagle, marqués de Torre Tagle, also defected to the royalists, dying soon after. Political unity was achieved only when Bolívar was vested with dictatorial power.

Bolívar's prospects brightened when the royalist forces split and one general withdrew his troops. In addition, international support came from the United States, which under the Monroe Doctrine stood as a guarantor for the independence of former Spanish colonies. Meanwhile, Europe decided not to intervene in America in spite of Spain's insistence to the contrary. Moderate Peruvian Creoles, who had envisioned the success of a liberal reform movement, lost all hope and realized Peru was on its own.

Bolívar financed the war against royalist forces with Peru's first international loan (from the United Kingdom), and without remorse or hesitation he expropriated all property, including that of the church, he could get a hold of. Similarly he imposed recruiting quotas on the liberated territories. The highland provinces of Cajamarca and Chota, Piura, and Huamachuco were most affected. Bolívar knew that the final battles had to take place in the Peruvian highlands among a population that had signaled strong pro-Spanish and even monarchical support. Thus, the central highlands, one of Peru's richest regions, bore the brunt of this war, which involved six military campaigns between the two biggest armies on the continent, plus the depredations of hundreds of loosely organized guerrilla groups (Manrique 1995, 64–65).

When he left Lima and advanced into Cerro de Pasco, Bolívar commanded 6,000 Colombian and 3,000 Peruvian soldiers. On August 4, 1824, he confronted the royalist army, commanded by General José de Canterac, at the Battle of Junín, which was fought on the Meseta de Bombón, 12,000 feet above sea level. The battle ended with a hurried retreat of Canterac's army. Although the royalist army had been soundly defeated, complete victory still eluded Bolívar. In the end Bolívar's second in command, General Antonio José de Sucre, won the final battle of the war at the Pampa of Ayacucho (which in Quechua means "the

PRAISE FOR BOLÍVAR

Diego de Choquehuanca, a *curaca* from the province of Azángaro in Puno, lauded Simón Bolívar during a visit by the Liberator to Puno.

Once God intended to build an empire with savages and He created Manco Capac. Manco Capac's race fell in sin and then God sent Pizarro. After three centuries of atonement, God had pity with America and He sent You. You are, then, a man imbued with a godly design. Nothing that has ever been done before now even comes close to what You have achieved. If there ever is someone able to follow your path there has to be another world to liberate. You have founded five republics that are destined to witness immense development, and these republics will glorify Your name as none other. With time Your glory will grow as does the shadow when the sun declines (García Calderón 1879, 281; translated by Christine Hunefeldt).

corner of the dead") on December 9, 1824, and triumphantly entered the city of Cuzco two weeks later. It was not for another 12 months that the final bastion of Spanish resistance in Bolivia (then known as Upper Peru) was subdued, and in January 1826 the few resisting Spaniards who had taken refuge in Callao surrendered.

After the battle of Ayacucho, Bolívar called elections for a new congress, which was installed on February 10, 1825. Congress proclaimed Bolívar leader of the nation. He stayed in Lima until September 1826, when political unrest demanded his presence in his native New Granada. During his brief command over Peru's political destiny Bolívar attempted to introduce several liberal-minded reforms, especially pertaining to Indians, who represented about 60 percent of the new nations total population. In particular he strove to eliminate the still-prevailing colonial institutions and the exploitation of the indigenous population. These reforms, however, encountered resistance and, more often than not, were simply ignored.

Political programs for the new nation-state were abundant. However, the very proliferation of such programs created uncertainty among political leaders and their followers. It also explains why many different ideological factions contended for power. All parties envisioned a better future for the newly independent Peruvian citizens, but there was no agreement on the overarching goals or how to implement this future.

To this day Peruvians (and non-Peruvian historians) engage in heated debate over the meaning of the wars of independence. Did the wars of independence mark a radical transformation of preexisting colonial ways? Were the wars carried on the shoulders of Peruvians and based on a Peruvian willingness to become independent? What does the participation of Indians and blacks tell us? What were the long-term effects of these wars?

Whatever the answers to these questions, the wars of independence did not end internal turmoil and unrest. To the contrary, political independence from Spain unleashed new confrontations and ways of expressing such confrontations. The result was not a more egalitarian and prosperous society. Indians continued living in peasant communities, paying tribute, and providing free personal services to individuals and governmental institutions. Slavery continued. The Catholic Church held on to its traditional privileges.

In spite of the signs of continuity of Peruvian society after independence, changes were visible in the larger economic and political areas. Commercial networks—linked previously through the Potosí-Huancavelica-Lima-Seville connection—now became more regionally fragmented. The former Spanish nobility lost its hold on governmental issues and most of their economic assets, either because they had been discredited or robbed or they had returned to Spain. The Indian nobility had been dismantled in the aftermath of the Tupac Amaru II rebellion. The financial resources of the state were in disarray and practically nonexistent. Most economic enterprises, such as haciendas, *obrajes,* and mines, had been dismantled in the wake of the wars of independence. This was the scene confronting the "new" Peru in 1826.

The Initial Lessons of Independence

Demographically Peru was still a small country. An often cited count of people based on a register of contributions in 1836 recorded 1.3 million people living in 10 administrative departments.

The first republican census, in 1876, would show 2.6 million people, an increase of barely 100,000 from the last colonial census, of 1792. The densest population concentration was in the southern highland departments, which also had the highest percentages of Indians. Within the southern departments, 94 percent of Puno's population was Indian. Indians were concentrated not only in the southern highlands but also

Population Distribution by Department, 1836	
Department	Number of Inhabitants
Amazonas	71,267
La Libertad	162,429
Piura	57,815
Ancash	121,462
Lima and Callao	151,718
Junín	144,243
Ayacucho and Huancavelica	159,608
Cuzco	216,382
Puno	156,000
Arequipa and Moquegua	136,812
Total	1,313,736

Source: Basadre (1983, III:173) and Manrique (1995, 66)

within peasant communities (sometimes called Indian communities) and on haciendas as *yanaconas*. Around one-fourth of Peruvians were classified as mestizos, and with some minor exceptions (most notably

A Peruvian "gentleman" about the time of independence from Spain. Many Spanish-born whites fled the country during or soon after the wars, but native-born Creoles took control of the government of the new nation, even though they were a small minority in a population of Indians and mestizos. (Library of Congress)

in Cuzco and the Mantaro Valley in Peru's central highlands), mestizos lived in Peru's coastal valleys and cities. A quarter of Peru's 50,000 slaves and 40,000 free blacks and mulattoes lived on the coastal haciendas and the sugar, cotton, and rice plantations. Three-fourths of Peruvian slaves lived in the department of Lima, most of them in the city of Lima as artisans and servants.

This was the demography of Peru in the early decades after independence. Throughout the 19th century this demographic distribution would greatly influence economic and political life in the new republic.

Fighting for the King? Rebellion in Iquicha

Independence did not bring the rebellions in the countryside to an end. A revolt broke out in Iquicha, in the northern part of the department of Ayacucho, that lasted from 1825 to 1839. It differed from the pre-independence rebellions, whose partisans were almost exclusively Indians, in that its leadership was made up of a mixture of whites, mestizos, and Indians. Furthermore, this continued unrest showed that peasants and rural elites wanted to participate in the shaping of the new nation-state in their own terms.

When the upheaval reached the city of Ayacucho in March 1825, the *prefecto,* or political head of the department (a post-independence administrator), sent a military force that temporarily subdued the rebels. However, during the next months there were new signs of insubordination. More troops were sent to put down the rebels. This time, however, a peasant army of approximately 1,200 overwhelmed the government forces, plundered haciendas, and seized the town governor. Skirmishes continued until May 1826, a year after the wars of independence had officially ended. At that point the *gobernador* of Tambo (now the head of a district within the larger province) reported to the *prefecto* that 50 rebels had been beheaded and many other participants shot. New uprisings nevertheless followed.

The power of the Iquicha leaders resided in their ability to appropriate the tithes. They were able to name their own collectors, especially in the local coca haciendas. With the tithes they paid for the organization and logistics of their rebellion.

General Andrés Santa Cruz, a right-hand man to Bolívar, went to Ayacucho to meet and negotiate with the rebel leaders. Santa Cruz eventually reached an agreement and promised to pardon the rebels. A brief period of peace followed, but in 1826 Spanish officials who had fought against the patriot army, along with members of the local clergy and some of the Iquicha rebels, prepared to strike at the newly created republic, encouraged by rumors that 22,000 French and Spanish forces were on their way to help. From headquarters at local haciendas the rebellion leaders, with the aid of *varayocs* (traditional Indian community leaders), recruited an army of experienced fighters, known as *montoneros*. The uprising in Ayacucho was unresolved by the time Bolívar left Lima. When Marshall José de La Mar became president, he promised the people in Iquicha exemption from tribute and military recruitment. Some Iquicha leaders gave in, but others continued to resist and on November 12, 1827, took the town of Huanta. A few weeks later they laid siege to the city of Ayacucho. Domingo Tristán, *prefecto* of Ayacucho, organized peasants from neighboring provinces, especially the Morochucos ethnic group, to fight against the rebel leaders. In this confrontation, hundreds of rebels were killed. Some leaders escaped but were taken prisoner a few months later after relentless persecutions and repressive campaigns. The only leader to escape was Antonio Huachaca.

Later, in 1833, the remaining rebels in Huanta played another role in the complex politics of the new republic when they sided with the liberal-minded general Luis José Orbegoso in ousting the conservative president Agustín Gamarra. By this stage the state needed *iquichanos* military aid, a turn of events that allowed the rebels to negotiate with the republic for the creation of an independent state. Throughout this period of rapidly shifting confrontation and intrigue, the rebels remained in control of the local tithe collection on the coca haciendas. Their ability to manage local resources allowed the *iquichanos* to become part of the new republic on their own terms. They developed their own economic and political projects by sometimes resisting and sometimes accepting the Lima-based programs of conservatives and liberals alike. It was an armed entrance into a new era, and as such this rebellion demonstrates the competing national agendas existing at the times of independence. Such conflicting ideas about change and alternative visions of the future permeated the following decades.

7

THE LONG STRUGGLE FOR STABILITY (1826–1843)

The main hurdles in the process of consolidating the new republic were the lack of physical internal infrastructure; deep-rooted distances and suspicions between social groups; the complete disorganization and disarray of public finances; and, last but not least, the absence of an accepted and legitimate group of leaders. All of these conditions made it difficult for the new nation to achieve political, social, or economic stability, and it was a long struggle during the first decades after independence to achieve some sort of balance and order.

The Obstacles

At the time of independence, in the 1820s, Peru suffered from a lack of basic physical infrastructure. It is an often-cited fact that by the beginning of the 19th century there were fewer passable roads than had existed during Inca times. Most inland transport was done on the back of llamas and mules over small dirt roads. Trains of mules and llamas carried their loads across the steep Andes from the highlands to the coast and back, and from highland town to highland town. Communication was somewhat easier on the coast, where most products were transported using vessels and ports on the shores of the Pacific Ocean. Maritime transport linked Peru's coastal valleys to internal and international trade routes. However, the cold water stream on Peru's coast, the Humboldt current, made upstream sailing from north to south very difficult. It was easier to sail from Peru's north to Guayaquil, in Ecuador, than to Lima. To solve transport and communication problems, successive Peruvian governments emphasized the need to build railroads, especially to link the highland to the coast. Not until the last quarter of the 19th century, however, was a railroad project carried out using revenues obtained from the

Because of the lack of adequate roads in much of the country, llamas were the principal beasts of burden in early 19th-century Peru. (Library of Congress)

export of guano (bird droppings, used as fertilizer) from Peru's coastal islands.

At the time of independence, social structure was clearly defined and rigid. Population growth was still low due to a low fertility rate, high infant mortality, military campaigns, the emigration of many Spaniards, and the separation of Bolivia and Ecuador from what had been the Viceroyalty of Peru. For several decades after independence Peru had a racially defined occupational structure. Most artisans were black, most peasants were Indians, most smaller merchants were mestizos, elites were predominantly white. As a part of the "colonial heritage," Peru began its republican life with a racially defined occupational structure.

Throughout the 1820s several peasant upheavals challenged the political goals of Lima's elites. Some of the uprisings had monarchist undertones or used monarchist language to propose alternative visions of the new republic. In some cases, such as the fierce resistance by

Iquicha rebels, an assembly of regional actors (Indian, mestizos, and whites) kept "liberated" areas out of Lima's control well into the 1830s. The fragmentation of the country after the wars of independence was a reality far removed from republican ideals, which had envisioned a country for all Peruvian people. Social fragmentation was, in fact, reflected in the constitution. In the first constitutions only a minority of literate male property owners had civil rights and could vote or hold office. This in effect gave all power to the Creole elite and excluded Indians, most mestizos, and blacks. Civil rights were defined in terms of race. However, Peru was not alone in its narrowly defined franchise. Even in England, it took until the end of the 19th century before voting and eligibility for office became universal for men.

Political Instability

Between 1821 and 1840 Peru had five different constitutions (1823, 1826, 1828, 1834, and 1839), and between 1841 and 1845 six presidents governed Peru. Two basic political models were debated and fought over with words and weapons by successive contending parties after independence: a constitutional monarchy versus a liberal republic. Each form of government had its supporters, and several presidents defended one model or the other. Partisanship and factionalism were the result.

Defenders of a constitutional monarchy clashed with liberal republicans over key issues such as incorporating Peru's indigenous populations in the electorate. For decades monarchists posited that Indians were ignorant and subject (as servants and serfs on haciendas) to the control of third parties; thus they had insufficient free will to be allowed to vote. Liberals counterargued that most Indians lived in Indian communities where they owned some sort of land and were thus independent agrarian producers, and that Indians paid taxes to the state—the former colonial tribute, now called *contribución de indígenas* or *contribución rural*. Between 1849 and 1895, under liberal dominance, illiterate men—thus, Indians—were actually allowed to participate in indirect elections.

Another topic of heated discussions and confrontations was the division of power between the executive (the president) and the legislative (congress) branches of government. The five constitutions approved between 1821 and 1840 contained a clause by which an intermediate entity between the executive and the legislative was instituted, the Consejo de Estado, which in a way was an extension of the colonial *audiencia*. The Consejo was a consulting rather than legislative entity. Liberals defended the predominance of the legislative branch to avoid political centralization and the concentration of power; conservatives envisioned a strong executive as the only alternative to confront the prevailing military anarchy, with the goal of establishing a centralized republic. However, political beliefs and wishes were not set in stone. More than once some of the most prominent liberal thinkers changed sides when confronted with social disorder and anarchy (Contreras and Cueto 2000, 75–79). And social disorder and anarchy were paramount during the first decades after independence. Some Peruvians even invoked the colonial era as a better time.

The most visible expression of political dissension and uncertainty and of social disorder was a form of politics known as *caciquismo* (derived from cacique, a local boss). Many contending factions were led by a

PRESIDENTIAL MUSICAL CHAIRS

As in most other newly independent countries of Latin America, Peru witnessed a rapidly changing procession of political figures in the years following the wars against Spanish control. In the four decades after the departure of Simón Bolívar in 1826, Peru had 34 presidents, all of whom sought to fasten their personal hold on the country. They all came from the elite sector of society, and four out of five were military officers, most of them veterans of the revolutionary wars. A few were lawyers, and several were big landowners. A quarter were native to Lima. Two-fifths of the presidents had previously served in the important office of *prefecto* in one of the large departments set up after independence. Surprisingly, only a minority of the presidents had experience as legislators or cabinet members before taking executive power.

Succession to the presidential office was hazardous, and several of those who tried and failed met their ends in front of firing squads. Only one-fifth of the presidents between 1826 and 1865 came to power by coups d'état, but the threat of coups and rebellions in the departments often unseated presidents and added to the record of short executive tenure. Only a small percentage of Peru's presidents came to office through election by the legislature or the electoral college. Most reached office through constitutional succession or appointment (Dobyns and Doughty 1976, 158–159).

cacique or caudillo (military strongman), and each of these men embodied a different idea of how to govern a country that had no citizens. Some caciques and caudillos cared only about lining their own pockets. They usually had absolute control in their respective regions and became the mediators between the central state and provincial societies. In a reference to the colonial era, some contemporaries jokingly commented that a strong king (the king of Spain) had been replaced by several mock kings. Their power was based on close networks of dependents, blackmail, and the distribution of favors and rewards often wrung from the state. Hacendados, powerful merchants, high bureaucrats, officials in the military, or a combination thereof could become caciques or caudillos. They consolidated their power throughout the 19th century in spite of sporadic attempts to centralize power and keep *caciquismo* under control. In hindsight caciques and caudillos were generally pro-indigenous and pro-nationalist local power agents who managed to hold the country together by guaranteeing if not the ideal form of social order, at least some kind of order in the transition from colony to republic.

Whatever their intentions or achievements, cacique/caudillo-presidents faced almost insurmountable obstacles. The long, intense wars of independence had destroyed much of Peru's economic infrastructure. Lima's port city, Callao, was in ruins, and most coastal and highland agrarian enterprises had been ravaged by foraging armies. The church, in turn, had lost not only assets but men. Many Spanish priests left the country, and the church's grip on people's lives and consciousness diminished accordingly. Military caudillism or *caciquismo* held strong under these conditions. Most historians today date the end of the first era of *caciquismo* at 1872, with the election of Peru's first civil president Manuel Pardo.

Fiscal Issues

Aside from leadership, much of what any government can do depends on its revenues. Between 1827 and 1845, the Peruvian state expended between 5 million and 6 million pesos every year. At the time of independence the main sources of state income were the taxes on internal commerce and exports, the Indian tribute, and the state's production and distribution monopolies over tobacco, mercury, gunpowder, and playing cards. In independent Peru, however, state monopolies—with the exception of the playing cards, a negligible source of state income—were abolished, following the new principle of nonintervention by the state in the economic life of the country. But the new state was in desperate need of money and had to carefully restructure the income side of its budget.

Mining remained an important economic state enterprise, albeit much reduced in scale and productivity from colonial times. Already in the late colonial period Peru's silver mining axis had shifted from Potosí to the central highlands in Cerro de Pasco and Hualgayoc (in the present-day departments of Pasco and Cajamarca, respectively). The mercury mines in Huancavelica were no longer productive, and mercury now had to be imported from Europe. Although Cerro de Pasco had seen the installation of the first steam engines to pump out rising water levels in mine tunnels in order to revive faltering mines, these machines were destroyed during the wars of independence. The mining industry could no longer count on the strong administrative and financial support it had enjoyed during colonial times. Mine owners instead had to depend on new market relationships to solve financial and technological hurdles, and the market proved exceptionally fickle. Mercury prices often doubled or quadrupled in times of scarcity. Mercury production worldwide was controlled by one company: In 1830, Spain—heavily indebted—transferred its mercury mines in Almadén to its creditors, the Rothschilds, who also owned the only other mercury-producing mines in the world, in Idria, and could thus set the price, at least until around 1850, when mercury from California became available (Contreras and Cueto 2000, 83).

Cerro de Pasco was the name of both a mountain and a major city in the region of the central highlands that became the center of mining activity after independence. (Library of Congress)

Under these new market relationships mine owners also had to find capital to finance costly mining production. In contrast to colonial times when the state bought silver bars from mine owners and granted credits on future production, after independence mine owners entirely depended on merchant capital to finance their enterprises. Often merchants proved to be less cooperative and reliable than the colonial state had been. More than one mine owner came to understand that free trade was not always beneficial. Mining, a risky venture, became riskier during times of political unrest. Many mine owners defaulted on the repayment of loans and after lengthy legal battles lost their mines to lenders. Anticipated foreign investments, especially from British entrepreneurs, failed to materialize in large measure because of inhospitable political, social, and geographical conditions.

In spite of these problems silver was Peru's main export product, composing between 82 and 90 percent of total exports, until 1840. The silver from mining paid for the growing imports from Europe; thus, Peru kept pace with its balance of trade by exporting silver. An unhappy counterpart of this process was that the internal market was left with diminished amounts of circulating money; no money was left to engage in market transactions inside the country. Slowly, debased coins coming from Bolivian mints replaced the strong Peruvian peso, and foreign merchants became suspicious of their trade relations with Peru. The debased coin, called the *peso feble* or "weak peso," in contrast to the *peso fuerte* or "strong peso," contained on average 40 percent less silver, replaced by less valuable metals such as copper or tin. In an economy with no paper money, lowering the content of silver in circulating coins was equivalent to inflation. Prices for imported goods rose accordingly.

The internal customs, or *alcabala*, was abolished, but the tribute paid by Indian peasants continued, and in fact the Indian head tax provided the state with larger sums of money than the internal customs. Both payments were colonial leftovers that did not fit well into more liberal and enlightened times; however, fiscal need prevailed. The rationale behind keeping the indigenous tribute was that Indians, the majority living in peasant communities and holding communal property in these communities, could not be taxed on landed property and that by being essentially self-sufficient they contributed nothing to the state through the consumption of imported goods. Thus they had to pay a *contribución única*, a pseudonym for the colonial tribute.

Until around 1850 the Indian tribute (under its new name) was the largest single income source of the Peruvian state. The most lucrative region for tribute payments was the densely populated southern highlands (Cuzco and Puno). The central highlands (Junín) paid an intermediate amount, and the coastal areas (Lima and Trujillo) provided relatively low amounts. Cuzco and Puno were where the largest numbers of indigenous peoples lived.

Tribute payments were temporarily abolished between 1854 and 1876, during the guano boom, but were restored between 1876 and 1895, when they were reintroduced in the form of a salt tax by President Nicolás de Piérola. The salt tax affected the same people who had been paying tributes before.

Another targeted population as a source of income were *castas*, or nonindigenous people from varied racial backgrounds. During the early 19th century the colonial state under Viceroy José Abascal had tried to impose a tribute on *castas*, aiming especially at the growing mestizo population. After independence the government launched a series of census projects in 1827, 1836, and 1850 primarily to attempt to account for the overall population growth but also to count potential non-Indian tribute payers. In spite of such efforts the contributions obtained from non-Indians were very limited and subject to continued questioning from non-Indians and local bureaucrats alike.

Thus, the revenues the early republican state depended on mainly came from departments with a high concentration of indigenous populations. The population count in 1827 showed that the southern highlands (comprising present-day departments of Ayacucho, Huancavelica, Cuzco, Apurímac, Puno, Arequipa, Moquegua, Tacna, and Tarapacá) had 52 percent of Peru's population and the central highlands (Lima, Ica, Junín, Pasco, Huánuco, and Ancash) had 28 percent. The northern region (La Libertad, Lambayeque, Cajamarca, Piura, Tumbes, and Amazonas), with 22 percent of Peru's population in 1827, had many haciendas and plantations, but very few Indian peasants. Regional development patterns over the following decades were closely connected to this regional population distribution.

Under newly independent Peru and its prevailing free-market ideology, a reduction of import taxes should have been expected. But as was the case with the abolition of the Indian tribute, lowering import taxes would have resulted in insufficient revenue for the state. The first opening of the international market came in 1821, in the wake of the protectorate of general José de San Martín. The import tariffs were lowered to 20 percent of the imported goods' declared value. Few imports were barred, and many imported items especially from Great Britain flooded Peru's market, soon saturating the market—in contrast to expectations. In response, in 1826, the Peruvian government increased taxes—to rates of up to 80 percent—on imported goods that competed with local production, such as oils and lard, hides, furniture, clothes, tobacco, candles, and spirits. In spite of increased taxes the revenues obtained from customs diminished. Such early experiences led to heated debates on overall economic development strategies. Was the way to success to open Peru to the international market, as Great Britain had done? Or, did the nascent industry need—as the United States had decided—some protection from external competition to gain time to consolidate?

Neither of these economic theories was translated into reality. Policies governing customs oscillated widely, to the point where unpredictability actually became an efficient form of protectionism. Post-independence Peru was divided along geographical lines into two camps on customs issues: a protectionist-minded north (including Lima) that was heavily engaged in trade with Chile, and a free trade–minded south that advocated an integration with Bolivia and increasing interaction with British merchants, who were buying locally produced wool, saltpeter, and bark. However, not all economic actors in southern Peru agreed to the free-market policies. Former *obraje* owners in Cuzco had been completely ruined by the opening of trade with Britain, and Cuzco had lost its dominant economic position to

In post-independence Peru, Arequipa, shown here in a later photograph, became the center for British merchants who traded in raw materials from the southern region. It was also the center of several separatist movements to break away from Peru. (Library of Congress)

Arequipa, a city where most British merchant houses had their head-quarters. Unable to impose a nationwide answer to the protectionism versus free trade debate, Peru's south instead adopted separatism and between 1836 and 1839 tried to establish the Peruvian-Bolivian Confederation under the guidance of General Andrés de Santa Cruz, a former independence fighter and then president of Bolivia.

National Identity and National Borders

After their successful revolutions, it was crucial that the newly inde-pendent Latin American republics establish national boundaries and their separate territoriality. The new boundaries would determine issues of military defense and commercial policies, and they would begin to determine the nature of continuing national interests. The 19th century witnessed many twists and turns that led to the boundary configuration of present-day South America.

Peru fought regularly throughout the 19th century: war with Colombia in 1829; war with Bolivia between 1829 and 1834; campaigns against Chile between 1835 and 1842; skirmishes with Ecuador in 1860; war with Spain in 1866; and a prolonged war (War of the Pacific) with Chile from 1879 to 1884. These conflicts were part and parcel of the process of constructing a national identity in a country that had never thought of itself as a distinct entity. With the exception of the skirmishes with Ecuador and the maritime battles with Spain, Peru lost all of these conflicts, and with each military loss came the loss of terri-tory. The construction of a national identity had territorial costs and, maybe even more important, psychological costs in terms of national pride and consciousness.

One important episode in this sequence of wars was the attempt to create the Peruvian-Bolivian Confederation. Had it been successful, this effort would have led to the establishment of a new country, integrating present-day Bolivia and the southern Peruvian departments. At issue was international trade—free trade versus protectionism—but the real issues were obscured by a merry-go-round of shifting alliances and changing presidents.

When General Simón Bolívar left Peru in 1827, the Peruvian congress selected as president one of his closest collaborators, Ecuadorean gen-eral José de La Mar, to replace Andrés de Santa Cruz, who had served in the interim. The new president briefly invaded Bolivia, forcing Bolívar's former lieutenant and Bolivian president General Antonio José de Sucre to flee after the Bolivian troops declined to fight the Peruvian invaders.

La Mar then marched north into Gran Colombia, the southern region of the composite nation presided over by Bolívar, and seized the city of Guayaquil. However, La Mar and his army were defeated by Colombian troops in the battle of Portete de Tarqui in 1829, and consequently Peru lost Guayaquil. (The borders between Ecuador and Peru were not clearly delineated until well into the 20th century and are still subject to occasional border skirmishes.)

Following his defeat, La Mar was ousted from the Peruvian presidency by the Cuzco-born general Agustín Gamarra, who had reached an agreement with General Santa Cruz and General Antonin de la Fuente. Gamarra became president of Peru, with La Fuente as vice president, and Santa Cruz took over the presidency of Bolivia. When Gamarra reached the end of his term in 1833, one of his supporters, Luis José Orbegoso, was appointed to succeed him. Whereas Gamarra had supported protectionist measures in an attempt to safeguard Cuzco's *obrajes,* Orbegoso implemented free trade. This change in economic policy deepened the existing antagonism between the protectionist northern coastal plantation owners and the free trade–minded south. A pro-Gamarra faction deposed Orbegoso, who was then restored briefly to the presidency after a short, bitter civil war. The situation became even more complex when the caudillo Felipe de Salaverry became president and allied himself with Gamarra against Santa Cruz, who hoped to unite south Peru and Bolivia. Santa Cruz won a series of battles and captured and executed Salaverry. Santa Cruz proclaimed the Peru-Bolivian Confederation with himself as protector in 1836. The confederation was short lived, however, ending three years later with the military defeat of the Peruvians and Santa Cruz by a Chilean army.

This sort of muddled political and military sequence was, unfortunately, all too typical of the early years of the Peruvian nation. Might seemed to make right, and few national leaders seemed to have the best interests of the country at heart—or at least they put national interests well behind regional interests and self interest. After the defeat at the hands of the Chileans and the disintegration of the Peru-Bolivian Confederation, chaos and anarchy took hold. Successive caudillos came to power, some of them lasting less than a few weeks. In the 19 years between 1826 and 1845, Peru counted 12 presidents and approved six constitutions. Executive powers were paramount; at the same time Lima's popular classes, tired and disgusted with unrelenting and dreary military coups, founded the first mass-supported proconstitution movements.

8

THE AGE OF GUANO
(1843–1879)

The extraction and export of guano, or seabird droppings that had been deposited for thousands of years and sedimented on coastal islands, dominated Peru's economic life for four decades. Pre-Columbian societies knew of the fertilizing benefits of guano; however, it was the German scientist Alexander von Humboldt (1767–1835) who through his writings alerted European readers to the value of guano. Demand for guano increased with the industrial revolution in the United Kingdom, where industrial workers in cities needed to be fed with higher agrarian yields.

The income from the guano trade was immense and might well have been spent to develop Peru into a model modern state. Unfortunately much of the guano wealth went into building a wasteful state bureaucracy or was frittered away on grandiose railway projects that were never completed. Worse still, the Peruvian government chose to borrow massively in the international financial markets, pledging future guano production as security.

There were some solid accomplishments, such as the use of guano income to end slavery through a program of purchasing freedom for the country's black slaves and to end the burdensome Indian tribute in 1854. On the whole, however, Peru failed to take full advantage of four decades of prosperity, from the 1840s through the 1870s, despite positive developments in wool and agricultural production in the south and central highlands.

Toward Political Maturity

Peru's first timid steps toward organizing the business of the state came between 1843 and 1844, when General Mariano Ignacio Vivanco attempted to organize a national budget and to implement a judicial and an educational system. Vivanco had lived as an exile in Chile, where he learned from its example of organizing state issues. Chile, under the leadership of President Diego Portales, was one of the most stable areas in a chronically unstable Latin America.

In 1845 a strong caudillo, Ramón Castilla, seized Peru's presidency. The Castilla regime, which coincided with a timely European demand for guano from islands off the Peruvian coast, provided Peru with two decades of relative economic growth and political stability. Castilla led Peru through most of the guano age. His social measures, such as the abolition of Indian tribute and slavery in 1854, as well as his attempts to control internal corruption provided him with vast popular support, which allowed him to fight off several challenges, most notably a rebellion led by José Echenique. (Castilla defeated Echenique on the battlefield in 1855. Castilla died on his horse in Tarapacá in 1867, on his way to quell yet another uprising.)

A constitution promulgated by Castilla in 1860 that was ideologically halfway between liberalism and ancien régime resulted in Peru's first elections. Under this constitution, all taxpayers, property owners, literate men, and workshop owners could vote and hold office. It was an indirect vote; that is, every 500 men chose one member of the Electoral College, which elected congressmen and the president. In the congress, senators represented the departments; deputies represented the provinces, and the number of deputies for each province corresponded to its population. To become a deputy one had to earn more than 500 pesos a year; to become a senator a candidate had to earn no less than 1,000 pesos annually. Congressional seats were thus reserved for the economic elites. Elections took place, for the first time, from 1871 to 1872. It took almost a whole year to tidy up the electoral process.

These elections prompted the founding of the Sociedad Independencia Electoral, which in turn became the Partido Civil in 1872, the political party through which Peru's coastal oligarchy remained in command of Peru until the beginning of the 20th century. In its inception the Partido Civil was a political counterforce to the military and caudillos. The head of the Partido Civil was railroad businessman Manuel Pardo. The *civilistas,* as the party members were called, were supported by big merchants, large financial interests, and many liberal intellectuals and professionals. Pardo's main opponent was Nicolás de Piérola and his followers, called *pierolistas* (Contreras and Cueto 2000, 143–145).

In contrast to Pardo, Piérola was more oriented toward the provinces and looked after the interests of medium-sized landowners and small merchants. He voiced his opposition to foreign interests and those who supported such interests, such as the coastal plantation owners. Disputes between *civilistas* and *pierolistas* would dominate the Peruvian political scene (and eventually the military scene) until the late 1910s. In 1872 Pardo won the elections, but only after a gruesome attempted coup rocked the nation. During the last days of July 1872 War Minister Tomás Gutiérrez, backed by his brothers, all of whom were army colonels, arrested President José Balta and declared himself president. The so-called rebellion of the colonels failed in large measure because it lacked popular support in Lima, and the Peruvian navy and key elements of the army sided with the *civilistas*. When one of the Gutiérrez brothers was killed by an angry mob in Lima, the coup leaders murdered President Balta in his cell, which set off a violent public reaction. A mob seized Tomás Gutiérrez, killed him, and hung his body along with the beheaded corpse of one of his brothers from the towers of Lima's main cathedral. A few days later Pardo became president.

Pardo's ascendancy to power was followed by several important reforms: He decentralized state administration, giving more power to municipalities; he made primary education obligatory for all Peruvians; he undertook several measures to promote European immigration; and he organized the first national census in 1876. This census counted 2.7 million Peruvians, of which 58 percent were Indians, a finding that signaled an increase in the nation's mestizo population. The census also found that 70 percent of the population were illiterate and that there were 4,400 haciendas, where one-fourth of Peru's rural population resided.

MANUEL PARDO

Manuel Pardo (1834–98) was a descendant of an aristocratic colonial family. His grandfather had been an official of the *audiencias* of both Lima and Cuzco. Pardo was educated in Europe, and entered—as did many of his peers—a career in commerce and finance. For health reasons he spent a whole year in the city of Jauja in 1858, and it was probably in the Mantaro Valley that he conceived his future railroad project. There he observed how, for lack of adequate transportation, the rich produce of Lima's hinterlands could not reach the urban market. Railroads and Pardo's presidency would go together in the Peruvian historical record, and the railroads are considered the main 19th-century achievement of his Civil Party (Partido Civil) (Contreras and Cueto 2000, 136).

Pardo's presidency was not without serious hurdles. He had inherited both an immense foreign debt, which inevitably prompted serious financial problems amid decaying guano revenues, and unending small rebellions in the interior, largely waged by caudillos and the *pierolistas*.

Guano

Between 1840 and 1880 Peru exported approximately 10.8 million metric tons of guano at an average price of £10 per ton. Thus, over the course of these 40 years, Peru earned around £100 million from the guano trade and became one of the wealthiest countries in Latin America. Moreover, guano was state owned; in other words, all the income from exporting guano went to the state coffers. Because these revenues were state administered, the Peruvian government had a unique opportunity to develop projects under its own auspices.

What did the Peruvian state do with the money obtained from selling guano to Europe? The answer to this question is complex and multilayered. It involves how guano was extracted, who participated in

Seabirds, seen here on one of the Chincha Islands off the coast of Peru, have flocked for hundreds of years on South America's coastal islands, leaving thick deposits of guano. In the 19th century guano was mined as a hugely lucrative source of agricultural fertilizer. (Photo by Alejandro Balaguer/Andes y Mares)

what ways in the guano exports, and how British and Peruvian interests merged or conflicted in this export venture.

In contrast to ores or agrarian produce, guano was easily accessible and needed no heavy equipment or high capital investment. Packing guano and loading it on ships bound for Europe required only men, bags, shovels, and transportation. The men were mostly convicts or Chinese immigrants known as coolies, who provided cheap labor that accounted for about 4 percent of total production costs. Bags were easily provided by small-scale textile workshops. Shovels were imported and paid for by money minted in Cerro de Pasco. The ships sailed under European flags.

Guano exports hugely enlarged the government's fiscal revenues. In 1846 revenues obtained from guano accounted for less than 10 percent of state revenues (513,000 soles of 6.113 million soles). (The sol was established as the national currency in 1863.) Only five years later this percentage had risen to more than 25 percent (2.194 million of 7.636 million soles), and by 1872, to about 50 percent (34.566 million of 67.987 million soles) (Manrique 1995, 121). Such financial windfalls made it easy to get loans on the international financial markets and allowed Peru to borrow against future guano production, although this practice would eventually lead to a deep financial crisis.

The Impact of Guano Exports

Many Peruvian and non-Peruvian authors have discussed at length why Peru—having access to the tremendous resources provided by guano exports—did not achieve economic and political modernization. Historians previously assumed that the guano revenues benefited mainly foreigners, but recently it has been convincingly argued that most revenues were retained inside the country. By analyzing state expenditures, U.S. economist Shane Hunt (1984, 51) has shown that 53.5 percent of the Peruvian budget was spent on expanding Peru's civil and military bureaucracy, 20 percent on the building of railroads, 11.5 percent on transfer payments to Peruvians and 8 percent to foreigners, and 7 percent to reduce tributary impositions on poor people. The nature of these expenditures tells the story about the lost economic opportunity.

At the beginning of the guano era the Peruvian governmental apparatus was small, amounting to only three ministries with a few dozen bureaucrats each. The demands of the guano boom, however, rapidly expanded almost all branches of the Peruvian government and added hundreds of state-employed workers. Both police and military forces, for example, were increased in numbers and had their powers extended to the provinces, which had the side effect of substantially reducing the autonomy and power of caciques. With money from the guano trade Peru became one of the strongest military powers in South America and one of the first nations on the continent to own armored steamships. The Peruvian navy was strong enough in 1866, for example, to fight to a standstill a Spanish fleet that had attacked Callao.

In addition to providing such benefits, however, the employment rolls of the expanding state apparatus were also used as patronage to recruit and reward followers. Such hiring abuses led to high levels of inefficiency and corruption. Investing more than 50 percent of state revenues in an inefficient state administration stifled progress.

Previous loans and the accumulated interest on them further drained state resources. In 1822 and 1824 the Peruvian state contracted two loans in London in the amount of £1.81 million. Succeeding governments were unable to repay them, and by 1848 these loans and the principal and interest had increased Peru's debts to £5.38 million—three times the initial loan. Recognizing Peru's sudden economic windfall, the British bondholders of the debt exerted great pressure to make Peru repay the outstanding loans. In 1849 the Peruvian government signed a treaty by which Peru agreed to repay these loans through new bond issues backed by future sales of guano. With this treaty Peru was readmitted to the international financial community and could obtain new loans. However, new loans soon had to be used to repay old loans and accumulated interest, and old loans and new loans eventually ate all available fiscal resources.

In 1869 the minister in charge of Peru's economics, Nicolás de Piérola, signed a contract with the French businessman Auguste Dreyfus by which Dreyfus became the only agent allowed to extract guano. Until then a large group of Peruvian consignment agents had been in charge. With the money he gained by exporting guano, Dreyfus made new loans to the Peruvian government. With £11.92 million loaned by Dreyfus to the administration of José Balta in 1870, the government began the construction of railroads. In the end guano deposits were greatly depleted; the railroads were left unfinished; and Peru faced an external debt of £35 million, an amount that required an annual interest and principal payment of £2 million, which then was the entire annual budget.

In addition to the British bondholders many native Peruvians held long-standing claims on the government. Under pressure from such claimants the Peruvian government recognized this internal debt. The government acknowledged the nation's obligations to its own citizens, such as those who had supplied funds for the patriot armies during the wars of independence. Over time more and more claimants presented larger and larger claims. In 1851 the state-recognized internal debt amounted to 4.88 million pesos; by 1858, it had grown to 23.2 million pesos, or five times the annual budget of 1850 (Contreras and Cueto 2000, 125). Governmental corruption lay at the heart of much of this drastic increase. The state also acted intentionally to transfer public savings to private hands in the hope of promoting investments. The state's recognition of an internal debt was intended to foster the development of an entrepreneurial middle class and to forestall suspicions harbored by nationalists about the government's relations with foreign capitalists.

Rather than becoming revenue producers, as hoped, Peruvians continued to receive money from the state. Peruvian historians Carlos Contreras and Marcos Cueto (2000, 133) have calculated that each Peruvian cost the state five times more a year than he or she contributed to the state. During the boom the gap was filled by guano revenues. Who gained from these state-earned distributions? According to Peruvian historian Alfonso Quiroz in his 1987 book, *La deuda defraudada,* a total of 2,028 people received state bonds; however, two-thirds of the total bond value was held by only 126 people, mostly large land owners and merchants and some state bureaucrats. Money thus obtained from state coffers was only marginally invested in productive ventures, such as a few banks and small textile and food industries. In large measure the money was reloaned to the state. For lenders this was a less risky investment with higher yields than investing in industrial development, at least until the Peruvian state went bankrupt. In a sense the Peruvian guano age suffered from what contemporary economists would call the "Dutch disease." Abundance of money lowered prices for imported goods and increased labor costs, whereas the high profitability of guano exports increased the borrowing price of money (that is, interest rates).

During the boom Lima and other coastal cities benefited most from guano revenues, sometimes through the internal debt mechanism but more often simply because more money entered the economy. For example, real salaries increased on average 3 percent annually. However, with more money circulating in the cities came inflation, and inflation further accentuated economic differentiation. Between 1856 and 1869 the accumulated price inflation surpassed 100 percent. As a result labor conditions and standards of living worsened. Lima's artisans were the first to react when in 1858 they marched through the

A public square in Lima, decorated for the July 28 celebration of independence day in 1868 at the height of the guano boom (Library of Congress)

city's streets protesting against elite consumption patterns. Suddenly enriched, Lima's elites resorted to imports. Doors, windows, pianos, shoes, and clothes came from Europe, leaving Lima's artisans (most of them descendants of former slaves) without work and income.

Slavery and Indian Tribute Reassessed

One important expenditure of the Peruvian government during the guano boom was money spent on effectively abolishing slavery. Seven percent of guano revenues were set aside, and the government bought the liberty of 25,505 slaves from slave owners for 300 pesos each. In theory there were no slaves in Peru, as slavery had been abolished by General José de San Martín in 1821. Shortly after San Martín's proclamation, however, former slaves were put under the tutelage of their owners. At first this tutelage lasted until the former slaves reached age 21, but in 1839 it was extended until age 50. Decrees, intentions, and reality were revealed in the state abolition expenditures. A simple calculation shows that the Peruvian government paid 7.65 million pesos to slave owners, money that was largely spent after 1854 on expanding sugar and cotton plantations.

The other component of social expenditure was the temporary abolition of the Indian tribute, which until around 1840 had represented 25 percent of state revenues. After 1840 the Peruvian state made several attempts to reform Peru's tributary system, but each met political resistance. No party or leader wanted to support such unpopular actions. President Castilla abolished the tribute in 1854. The reform implemented in 1866 by Manuel Pardo, Peru's minister of economics (and later its first civil president), was short lived. Pardo wanted to make tax collection uniform by taxing all Peruvians, not only Indians. According to his plan all male Peruvians between the ages of 21 and 60 were to pay the equivalent of 12 days' labor in a year in taxes. The experiment lasted less than a year and ended with the ouster of President Mariano Ignacio Prado.

Despite attempts, the Indian tribute was not replaced with a more efficient and ethnically neutral taxing system. To the contrary, the same Indian tribute abolished in 1854 was reintroduced in 1885. Between 1854 and 1885, however, abolishing the tribute had long-term consequences for mining and agriculture in the highlands. It also at least partially explains why coastal plantation owners could not use Indian labor and resorted to importing Chinese laborers to work on their fields: Once the Indians had no need for cash to pay their tribute, they largely could engage in their own endeavors.

One of the peasants' few monetary needs was money to fulfill communal religious duties, including buying candles, providing dresses for statues of the local patron saint, and paying the services of a priest. Many hacienda and mine owners were aware of this cyclical need for money and visited the peasant communities (or sent a hired intermediary) knowing when such festivities were scheduled to take place. Subsequently hacendados or their agents would entice the peasants involved to accept gifts or money. In exchange the ensnared peasants would find themselves obligated to work off the value of the gifts or loans by laboring in a mine or on a hacienda. This form of hiring laborers has been called *enganche* (meaning a "hook"). Often such practices were endorsed by or even organized with the help of local political authorities. Once entrapped by this system, workers saw their debts constantly increase.

The abolition of both the Indian tribute and slavery meant a retreat of Indians and former slaves from the labor market, leaving plantation owners on the coast and hacienda owners in the highlands with a labor shortage, and the state with lower income from internal taxation. As landowners' complaints became louder, the Peruvian government

WAR WITH SPAIN

The causes of a mostly maritime war with Spain, fought in 1865 and 1866, could be traced to an 1859 policy of the Peruvian government to promote the immigration of Spaniards as a way to help Europeanize the Peruvian population. Among the immigrants were 175 Basques, who were settled in a northern coastal estate to grow cotton on shares. The estate owner treated them poorly, and tensions eventually resulted in armed violence in 1863. The Spanish government protested when the Basque workers were arrested, and the conflict escalated over the course of the next two years.

In 1865 Spain occupied the guano-rich Chincha Islands, thereby depriving Peru of its principal source of revenue, and landed a small force of sailors in Callao, where one Spanish sailor was killed in a fight with local Peruvians. In May 1866 a Spanish fleet opened fire on Callao and was subsequently attacked by several modern, well-armed and well-trained Peruvian warships. The Peruvians disabled the principal Spanish ship and forced the Spanish forces to retreat (Manrique 1995, 131).

The Chincha Islands, temporarily seized by Spanish forces in 1865 (Photo by Alejandro Balaguer/Andes y Mares)

sought to replenish the labor supply. First Peru invited European immigrants, who according to contemporary thinking would also improve Peru's racial profile. Then—once it became clear that Europeans were a demanding rather than obedient labor force—Peru organized, in conjunction with Chinese consular representatives, the importation of unskilled Chinese workers from Macao and Canton (Guangzhou).

Several factors converged to lay the groundwork for the expansion of coastal plantations in the 1860s: money paid by the state for the manumission of slaves, fresh labor in the form of Chinese coolies, high prices in the international market, and capital from merchant houses and the newly created banks. Sugar production reached unprecedented heights in the 1870s—growing 495 percent between 1871 and 1878—and by 1879 sugar exports accounted for 32 percent of all Peruvian exports. In the wake of this expansion many wheat-producing haciendas in valleys near Lima switched to sugar production, and Peru imported wheat from Chile. Coastal valleys between Lambayeque and La Libertad contained the most important sugar-producing plantations. Cotton production did not lag far behind, especially during the years of the U.S. Civil War. Piura contributed 14 percent of all cotton exports, Lima 38 percent, and Ica (south of Lima) 42 percent (Manrique 1995, 130–131).

Chinese Immigrants

Between 1840 and 1874, 100,000 Chinese immigrants, mainly men, arrived in Callao. The Pacific passage caused high death tolls. Estimates indicate that between 10 and 30 percent of people who embarked in China died during the trip. Once these Chinese laborers were in Peru, their living conditions resembled those of former Peruvian slaves. Publicity about the deadly shipboard passage and labor conditions on the guano islands and on coastal plantations led to diplomatic protests, followed by an influx of Chinese laborers between 1870–74 before the looming abandonment of "importing" this labor supply. Chinese laborers were reportedly subject to harsh mistreatment, including whipping, incarceration, overwork, and even forced celibacy. The largest Chinese populations were in Lambayeque and La Libertad, where historian Humberto Rodríguez Pastor, using the 1876 census, counted 15 Chinese women and 12,864 Chinese men (1989, 68).

Since it was the landowners who provided the Chinese immigrants with the money to pay for the trip from China to Peru, these workers were indebted to and completely dependent on their employers. Once settled on the hacienda, Chinese laborers had to repay their travel money out of their wages in addition to feeding and clothing themselves. Hacendados would lend workers more money to meet their living

Chinese immigrant workers picking cotton in an irrigated field near Vitarte. Many Chinese agricultural laborers were brought to Peru in the 1870s and faced harsh conditions and treatment. (Library of Congress)

expenses, thus continually extending the initial labor contract. Chinese laborers were unable to leave their "owners" because of this continued indebtedness. Very gradually, however, Chinese laborers managed to rid themselves of their initial labor contracts to become small merchants, first in provincial cities and then in Lima. The common saying in Lima *el chino de la esquina* ("the Chinese on the corner"), which came to mean the small neighborhood grocery store, was testament to the role of Chinese merchants in this period, even after such stores were no longer in Chinese hands.

The Railroads

The building of Peru's railroads absorbed about 20 percent of the guano revenues during the decade between 1868 and 1878. Peru built its railroads in the hope of promoting development, integrating the country's economy, and linking the country to international trade. In the long run the only goal achieved was joining Peru more closely to the international market through the export of raw materials: wool, silver, copper, sugar, and cotton. Railroad construction closely coincided with the location of the main production sites of these raw materials.

In 1860 Peru only had two railroad lines: One linking Tacna and Arica in the south, and another (12 miles long) linking Lima to its port city, Callao and the elite vacation resort of Chorrillos. In 1872, president Manuel Pardo campaigned for the urgent need to massively expand the railroad system. He was certain that train whistles would awaken the country to the benefits of modernity. But dreams of modernity confronted an almost impossible geophysical landscape. To reach the highlands locomotives had to climb to 12,000 feet above sea level, and technological knowledge of this time was not up to the challenge.

It was an engineer from the United States, Henry Meiggs, who convinced the Peruvian government to launch a railroad-building program. Between 1869 and 1872 the Peruvian government borrowed £36 million to start building railroads. Ten new lines were built, though not all 10 were state initiated. The Lima-Chancay, Pimentel-Chiclayo, and Pisco-Ica lines were in private hands. Few of these large projects ever reached their final goal. For example, from 1868 to 1878, about 700 miles of railroad were built; this represented only about 10 percent of what had initially been planned. An economic crisis in the 1870s brought railroad construction to a halt. Meiggs died in 1877 leaving behind muddled and illegible plans and unpaid bills (Contreras and Cueto 2000, 139). His unfinished railroad network, which ended in isolated peasant communities, was virtually worthless. The evaporation of state resources with the end of the guano boom and the War of the Pacific (1879–83) between Peru and Chile postponed all railway endeavors for several decades.

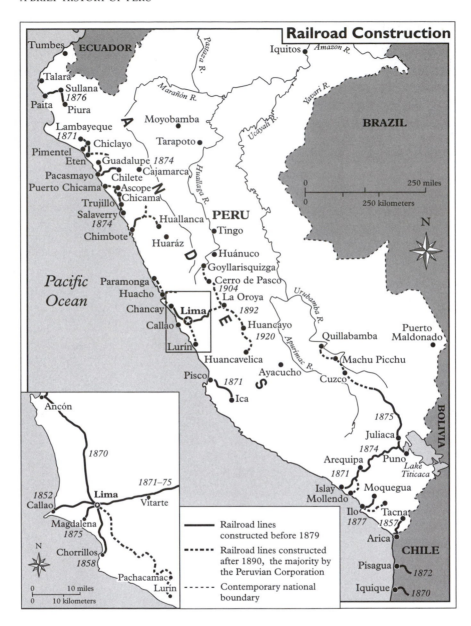

Railroad Construction

Historical Processes in the Regions

While historians have devoted much energy to explaining Peruvian national development during the 19th century, the historical processes and economic development of the distinct regions have been much less examined. Much is known about the overarching economic cycles in these regions, but the repercussions of these cycles within the regions remains relatively obscure.

Three economic regions in Peru are discernible during the 19th century. The economy of Peru's Andean south revolved initially around sheep and alpaca wool exports but eventually came to include copper and iron. The central highlands depended first on silver production, but by mid-century cattle production became important, as did production of *aguardiente* (brandy) by the 1890s. The third region, comprising Lima and Peru's central and northern coasts, rested on two pillars: guano exports and sugar and cotton production.

The Andean South

During colonial times before the establishment of the Viceroyalty of Río de la Plata in 1776, the cycles of the Andean south were closely knit to the mining industry. The loss of Potosí to the new viceroyalty launched the southern provinces into several decades of economic depression until a new product—sheep and alpaca wool—pumped money into the region. In step with the British industrial revolution, which created demand for the raw materials, exports of sheep and alpaca wool grew steadily.

Wool exports brought about dramatic changes in the region but did not benefit everyone. Indian peasants, for example, did not voluntarily participate in the wool trade. More often than not, a wool merchant's agent, called a *rescatista,* visited a peasant's hut, left a "loan," and specified how much wool he expected to collect during the next shearing season. When collection day came, these agents, sometimes backed by armed mestizo guards, returned to the peasant's hut and confiscated the wool. The agents often fabricated loans or attached astronomic interest rates to the amounts of money left with the peasant. Consequently peasants found themselves unable to repay a loan and often lost their animals and land. The wool trade, therefore, became a mechanism by which much peasant-owned land was acquired by aggressively expanding haciendas. Merchants, hacienda owners, and political and ecclesiastical authorities were conveniently silent witnesses to these extortions. Merchant capital obtained high returns, and Peru's pattern of servile, forced labor relations was perpetuated. The higher the prices of wool went on the international market, the hungrier for land hacendados became. This pattern also explains the almost complete absence of important technological innovations.

As happens with most raw material exports, the benefits derived from south Andean wool exports did not necessarily return to the region and the people who produced it. Moreover, single-commodity exports make regions highly dependent on international price fluctuations. The southern Andes curve of growth and decline depended more on price fluctuations on the international market than on the ups and downs of the Lima-based economy or events in other Peruvian regions. A telegraph installed in Arequipa brought price fluctuations into Puno's hinterlands, and wool was traded day to day accordingly. A price drop in Liverpool, therefore, had larger regional repercussions in the Andean south than a change of presidents in Lima or the flooding of a copper mine.

Until 1854, during Rámon Castilla's second presidency, Indians continued paying tribute to the republican state. Tribute payments meant that Indian peasants had to participate—in one way or another—in market relationships to obtain money to pay the tribute. The abolition of tribute payments in 1854 meant that Indian peasants could revert to a

RAW MATERIALS AND INVESTMENTS

Study of the historical processes in the southern Andes raises an important question: Can the successful export of raw materials promote development?

Peasants of the Andean South—a large majority in the production-commercial cycle (via the wool trade)—earned no benefits and were unable to accumulate money. With no money in their pockets, peasants had no purchasing power and, thus, could not participate as buyers in the internal market. On the other end of the wool cycle were those who did benefit from international trade: the landowners, merchants, and British buyers. More often than not, beneficiaries of the wool trade spent their money on luxury goods and on travel.

Reinvestment of this money in the region could have spurred economic growth or development—for instance, by developing a textile industry. This did not happen. The only textile factory opened, the Nadal Garmendia, was the single-handed effort of one Cuzco family in 1861. The imported French machinery to open this factory had to be carried on mules and llamas from the coast to Cuzco. However, even this "modern" industry did not have salaried laborers; it used the hacienda's servile labor force. Exports alone could not promote development, and in the end the experiment failed for lack of buyers, a salaried labor force, roads and transport, and demand.

natural economy—that is, to self-sufficiency. This also meant that hacendados and wool merchants were left with no arguments to coerce Indian peasants to produce or sell wool. Landowners responded by expanding their haciendas still further to incorporate entire peasant communities and then forcing Indian peasants to work on hacienda lands.

Peasant Reaction

Indian peasants, with no salaries, even if they had wanted to, were unable to buy textiles to clothe themselves. Cuzco, the city that during colonial times was an important center of textile production, had lost its preeminence within the southern Andes, and Arequipa became the new regional center. Between the end of the 18th century and the end of the 19th century, Cuzco's population dropped from 40,000 to around 13,000. Thus, the wool trade produced not only a higher level of social demarcation between the haves and have nots—merchants and landowners versus Indian peasants—but also stark inequalities within regions. Cuzco's large markets (*ferias*) to which thousands of people had come from all over the south of Peru as well as Bolivia, Chile, and Argentina simply disappeared. Prominence had shifted to the city of Arequipa and to British merchants.

These economic developments had a dramatic social counterpart. Indian peasants did not sit back and watch when landowners and merchants intensified their attempts to expropriate peasant land. Peasants responded. During the 1850s and 1860s, rapidly spreading peasant revolts arose in several communities in the department of Puno. The center of this revolt was the province of Huancané. Beginning in October 1866, the revolt spread to the districts and communities in Taraco, Caminaca, Samán, Achaya, Vilquechico, and Moho. In 1867 Indian peasants fought against state troops in Capachica, leaving 57 soldiers dead. After this initial success, Azángaro's *subprefecto* and Puno's military commander-in-chief, Andrés Recharte, requested military help from neighboring Bolivia. The Bolivian troops never arrived, in large measure because government leaders in Lima soon recognized the international implications of Recharte's request. Instead reinforcement troops came from Lima under the command of General Baltazar Caravedo, who succeeded in avoiding more bloodshed through negotiations. As soon as Caravedo left, however, Puno's mestizo elites renewed the conflict in order to punish what they perceived as Indian insolence. These episodes resonated in Lima when Puno's three deputies to congress called for a punitive expedition to Puno to capture and punish the leaders of the peasant movement and confiscate the land from those communities involved in the rebellion. The expedition never left Lima, but the attempt to use state power to repress Indians and take their lands defined the objectives of landowners and local power holders and the growing ethnic-racial conflicts in the region.

Colonel Juan Bustamante, an itinerant merchant, became the leader of Puno's Indians. He was also the founder in Lima of the Pro-Indian Society (Sociedad Amiga de los Indios), an organization that sought to improve Indians' living conditions. Bustamante was a supporter of the new president Mariano Ignacio Prado, whose presidency had been challenged by an Arequipa-based caudillo, General Diez Canseco amid the Spanish siege of Callao in 1866. Bustamante's participation in the Puno peasant upheaval was therefore probably motivated by both national and local issues. Accused by local power holders of fomenting a caste war, Bustamante had to face Recharte's troops in January 1868. His poorly armed and equipped Indian troops were defeated, and he was taken prisoner and decapitated. Sixty Indians were executed with him.

The Central Highlands

During colonial times Huancavelica, located in the central highlands, was the source of mercury and therefore the key to silver production in Potosí. By 1840 Huancavelica was a ghost town. The mines of Cerro de Pasco became the economic focus of the central highlands in the 19th and 20th centuries. Silver in Cerro de Pasco was first discovered in the 17th century, but it was in the 18th century that silver production gradually increased. At the end of the 18th century Cerro de Pasco had already surpassed silver output in Potosí.

Silver Production in Cerro de Pasco (In Pesos)	
Years	Amount
1784–1788	531,921
1804–1808	1,472,543
1814–1818	837,716
1839–1843	1,690,328
1879–1883	761,075
Source: Manrique (1995, 104)	

Between 1820 and 1840 Peru's economy largely depended on silver exports from Cerro de Pasco. Without the silver from Cerro de Pasco, Peru would have been unable to engage in international trade. In contrast to the merchant houses in Arequipa, the silver mines belonged to Peruvian owners, and Cerro de Pasco, in spite of its inaccessible location, became by contemporary standards a large city. Outlying areas—from Huanuco and Tarma to the fertile Mantaro Valley and Lima—were integrated into Cerro de Pasco's economic life. Laborers from these adjacent departments became the permanent and seasonal laborers in the mines. Tayacaja was the only province in Huancavelica that maintained some economic link with the new mining site by selling, toward the end of the 19th century, large numbers of llamas to Cerro de Pasco mine owners. When the rail line between Pasco and La Oroya was finished in 1893 and the minerals could be transported directly from Cerro de Pasco to Callao, even this small trade between Huancavelica and Cerro de Pasco was doomed to disappear. Huancavelica and nearby

BRITISH INVESTMENT

In the early 19th century Peru's image in Europe was one of unlimited wealth based on vast reserves of silver and gold. British investors were therefore eager to see the dissolution of colonial links between Spain and its colonies and became aggressive investors in mining shortly after Peru's independence.

Five British enterprises invested a total of £4.6 million in Peruvian mining ventures. However, these enterprises failed. British investors found it difficult to obtain labor for their mining enterprises, and without a labor force the initial investments promptly collapsed. When they tried to bring in laborers from the United Kingdom, British investors soon found out that these laborers were very unwilling to work under the hard conditions and for the low pay Indians usually received.

These investment disasters provoked a financial crises in London that had international repercussions. These early experiences curtailed further direct British investment in Peruvian mining until the late 19th century. Even then, the British were more cautious and decided to engage in commercial transactions rather than direct investments. The great and unexpected opportunity to expand commercial activities came with guano, a natural fertilizer much needed to improve agrarian output in the United Kingdom and the rest of Europe.

Ayacucho were left out of the surging economy of the central highlands and forced to revert to self-sufficiency.

Throughout the 19th century mining witnessed only minor technological improvements and was basically a small-scale activity, each mine owner working together with four or five workers in thousands of small sites stretching over hundreds of square miles. Among other things this dispersal avoided a concentrated destruction during periods of political unrest. But it also required a complex logistical and transportation system to carry the ore to the smelting sites. Thousands of mules crossed the Andes coming from as far away as Jujuy, Salta, and Tucumán in present-day Argentina to solve the transportation problems.

The fertile lands in the Mantaro Valley flourished in tandem with the expansion of mineral production in Cerro de Pasco and the growth of Lima. From the Mantaro Valley came the food for an increasing number of people in both cities. Contrary to what happened in other regions, this rich 40,000-acre landscape had few haciendas and many peasant communities. This land tenure pattern was probably a result, of the initial alliance between Francisco Pizarro and the local ethnic group, the Huancas, to fight against the Incas. In the wake of this alliance, *curacas* obtained privileges and land that they were able to keep throughout the colonial period. Also unique to the Mantaro Valley was the high level of market involvement of its indigenous populations. The Huancayo market began as early as 1572 and promoted a highly developed labor specialization in the region, including a rich tradition of artisan textile production. Agrarian and artisan produce from the Mantaro Valley went to distant places all over the region. Still, agrarian and manufacturing tools were little developed. Peasants still used the Incan hoe and, not having irrigation systems, heavily relied on rainfall.

The wars of independence had relatively little damaging effect on Cerro de Pasco's mining, in spite of the fact that patriotic and royalist armies alternatively occupied this region and the final battles for independence took place here (precisely because it was where the silver mines were located). Agrarian production suffered much more from these military incursions, as communities and haciendas lost cattle and crops to feed the armies. Many Spanish hacienda owners left the region following the defeat and withdrawal of royalist soldiers. Land became cheap and an easy acquisition for those who had the money to buy it: merchants and mine owners.

Thus, as opposed to land patterns in the southern Andes, haciendas expanded not at the expense of peasant communities but at the expense of other haciendas while maintaining an independent and market-ori-

THE VALLADARES

Manuel Valladares Pérez was a successful mine owner in Cerro de Pasco. In the 1830s he migrated to the Mantaro Valley and married a local woman. After settling in, he began purchasing land, and his sons continued to do so well into the 1850s. Valladares managed to concentrate 19 haciendas in his hands, covering 121,000 acres, from Tayacaja to Cerro de Pasco. This pattern was followed by other families in the region and led to the formation of a new economic elite that based their fortunes on a combined mining-merchant-landowning enterprise (Manrique 1995, III).

ented peasantry. Such an equilibrium of social forces explains the relative peace in the central highlands, at least until the end of the 1870s.

When silver prices dropped on the international market, mine owners shifted their investments toward agriculture, showing a great flexibility in terms of entrepreneurship and in the ability to manipulate capital and investments. This turnaround went hand in hand with an improvement of stocks and seeds and improved labor productivity (levels of specialization according to ecological requirements). Confronted with an independent peasantry, land and cattle owners had to adjust to labor scarcity. The success of this endeavor went beyond technological and labor organizational improvements. Independent of international price fluctuations, the agrarian produce from the central highlands fed an internal market, especially Lima, where prices for food kept rising following the guano boom, to the benefit of food producers.

The region's economic success was further boosted with the acquisition of land in the Amazons, east of Cerro de Pasco. In 1848 President Ramón Castilla sent a military expedition under the command of Junín's *prefecto*, Mariano Eduardo Rivero y Ustarriz, to "reconquer" the Chanchamayo Valley and its surroundings. This territory had been ruled by a local tribe, the Ashaninka, ever since Juan Santos Atahualpa retreated to this area in the mid-18th century. After massacring the indigenous inhabitants, Castilla's government promoted the settlement of colonists in this area and established a fort in San Ramón to prevent further incursions by Amazonian Indians. Soon, tropical products such as coffee, fruit, and sugarcane from the

Chanchamayo Valley enlarged the agrarian regional exports from the central highlands. Sugarcane production led to the building of distilleries that supplied liquor to workers on coastal plantations and to Peru's growing urban populations. Based on these diversified regional exports, central highland elites successfully participated in new, often Lima-based, economic ventures.

Beyond Guano

It is through the lens of state expenditures that one can view the failure of the Peruvian government to use to advantage the large revenues obtained from guano exports, in spite of substantial shifts in governments. A more stable, more liberal, and more development-oriented government had envisaged Peru's path toward development, had observed those developments in other countries (especially in the United States), and had shown a willingness to engage in large national projects.

A local cultural elite emerged during the guano boom, some of whom had studied in Europe with scholarships provided by the Peruvian government. Many of these intellectuals promoted the creation of a national identity through their various works. For example, some of them drew the first territorial maps of Peru. Others studied and wrote about key events in Peru's history or about Peruvian customs and landscapes. Enterprising archaeologists uncovered pre-Hispanic ruins. The knowledge and art of this group reached audiences in Europe and the United States.

This flourishing of culture was paralleled by the expansion and consolidation of universities and the secularization of Peruvian society. In the wake of the guano boom priests began to receive salaries from the state, an arrangement that subordinated the Catholic Church to the state. Overall the visibility of the state increased, laws were debated in congress and in journals, and more people participated in elections.

Similarly the state expanded its hold on Peruvian territory through colonization projects into the central Amazon basin. Most colonists were central European immigrants. The colonies of San Ramón and La Merced were inaugurated in 1847 and 1869, respectively. Pozuzo, a German colony, was founded in 1857. By 1876 Peru had increased its population with 18,078 Europeans (mostly from Italy, France, Spain, and Germany) and 92,130 Chinese.

In spite of the misuse of guano revenues, these were signs and symptoms of progress in a country that had struggled hard to come to grips with its political, economic, and social future after independence.

Unfortunately in 1879 once more a war brought all indicators of progress to a disturbing standstill, if not reversal.

The Collapse

When it finally came, after four decades of prosperity, the collapse of the guano boom was rapid and devastating to the national economy. In 1872 Peru received loans in the amount of 21.167 million soles; the following year it received only 6.936 million soles. Two reasons explain this abrupt change: a decline in the overall European need for agricultural fertilizer and the discovery of synthetic fertilizers that began replacing Peru's bird droppings. Moreover, guano prices plummeted at a time when state debts had multiplied by eight. In 1876 the Peruvian state announced bankruptcy.

However, well before 1876, the Peruvian government had anticipated the need to replace guano with exports of nitrate. Nitrate mines were located in what still was Peruvian territory in the southern province of Tarapaca. Nitrate was a promising export product as it was a key ingredient in the production of synthetic fertilizers and gunpowder. The nitrate mines were owned by Peruvian, Chilean, and British citizens. In 1873 President Manuel Pardo created the state nitrate monopoly (Estanco del Salitre), and signed a mutual defense treaty with Bolivia. From then on, nitrate producers were forced to sell their produce to the Peruvian state. The defense treaty with Bolivia was meant to restrain Chile from interfering with the saltpeter mines in southern Peru. Two years later Pardo's government expropriated the nitrate bureau (*oficinas salitreras*), and the need to pay for this expropriation led to unplanned issuance of paper money and to inflation. Chile, on the other hand, in association with British and other European enterprises, was unwilling to comply with the new taxes imposed by the Peruvian state. When the Peruvian government announced its intention to nationalize the nitrate mines, Chile—prodded by British and Chilean producers and merchants—declared war on Peru. The War of the Pacific that confronted Peru and Bolivia on one side, and Chile on the other, lasted for five years and had devastating effects on Peru.

9

THE WAR OF THE PACIFIC
AND AFTER (1879–1900)

One of the most destructive events in modern Peruvian history was the nation's ill-advised and ultimately catastrophic involvement in the War of the Pacific from 1879 to 1885. Not only did Peru lose militarily, it suffered a prolonged and aggressive invasion and occupation by Chilean forces, which in turn fragmented the Peruvian political leadership and economy even further. When the war finally ended, Peru had lost its southernmost nitrate-rich provinces, it had given up its guano income, and its remaining economy was shattered. Yet, in spite of the devastating consequences of the War of the Pacific, the nation recovered, and the final two decades of the 19th century brought Peru closer to its goal of modernization by establishing new patterns of trade and regional economic production.

The War of the Pacific

When Bolivian president Hilarión Daza in 1878 impetuously attempted to seize Chilean-owned nitrate producing companies in the Antofagasta region of the Atacama desert, he plunged his nation and Peru into a war with their powerful neighbor to the south. Bound by a mutual defense treaty with Bolivia, Peru entered the war. Neither Peru nor Bolivia had serious armed forces. Most commanders on the Peruvian and Bolivian side had no rigorous military training, and most soldiers were recently recruited Quechua-speaking Indians. Peru had what still appeared to be a strong navy, but advancing technology had made most of her warships obsolete and ineffective against the Chilean navy's better-armed and better-protected ironclads. Moreover, as one historian has written, Chile was a relatively cohesive country with a strong national tradition, whereas Peru and Bolivia were "fractured nations" where mountain barriers divided their people physically "while an almost unspannable

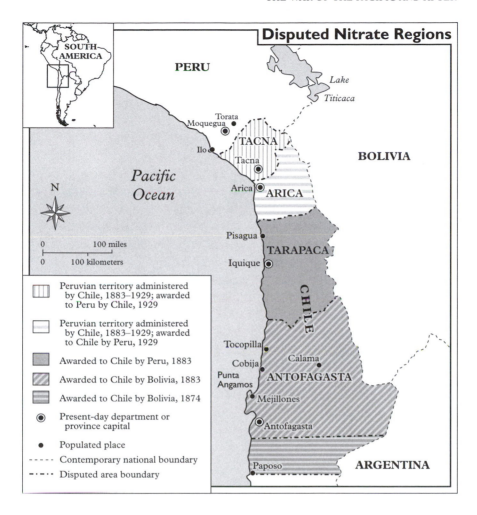

Disputed Nitrate Regions

cultural chasm separated their Indian and non-Indian citizens"
(Wehrlich 1978, 112).

The military campaign opened with a series of naval engagements,
the most serious of which was the Battle of Iquique Bay in May 1879
when the Chileans defeated the Peruvian flotilla. Though the Peruvian
navy's most powerful vessel, the *Huascar,* escaped to fight on for a while
as a raider, this victory allowed Chile to control the sea routes along the
Pacific coast. These were vital to fighting the land war, since supplying
or transporting armies on inland roads was nearly impossible. The
Chilean navy could enforce a blockade when and where it wished from
this point forward, and it could land and supply its own armies wher-
ever it desired.

The harbor at Callao, shortly before it was invaded and occupied by Chilean forces (1881) during the War of the Pacific (Library of Congress)

The first battles of the land war also proved disastrous for the Peruvian and Bolivian armies that attempted to defend the contested southern nitrate provinces of Arica, Tacna, and Tarapacá. After temporarily checking the Chilean forces in Tarapacá in November 1879, the Peruvian and Bolivian armies were crushed in a series of losses to the much better equipped and trained Chileans in Tacna and Arica. The victors took complete control of what had been Peru's southern provinces, and all resistance there collapsed. President Daza of Bolivia deserted his armies, forfeited his office, and fled the country. Peruvian president Mariano Ignacio Prado (1826–1901), elected in 1876, fared scarcely better. After commanding troops in the south, he returned to Lima, handed over the government to Vice President Antonio de la Puerta, and left for Europe, claiming he was going to seek help in the war effort; in fact he deserted, too.

Peruvian national leadership disintegrated with the military defeat at the hands of the Chileans and, over the following months and years, became a tangle of competing figures who tried to seize office. Nicolás Piérola, for example, ousted the vice president and proclaimed himself president in December 1879. After peace talks arranged by the United States failed, the Chileans landed a large army south of Lima and advanced on the city, which surrendered in January 1881 after two bloody Peruvian losses in the suburbs of San Juan and Miraflores. Piérola fled to the mountains, and the Chileans occupied Lima, bringing havoc and destruction. They looted the national library and even carted off the animals from the zoo in addition to seizing property and extorting cash from the residents.

Fragmented Leadership

The degree to which Peru's popular classes participated, willingly or unwillingly, in the war is a matter of debate, and so is the role played by the military and political leaders. Chilean officials received strict orders not to interfere with Peruvian Indian peasants, letting them know that this was not *their* war, thus avoiding that Indians sided with regional and national white elites. How deep-seated racial cleavages still were after more than a half century of political independence from Spain is evidenced by the conflicts between racial groups during the

A POLITICAL CRITIC'S VIEW OF WAR

Peru's defeat in the War of the Pacific provoked many reactions among Peruvian intellectuals, none more somber and scathing than these comments by Peruvian writer and reformer Manuel González Prada, published in 1894.

> *What is bad in the individual we judge to be good in the collectivity, reducing good and evil to a simple question of numbers. The enormity of a crime or vice transforms it into a praiseworthy action or into virtue. We call the robbery of a million "business" and the garroting of entire nations "a glorious deed." The scaffold for the assassin; apotheosis for the soldier. And, nevertheless, the obscure laborer who kills a fellow worker, whether in revenge for some injury or to take his money or his wife, does not deserve so much ignominy or punishment as the "illustrious soldier" who kills twenty or forty thousand men to gain glory or to win the field marshal's baton . . .*
>
> *When man leaves behind his atavistic ferociousness, war will be remembered as a prehistoric barbarity, and famous and admired warriors of today will figure in the sinister gallery of the devil's children, by the side of assassins, executioners, and butchers (1966, 46–47).*

War of the Pacific. The collapse of national order brought on domestic chaos and violence, most of it motivated by class or racial divisions. Chinese and black laborers took the opportunity to assault haciendas and the properties of the rich in protest of the mistreatment they had suffered in previous years, Lima's masses attacked Chinese grocery stores, and Indian peasants took over highland haciendas.

The lack of national cohesiveness was most sharply demonstrated in the confusion and confrontations among Peru's would-be wartime leaders. Over the course of the next 10 years (1879–89, approximately), they often were as much in conflict among themselves as with the invaders. Piérola, for example, withheld support from some Peruvian troops and commanders in order to forestall future challenges to his own power. In some places, however, such as the central highlands, opposing racial-ethnic groups joined forces to fight for Peru, resisting Chilean troops with a more united front. As a result, an incipient sense of nationalism emerged in the wake of the war.

Since they did not want to negotiate with him, the Chilean occupiers did not recognize Piérola's claim to the presidency. Instead, with the assistance of a group of "notables" from the Partido Civil, they designated the lawyer Francisco García Calderón (1834–1905) as the new president. The Chilean generals declared the Lima barrio of La Magdalena as neutral territory and allowed García Calderón to set up a government there. García Calderón's nomination deepened civil strife: Piérola had widespread popular support as well as support from among the Civilistas. In the following months neither president showed much interest in facing the enemy. They were more concerned with their own power struggle, while the Chilean army controlled the capital and most of the Peruvian coast.

García Calderón failed to win support outside his small enclave, but he did manage to obtain diplomatic support from the United States, which offered to help him attain peace without territorial concessions to Chile. This offer mainly was prompted by the belief of the U.S. ambassador to Peru that the country might be ripe for U.S. annexation; furthermore, U.S. Secretary of State James Blaine believed he could benefit financially from a settlement. Both U.S. officials were frustrated in the end, and U.S. involvement in the negotiations collapsed (Manrique 1995, 167).

García Calderón initiated peace talks with Chile, and he proved to be a tough negotiator. He was willing to pay for a lost war; however, he was unwilling to cede any territory to Chile, although Chile claimed by right of conquest the southern province of Tarapacá, where Peru's richest nitrate fields were located. In response to García Calderón's hard line, the Chileans in November 1881 dissolved his government and exiled him to Chile. After much maneuvering from his position in the highlands, Piérola gave up and left for Europe. In their places Admiral Lizardo Montero declared himself president from his base in Arequipa. His authority was challenged, however, by General Andrés Cáceres (1833–1923), who had organized resistance forces in the highlands.

Emergence of Cáceres

Cáceres had hidden for three months in Lima after the Chilean invasion, nursing wounds suffered in the Battle of Miraflores. He escaped to the central highlands in April 1881 to join Piérola. Piérola feared Cáceres as a rival for power but named him the military chief of the central departments before fleeing to Europe. Over the next two years Cáceres created a 5,000-man army and won a sequence of victories against the Chileans in the Breña Campaign in July 1882 in the Mantaro Valley at Pucará, Marcavalle, and Concepción. The Chilean army lost 20 percent of its soldiers and Chilean troops were forced to retreat to Lima.

Cáceres's successes in the central highlands had much to do with how the relationships between haciendas and peasant communities had developed in earlier decades, and the relative strength of its peasant population. The Mantaro Valley was ethnically more heterogeneous than other places in Peru, and it was more commercially advanced, with long-standing links to urban cities, especially Huancayo and Lima. Cáceres's military talents were also a part of his success. He was a skillful strategist, and, perhaps more important he was a landowner and fluent Quechua speaker. Peasants referred to him as *tayta* ("father" or "protector" in Quechua).

In spite of his promising start, Cáceres was unable to stand up to new Chilean offensives, in part because of the emergence of a new claimant to Peruvian leadership, the northern hacienda owner Miguel Iglesias (1830–1909) from Cajamarca, who had lost a son in the battles for Lima. The Chileans recognized Iglesias as president because they thought he would negotiate with them for peace. This turned out to be correct, and in October 1883 Iglesias signed the Treaty of Ancón, which technically ended the War of the Pacific. Under the terms of the treaty Peru gave up Tarapacá province immediately. Chile was to administer Tacna and Arica for 10 years, at which point a vote of the people of these provinces would determine which country they belonged to; the loser would receive 10 million pesos as compensation. Through the treaty the Chileans not only got Peru's rich nitrate fields but also its remaining guano reserves.

Iglesias was able to represent himself as the sole negotiator for Peru because at the time Cáceres was not in a position to contest his claims. When the central highland provinces had begun to show signs of economic exhaustion and it became increasingly difficult to sustain a standing army, Cáceres had decided to march north to attack Iglesias, in an attempt to restore a unified political leadership. However, Chile had mobilized all its available resources to simultaneously defend Iglesias and attack Cáceres's remaining troops in the central highlands. Iglesias had not hesitated to provide the Chilean army with all the information and resources they needed in order to administer a crushing defeat to his rival Cáceres at the Battle of Huamachuco in July 1883.

Meanwhile Admiral Montero had installed his government of Peru first in Cajamarca and then, in August 1882, in Arequipa, where he stayed until 1883. He refused support to Cáceres, in spite of promises to do so. In fact, when the victorious Chilean army reached Arequipa after the Battle of Huamachuco, it found a large cache of arms and other

The main plaza in Arequipa, the city where Admiral Lizardo Montero established his headquarters and proclaimed himself president of Peru during the Chilean occupation.
(Reproduced with permission of the General Secretariat of the Organization of American States)

military items sent from Bolivia that Montero had withheld from Cáceres; consequently Cáceres's men fought the invaders wearing *ojotas* (Indian sandals) and brandishing obsolete rifles. With the arrival of the Chilean army Montero fled Arequipa across Lake Titicaca, going first to Argentina and then to Europe. While crossing the lake he appointed Cáceres president.

In June 1884 Cáceres finally recognized the peace treaty signed by Iglesias, and this meant new civil strife. Cáceres and Iglesias led their armies against each other until Iglesias, still the president, was defeated in December 1885. Cáceres, then, won the elections in June 1886. War against Chile was no longer feasible. Cáceres demanded that Chilean troops leave Peru and allow Peruvians to resolve their disputes themselves without foreign interference. Chilean occupation had lasted three years, during which coastal hacienda owners and city-based merchants had had to pay *cupos* (cash reparations) to the Chilean army under the threat of destruction of their properties. Chilean generals drew up a list of the 50 most prominent members of Lima's society and forced each to pay 20,000 pesos a month, an amount that was six times the monthly salary of Peru's president. The last Chilean troops pulled out of Peruvian territory in August 1884, leaving the Peruvian state economically and politically bankrupt.

The Postwar Era

The war against Chile was followed by civil war. Cáceres and Iglesias continued fighting each other, in spite of the fact that they represented the same economic interests, namely highland hacendados. Iglesias was defeated in 1885, and in 1886 a provisional government called for elections. Cáceres—now transformed in the public mind into the hero of the resistance against Chilean troops—was elected president. The Partido Civil supported Cáceres, and the *pierolistas,* now folded into the Democratic Party (Partido Demócrata), boycotted the elections.

While *pierolistas* and supporters of Cáceres were waging their war, a peasant uprising again shook Peru's highlands beginning in 1885. Its leader, Pedro Pablo Atusparia (1840–87), was a *varayoc* (ethnic leader) in Huaraz who protested the arbitrary reimposition of the *contribución única*—the Indian tribute—amid economic devastation. A "pacification" force sent from Lima defeated the rebels and forced Atusparia to surrender, but some of Atusparia's more radical followers who advocated the extermination of all whites continued to resist. Colonel José Iraola, the commander of the suppression forces, obliterated entire peasant villages. The final death toll was in the thousands. Atusparia himself was spared, and when he met with Cáceres in 1886, two days before his election as president, Cáceres promised Atusparia schools, relief from head taxes, and protection of community lands as well as a government scholarship for Atusparia's son. None of these promises, however, materialized.

After the peasant unrest subsided, Cáceres faced an accumulated external debt of £51 million. Peru had not made payments on its external debt since 1876. The annual interest payments amounted to £2.5 million, but Peru's annual budget had dropped to £1 million, approximately one-fifth of what it had been prior to the war (Contreras and Cueto 2000, 165). The internal financial situation did not look any better. Beginning in 1875 the Peruvian government had massively printed money to pay for the expropriation of the nitrate fields, and during the war itself, more paper money (now briefly known as "incas") was printed. As a result, paper money had completely devalued, and no one wanted to accept it. Only two private banks had survived the war. The Peruvian government had to find ways to solve these dire financial problems in order to reintroduce Peru into the international financial market.

One of the first steps was to try to reestablish—yet again—the Indian tribute, in the form of a personal contribution" (contribución personal) and only in one of Peru's 18 departments, namely Puno. In other places the dislocation brought about by the war had greatly diminished the power of local landholders and had undermined their ability to coerce local peasants to accept state demands. Confronted with this situation, the Peruvian state attempted to introduce fiscal decentralization but with little success. Decentralization depended—in an almost circular and contradictory way—on the tributes paid by peasants. In the attempt to reconstruct the country on the local and regional level, the revenues obtained from the contribución personal were turned over to the departmental boards (juntas departamentales) to be used to implement local infrastructure projects. Access to these fiscal resources provoked often-violent confrontations between local power holders. What was meant to give provinces a higher level of autonomy in the decision-making process actually created tenser political relations in the countryside, where overall poverty provoked widespread banditry.

The Grace Contract

In 1889 President Cáceres signed a remarkable document, the Grace Contract, the result of three years of hard and intense negotiations. The agreement was named after Michael Grace, the appointed representative of the British bondholders who held most of Peru's huge debt. The creditors organized themselves as the Peruvian Corporation, and Grace claimed that his clients were the actual owners of Peru's infrastructure. It had been their loans that had been used to build the nation's railroads, irrigation systems, and public buildings, for example. Since Peru lacked liquidity, Grace argued, his clients should be given use for 99 years for their own benefit of Peru's resources, such as mines, land, railroads, ports, and customs. He left open the questions of what would be left to Peruvians to pay for their own recovery after the war or how Peru could be, quite literally, managed from London.

President Cáceres encountered stern congressional opposition to these propositions, so he dissolved congress and continued his negotiations with Grace. At the end, in return for canceling Peru's external debt, the Peruvian Corporation took control of Peru's railroads for 66 years, became owner of 810,000 acres in the Amazon basin, was granted free navigational rights on Lake Titicaca, and received an annual payment of £80,000, which was approximately 10 percent of the national budget, for 33 years.

In spite of the draconian sound of these terms, the Grace Contract ended up being quite beneficial to Peru. As a result of the contract the Peruvian railroads were repaired and expanded from Callao to Cerro de Pasco in 1904, as was the line from Mollendo to Puno and to Cuzco in 1908. Moreover, only relatively few acres of Amazonian land were actually delivered, and the £80,000 was only paid the first year (Contreras and Cueto 2000, 168) (although later on, in compensation for Peru's default on this payment, the ownership of the railroads was granted in perpetuity).

Overall the aftermath of the War of the Pacific marked a changed foreign involvement. Whereas before the war foreign presence came in the form of credits and commercial deals, afterward there were direct foreign investments in key economic undertakings. After an initial slowdown of Peru's economy following the worldwide economic crisis in the early 1890s, fresh, direct foreign investments reached Peru to pay for the modernization of its ports and the expansion of mining production and the refining of ores. Between 1897 and 1903, the world (including Peru) turned to the gold instead of silver standard, and after 1897, only the state (no longer state-overseen private banks) could mint money. The new currency was the libra peruana (Peruvian pound), equal in value to the British pound and valued at 10 silver soles.

Another important task Cáceres had to face was to end Indian resistance in Peru's central highlands, a movement he himself had initially helped organize. By 1888, 45 of the most important haciendas in the central highlands (about 10 percent) between Cerro de Pasco and the province of Tayacaja (north of the Department of Huancavelica) were still held by armed Indians. This occupation had begun in 1882 by a decree issued by Cáceres, holding that Indian guerrillas were to punish all those attempting to collaborate with the Chileans by occupying their properties. Even after the war came to an end Indian guerrillas continued to take over more and more haciendas. What had begun as a patriotic effort had turned into a class confrontation. As president, Cáceres now sided with landowners. Through negotiation and force the Peruvian government sought to return these haciendas to their former owners. It was not until 1902 that the last haciendas were recovered. The reintroduction of the *contribución personal*—meant to replenish empty state coffers—was another attempt to strengthen the hand of landowners. Soon caudillo tactics were back in place. Cáceres had gradually changed from the hero of resistance to an old-fashioned strongman. Having defended territorial integrity during the war, afterward he handed over Peru's most vital resources to the Peruvian Corporation.

Only 10 years after the Treaty of Ancón had been signed, new disturbances were on Peru's political horizon. Cáceres's presidency ended in 1890, but he had no intention of giving up power. He stage-managed the selection of General Remigio Morales Bermúdez as his successor. Shortly after taking office, however, Morales Bermúdez died in 1894. A provisional junta organized new elections, and Cáceres again won. Nicolás Piérola, the leader of the Democratic Party and a long-standing opponent of Cáceres, objected to the results of the 1895 elections, and after a short civil war, Piérola took power in March 1895. Because of his measures in the aftermath of the War of the Pacific, Cáceres had lost his support among peasants in the central highlands. Many earlier *tayta* followers now sided with *tayta's* enemies. The Partido Civil, which had earlier supported Cáceres, now supported Piérola. The old war hero was on his way into permanent exile.

Modernizing Peru

In the wake of the War of the Pacific, Peru needed economic and political uplift, and fortunately, a new generation of positivist thinkers with much common and practical sense emerged. They added a new dimension of technical knowledge to politics and the organization of eco-

Lima in the late 19th century, following the War of the Pacific (Christine Hunefeldt)

nomic life by collecting and evaluating data on economic performance and, perhaps most important, showing that successful politics need not follow the whims of unversed individual strongmen. This new group of technocrats was organized as the Geographical Society of Lima (Sociedad Geográfica de Lima), founded in 1888 in imitation of similar organizations in Europe and the United States. Aside from regularly publishing a journal, the *Boletín de la Sociedad Geográfica,* the society had a strong influence on natural resources research, evaluation of economic feasibility projects, new scientific discoveries, and, last but not least, the discussions on territorial boundaries. Prominent intellectuals from the society and from the universities supported and often spearheaded the government's efforts to push Peru toward modernity.

The "Indian question" remained high on Peru's government agenda. There were two general opinions on this matter. The first was based on social Darwinism, which held there was a parallel between the biological process of natural selection and the social process: The "strongest" and "best" of humans were meant to survive and move forward. Under this viewpoint the white race and culture were believed to work together to achieve development, whereas Indians were doomed to cultural—if not physical—extinction. Therefore, social Darwinists believed that in order to develop, Peru needed to improve its racial stock by bringing in European immigrants. In 1894 a law to encourage immigration was passed, but the results were dismal. Few European immigrants reached Peruvian shores, and those who did and were settled in the Amazon basin soon departed when they found themselves cut off from any governmental help. Although the Peruvian government had promised to build roads to connect these outlying areas to markets and cities, these promises never materialized. Europeans wishing to immigrate to the Americas had better options in the United States, Brazil, Argentina, and Chile.

The second theory concerning Indians aimed to "redeem" the indigenous race by teaching Indians to read and write, which would "raise" them to Western cultural standards. According to this theory, Indians were behind in their evolution but not unable to learn. The best ways of making Indians learn, in this view, were obligatory military service, inclusion into the tax system, and educational reforms.

While grand reforms and intentions regarding Peru's natives were laid out, the economy needed cheap labor, and white landowners wanted to expand current estates and create new ones. Cheap labor meant Indian peasants, and more land meant Indian land. Indians were indeed fundamental to the expansion of coastal haciendas and plantations. By the century's end they would be joined by another cheap labor force, Japanese immigrants. Still, none of these laborers joined this labor market of their own free will. Through indebtedness, Indians from the highlands were dragged to the coastal haciendas, and many Japanese immigrants did not have the faintest idea of what would become of them once they left their homeland.

Rebuilding the State

Peru managed to rebuild its finances by resorting to indirect taxation. Tobacco, opium, matches, and salt were widely consumed, and new taxes on them, in addition to the existing alcohol tax, provided the Peruvian state with a substantial portion of its income. The success of this form of taxation allowed the Peruvian government to reduce taxes on exports, thus greatly expanding exports. It also allowed the abolition—once again—of the *contribución personal* in 1895. By the end of the 19th century the Peruvian state had doubled its income since the end of the War of the Pacific, and income would climb further over the following years. The state no longer depended on private enterprise to determine its budget, and private enterprise no longer depended on a single export product such as guano but had diversified its investments into sugar, cotton, wool, rubber, copper, silver, and eventually also petroleum. The Peruvian state had gained a certain level of independence in its decision-making processes and could use key institutions to further sponsor economic development.

During Cáceres's presidency (1886), organizations such as the Chamber of Commerce of Lima and the Register for Real Estate (Registro de la Propiedad Inmueble) came into being and promoted internal credit transactions. The Lima's Bolsa de Valores (stock exchange) showed signs of economic impetus around 1896 and allowed for new patterns of investment and the creation of new enterprises. Economic progress was further enhanced by the opening of several banks: the Banco Italiano in 1889, the Banco Alemán Transatlántico in 1897, the Banco Internacional in 1897, and the Banco Popular in 1899. Separately, the establishment of civil registers for baptisms and deaths, which took such functions out of the hands of the church, completed a century-long secularization process.

When Piérola came to power in 1895, the push toward decentralization came to an end, the *contribución personal* was abolished, and local administration costs were carried by a Lima-based budget. Only education, health, and public works remained under the aegis of local state dependencies, the departments. Piérola also created a professional army under the guidance of French advisers.

Piérola's initiative to create a salt monopoly in 1895 provoked some Indian upheaval in the highlands. Until then, salt had provided many peasant communities with a source of supplemental income. It was also

THE "DEMOCRATIC CAUDILLO"

President Nicolás Piérola was known as the "Democratic Caudillo." U.S. historian Peter Klaren has noted that Piérola believed only a strong hand at the helm of an authoritarian central government (guided in measure by the tenets of Catholicism) could hold Peruvian society together in the face of the nation's geographical diversity and class and racial divisions. A weak government would be doomed to failure when confronted with these forces. Piérola was convinced he reflected the popular will, but he insisted on firm control. Endowed with high energy and possessed of an engaging personality that allowed him to appeal successfully to the masses, he was well suited to the task of governing in such a fashion as a devout Catholic (Klarén 2000, 201).

tied into Indian religious practices. The most dramatic Indian uprising occurred in the northern part of the Department of Ayacucho, when about 1,000 men from Huanta killed their mayor and the *subprefecto.* Future president Oscar Benavides—at the time a lieutenant—led the military expedition against this rebellion and captured its leader, Juan Sánchez. Other reasons for these scattered rebellions were Piérola's monetary reform, which aimed to regularize the money circulating within the economy; the rejection of governmental bonds to pay taxes; and the labor drafts imposed on the indigenous population to carry out governmental tasks (the *faenas de república,* or "work of the republic") without pay—for example, as messengers, police, carriers, and construction workers. Even after Piérola's presidency ended, successive governments tried to prohibit the free use of Indian labor but failed, in large measure because the state lacked the financial resources to pay for these services.

Overall, during 1895–99, Piérola followed in the footsteps of the earlier *civilista* political and economic program. However, unlike the Partido Civil, he could not count on the abundant revenues obtained from guano and nitrate. As president, Piérola concentrated power in Peru's capital city but left the more traditional highland provinces in the hands of local powerholders known as *gamonales;* Lima's government depended increasingly on coastal plantation owners and foreign loans and investments.

In a sense Peru shared in Europe's belle epoque, when many Latin American intellectuals and politicians looked to London and Paris for examples to follow. For decades many more *limeños* traveled to London and Paris than to the imperial capital of the Inca, Cuzco. This orientation went hand in hand with a neglect of domestic matters and a disdain for the common people, especially Indians.

In 1899 Eduardo López de Romaña (1847–1918) became president based on a coalition between *pierolistas* and *civilistas.* Election results in those days were usually decided well before election day. Candidates and their supporters would rally people, often imposing their candidacies by force, blackmail, or outright intimidation. Under the new electoral law passed in 1895, illiterate citizens could not vote. Thus, in 1899, only 108,597 people, or around 2.5 percent of Peru's population, were eligible to vote. Only about half of these eligible voters actually voted, and López de Romaña got the most votes by a very large margin.

López de Romaña's successor in 1903 was Candamo, also a *civilista.* Candamo died eight months after taking over the presidency, and the Partido Civil imposed its chosen candidate, Augusto Bernardino Leguía

VIEWS OF INDIANS

Ventura García Calderón, a son of the former president Francisco García Calderón, exiled to Chile at the end of the War of the Pacific, and a candidate for the Nobel Prize in literature, described Indians in his compilation of tales *La venganza del cóndor* (1923) as a species of aliens with prominent cheeks and dark skins, who ate one another's fleas and fornicated with white llamas. His work was published in several languages around the world. Yet García Calderón had had little if any contact with Indians during his life.

In the view of Lima's elites, Peru's Indians were considered part of the rich natural resources of the country. At the same time, however, they were the source of all the country's woes. In 1901, for example, Manuel Candamo (1842–1904), president of the Peruvian senate and future president of Peru, was convinced that Peru's problems had nothing to do with legislation but rather with its people, a challenge that would eventually be resolved through race mixing (Bosadre 1983, VIII: 102).

(1863–1932) in 1908. Leguía was followed by Guillermo Enrique Billinghurst (1851–1915) in 1912 as a result of Peru's first workers' strike in Lima. It was the first time Peru's masses had been sufficiently organized to intervene in Lima's "aristocratic" politics. Billinghurst was not part of the oligarchy but a representative of the emerging middle class. *Civilistas*, however, did not silently accept this turn of events, and they orchestrated a military coup in 1915 that put in power Oscar Raimundo Benavides (1876–1945), restoring *civilista* dominance.

Another general strike over increased costs of living in 1919 brought Augusto B. Leguía back to power, in spite of his failures during his first presidency. This time he used popular discontent to gain the presidential chair. Although *civilistas* had brought him to power in 1908, Leguía now faced *civilista* opposition in parliament. Claiming there had been electoral fraud, he closed down the parliament and governed Peru until 1930 with only a perfunctory bow toward democracy. When Leguía exiled opposition *civilistas* in 1919, the Partido Civil disappeared from Peru's political map.

Those in power between 1900 and 1919 were inclined toward liberalism and modernization. They intended to turn Peru into a more European-like country, that is, into a better-organized, more prosperous, and better-educated nation. Several important measures were taken in order to implement these progressive ideas. In 1900 the Mine Code replaced the Old Ordinances of 1786. The new code guaranteed secure investments and promoted more investments and the concentration of mine ownership as well as the expansion of commercial agriculture. Also encouraging this process was an 1890 decree that froze taxes on exports for 25 years. Foreign experts were invited to help improve Peruvian mines, agrarian technologies, and irrigation projects. In 1902 the Peruvian government established the National School for Agriculture (Escuela Nacional de Agricultura).

The founding of new governmental agencies to promote progress went hand in hand with a denationalization of national resources. More enterprises became foreign owned. As more regions became specialized in more export products, the earlier regional division of labor also changed.

Economic Changes

Shifts in Ownership of the Mines

Many smaller Peruvian mines passed into foreign hands, especially the rich silver and copper mines in the central highlands of Cerro de Pasco, which became the property of the U.S. Cerro de Pasco Corporation, founded in New York in 1901 with money from some of the biggest U.S. fortunes, such as the Vanderbilts, Hearsts, and Morgans. In less than three months, these interests bought up to 80 percent of the mines. Other foreign companies followed suit. The Vanadium Company, for instance, began monopolizing resources around 1907, and the Peruvian Corporation alone, with a working capital of £19 million, only £2 million less than Peru's national budget, demanded preferential treatment in the use of railways to lower transportation costs and monopolized mineral refineries.

By 1920 the Cerro de Pasco Corporation and Northern Peru Mining, another U.S. company, working in La Libertad, controlled almost all Peruvian copper, silver, and gold. Through purchase, fraudulent legal maneuvering, and manipulation of their refining monopoly, U.S. companies gradually became the owners of most mining enterprises. Moreover these mining companies bought large tracts of land as a way to solve the labor problem. By depriving peasants of their small plots of land, the companies gave them no choice but to sell their labor to the mines. Total copper production rose from 275 tons in 1890 to 12,213 tons in 1905 and to 32,981 in 1920.

A similar chain of events happened to the oil fields in northern coastal Peru, where they became the property of British and U.S. companies. The International Petroleum Company, founded in 1913, bought the oil fields in Brea and Pariñas (Piura), which later came into the hands of Standard Oil of New Jersey. Between 1905 and 1919 the labor force working on Peru's oil fields more than doubled, from 9,651 to 22,000 men, and oil exports came to represent around 10 percent of Peru's total exports. These companies worked as enclaves in the Peruvian economy; that is, they had little effect on Peru's internal economy, and technology and engineers came from abroad.

Agrarian Enterprises in the Central Highlands

Economic concentration also occurred with the once highly productive agrarian enterprises in the central highlands. After the disasters of the war many hacienda owners looked for support from Lima's plutocracy to overcome the nation's crisis in the countryside. An alliance led to the formation of large cattle-raising associations (*sociedades*), but soon the provincial land and cattle owners found themselves excluded from the boards of these associations, replaced by the most powerful families in Lima (Prado Ugarteche, Mujica y Cavassa, Gallagher, Gallo Porras, Barreda y Laos, and Alvarez Calderón, among others). By 1914 the rail line to Huancayo was complete, and the international demand for wool was at its peak. Consequently, just when rewards were highest, most if not all properties had been transferred to outside hands. Gradually these owners aggressively sought community-owned lands in an effort to increase revenues still further and to augment the number of available laborers. In and around the La Oroya refinery toxic fumes and river contamination poisoned peasant lands and animals. Peasants without land became peasants who had to sell their labor to survive. Land, mines, and regional commerce were now in the control of investors in Lima and New York. Cerro de Pasco, once a part of the Department of Junín, lost its intraregional links with the Mantaro Valley and in 1931 became administratively a separate department.

Plantations on the Central and Northern Coast

The War of the Pacific had devastated small and medium-size agrarian enterprises on Peru's central and northern coast. Chilean troops had imposed high assessments on these properties, and the Chinese laborers had fled the countryside. The destruction of agrarian properties in these regions required high investments to restart production. Domestic capital was scarce, and the only source left was external credit. So in the aftermath of this war land became concentrated in few hands, and most landed property became foreign owned. Big money came from Germany (Gildemeister), England (Grace), and Italy (Larco), as well as from commercial enterprises (Duncan & Fox, Graham & Rowe, Prevost, and Kendall). Foreign owners had the necessary international contacts to obtain money to rebuild, expand, and modernize their properties. Most of these huge enterprises encompassed hundreds of square miles, some extending well into the Peruvian highlands, often for the single reason of obtaining cheap labor. They expanded irrigation systems and railroads and used steam engines to transport their sugar and cotton to the Pacific ports.

Some smaller landowners tenaciously resisted handing over their properties; however, few could in the long run keep their properties. Often, larger landowners resorted to violence to convince their smaller counterparts to sell their land. Cutting off the water supply and harassing the field laborers were common methods to obtain a property transfer. When Peruvian nationals retained ownership, they often depended on the larger enterprises to process their sugarcane. The results of these events were the consolidation of large haciendas and the building of strong agro-industrial enterprises on these haciendas. A new elite emerged, the so-called sugar and cotton barons. There were also regional shifts. Whereas during most of the 19th century, Lima had been the main sugar-producing department, the Department of La Libertad on the northern coast gained preeminence toward the turn of the century. Between 1894 and 1912 Lima's sugar production decreased from 37.2 percent to 22.3 percent in terms of total national production, whereas La Libertad increased its share from 30.8 to 43.8 percent.

Cotton production and commerce also depended on foreign capital. Foreign merchant houses loaned short-term money to producers with future harvests as the guaranty for repayment. If harvests failed, merchant houses took over the land. It was only in the 1930s that cotton producers finally gained access to internal financial resources. In smaller coastal cities, such as Pisco, Chincha, and Cañete, commercial enterprises processed raw cotton from local haciendas into exportable cotton fiber and oil. Rice production during this time period was mainly oriented toward the internal market, and rice became one of the most important ingredients in Peruvians' diet.

During World War I (1914–18), sugar and cotton prices rose dramatically, as did most other raw materials, providing further incentives to expand production and production sites, even after prices leveled out

Cutting sugarcane (Reproduced with permission of the General Secretariat of the Organization of American States)

in the early 1920s. By 1918 Peru had surpassed the productivity levels of Hawaii, the most advanced sugar-producing site. Expansion continued well into the 1930s. Gradually some of the revenues obtained from sugar, rice, and cotton exports was invested in urban financial ventures, such as banking and insurance companies. The Banco Internacional del Perú, the Banco Alemán Transatlántico, the Banco Popular, the

Compañía de Seguros Rímac, the Compañía de Seguros Nacionales, and Porvenir opened their doors between WWI and 1920.

One problem these large agrarian enterprises faced was shortage of labor. The Chinese coolies were no longer available, and the indigenous population in the highlands resisted migration to the coastal plantations so completely different from their accustomed altitude and climate. Landowners thus resorted to coercive means to convince these Indian peasants to work on their fields. They hired *enganchadores,* men who visited peasant communities in the highlands and awaited a proper moment to hand a cash advance to peasants in need of money, such as for community duties or religious and patron saint festivities. Such festivities required that the individuals involved not only take care of processions and dressing the respective saint or virgin but also feed the whole community. Often, this was only possible for the chosen individuals when they obtained extra cash. But once a peasant had accepted money from an *enganchador,* he was obliged to work for a certain amount of time on a coastal plantation to repay the loan. Landowners and *enganchadores* made sure, however, that these individuals were unable to repay the loan and were thus doomed to remain at the plantation for extended periods of time. The primary mechanism used to retain laborers was the estate-owned general store, where fraudulent accounting assured that the initial debt would never be repaid. A more stable and better-paid labor force emerged only gradually over the course of the first decades in the 20th century. In the 1920s sugar and cotton workers on Peru's coastal plantations became the backbone of very strong unions. In the 1930s these same laborers led to the formation of the Alliance for Popular Revolution in America (APRA) in conjunction with a newly emerging leftist intellectual community.

The Southern Highlands

The region that suffered least from the War of the Pacific was the southern highlands. Although Tarapacá and Arica on the southern coast suffered the brunt of early fighting in the war, the highlands only saw smaller skirmishes late in 1883, when the war was almost over. Cuzco, Arequipa, and Puno surrendered to Chilean troops without resistance, and collaborators helped Chilean officials establish control. The region was affected by the war only indirectly when the blockade of the port of Mollendo kept imported goods out of the south, eliminating competition with British textiles. As a result Arequipa, the center of southern textile production, exported four times as much wool in 1884 than it had in the years preceding the war. Also, thousands of tons of food had to be provided from this region to feed the armies.

As usual, Indians paid the bill. Not only were they expected to produce the crops and the wool, but they served as the soldiers and continued to pay tribute. The result was the strengthening of hacienda owners and a new brand of local powerholders called *gamonales*. In the departments located at higher altitudes, such as Arequipa and Cuzco, where there had been essentially no haciendas prior to the war, in the decades after the war they multiplied into the hundreds. In Puno the number of

THE WOOL TRADE

Trade in wool produced in scattered regions was concentrated in British-owned merchant houses in the city of Arequipa. William Ricketts, a British immigrant to Peru in 1852, founded one such house in 1896. Ricketts invited the powerful British company Gibbs & Sons to become his financial and commercial agent in Europe. Gibbs & Sons opened an office in Arequipa and was able to secure a loan from the Banco del Callao, owned by a Cuban financier, José Payán. Ricketts and Gibbs & Sons planned to distribute goods imported from Europe throughout Peru's south, using the railway between Puno and Sicuani (finished in 1891); however, they soon discovered that their potential customers had little money and found themselves accepting wool instead of money as payment for merchandise. This persuaded Ricketts and his British counterparts there was an opportunity to profitably export wool.

They quickly organized a large network of intermediaries to purchase wool throughout the southern Andes. Next they established a network of company agents near the wool production sites. These employees bought wool in advance by providing producers with credits of up to 75 percent of their expected wool production. The credit, in turn, was handed out in the form of cash or purchase bills for the imported goods from Europe that Gibbs & Sons provided. In more remote areas the company's agents traveled on muleback to buy wool from peasants and to sell imported merchandise, transactions that often involved bartering rather than purchasing. Often—as the *repartos* in colonial times—peasants never really had money in their pockets.

Wool exports grew constantly throughout the final decades of the 19th century and the first decades of the 20th century, especially during World War I (Based on Burga and Reátequi 1981).

haciendas rose from 705 to 3,219 between 1876 and 1915, and this increase took place on former communal properties that had belonged to the indigenous population. The basic mechanism used to expropriate communal land was the advancement of money to purchase wool from peasants. A predictable strategy based in paternalism and violence forced Indians off their lands and reduced them to a servile relationship. It took about 20 years before Indian peasants found the strength to resist *gamonalismo,* and it was not until in the late 1950s that peasants mobilized on a national scale.

The Urubamba Valley, near Cuzco, saw a peculiar kind of development in the aftermath of the War of the Pacific. Commercial crops were produced there as a result of colonization laws from 1898 and 1909 and the expansion of the railroads to Urubamba. Haciendas with little capital or technology were the main production sites. Owners—comfortably living in Cuzco—hired administrators to take care of their properties. The produce from these haciendas provided a high standard of living to owners and coca, sugar, coffee, tea, and other goods to people in Puno and Bolivia. These were some of the few commercial crops that reached what could be considered an internal market. When Indians from the Machiguenga tribes successfully resisted becoming laborers on these haciendas, the hacienda owners and local administrators established colonies of imported highland peasants on nearby plots of land. This strategy lowered the costs of labor, and the proximity of the labor force allowed the owners control over these laborers. Colonizers would, in turn, subcontract smaller portions of land to other peasants. Thus, the colonized peasants fulfilled their work assignments with the hacienda owners by drawing on peasants even humbler than themselves.

Cattle Raising and Exports

Large stretches of highland lands (from Cajamarca to Puno) were cattle-raising areas. Beginning in the years after the War of the Pacific, and more intensely toward the beginning of the 20th century, cattle producers imported breeding stock from Europe and provided Peru's export economy with hides, meat, milk, butter, and cheese. They also sent their produce to feed the growing labor force on coastal plantations and cities. Between 1905 and 1910, the larger cattle-producing haciendas, in alliance with Lima-based capital providers, founded associations, or *sociedades,* of cattle producers in Junín and the center of the country. In 1920 these organizations held 46,000 acres and 90,000 acres of land, respectively. In the Department of Pasco, the Eulogio Fernandini

The Urubamba Valley (Photofrenetic/Alamy)

Agriculture and Cattle Enterprise, which also owned mines, amassed more than 171,000 acres of land between 1903 and 1931. The concentration of land followed patterns common to other enterprises, especially mining. After Peruvian owners modernized their properties and invested in new technology and infrastructure, foreign enterprises offered to buy their properties at what national owners considered very good prices. Thus the Peruvian elite in a sense became less committed to national interests.

Changes in the Amazon

In the 20th century booming electricity and automobile industries in Europe and the United States, with their large-scale demand for rubber, had the effect of ending the peaceful lives of the Amazonian tribes. Rubber harvesting in Peru began at the end of the War of the Pacific and witnessed a peak in the first decade of the 20th century. Rubber was transported on Amazon rivers to the city of Iquitos, and from there to European and U.S. markets. Smuggling was rampant, making it difficult to quantify the amounts of rubber exported; however, it has been calculated that by 1910 rubber exports amounted to about 30 percent of total Peruvian exports.

Some owners of rubber fields were larger-than-life characters. They dominated the region of the Ucayali River, and the Putumayo region and amassed enormous fortunes in a very short time, spending their money on luxury goods from Europe and Brazil. During the height of the rubber boom, these regions grew so strong and powerful that Lima was confronted with several separatist uprisings, initiated by profiting elites in the Amazon. Through fiscal manipulation and military intervention—it took an armed expedition a year to get to the site of one rebellion—Lima's government prevented the disintegration of Peruvian territory.

Rubber harvesting not only depleted this resource but also brought epidemics to the region and imposed harsh working conditions and even enslavement on the native populations, resulting in the death of 80 percent of the indigenous peoples, especially along the Putumayo River. The treatment of Indian workers by the Peruvian Amazon Company was the cause of an international scandal between 1908 and 1912.

Rubber turned out to be another boom industry that disappeared as quickly as it had appeared when British investors took Amazon rubber seeds with them and found more profitable and secure resources in their colonial plantations in Java and Borneo. The rubber boom ended around 1912 when Asian producers inundated the international market and prices fell.

Another important crop from the Amazon basin was coffee. The Peruvian Corporation, operating under the Grace Contract of 1889, formed the Perene Colony, which was administered by a small group of British employees and included an area of 202,000 acres called the Valley of Chanchamayo, with its capital city at Tarma. The laborers were Ashaninka Indians. The Peruvian government had hoped to turn this region into a prosperous colonization project; however, declining coffee prices in the international market frustrated such expectations.

From a global perspective, therefore, in the aftermath of the War of the Pacific, Peru found itself more fragmented than before. Lima's importance grew, but the regions became weaker. Within the regions, power also became more centralized, most markedly in the south, where Arequipa came to dominate large areas that incorporated Puno, Cuzco, Andahuaylas, and Apurimac and saw a dramatic increase of its urban population. The locus of power became the coast, not the highlands, a tendency that continues to this day. Presently, one of every three Peruvians lives in Lima. In 1876 it was one out of every 12.

The 1900 Generation

Paralleling these developments, a new group of intellectuals, small merchants, and state bureaucrats began cracking open Peru's still rigid—almost feudal—social structure. Cultural and intellectual endeavors at the turn of the century focused on how to achieve progress, how to establish a legitimate political authority, and how to achieve social integration. These groups were linked to prominent educational institutions, such as the College of Education (Colegio de Educandas) in Cuzco and the universities in Cuzco and Arequipa. It was in these locations that *indigenismo* came into being, a movement of socially oriented concerns, especially on behalf of Peru's Indians. However important this movement was, there is little evidence of its effecting change for Indians. One of the few initiatives taken was to teach the Spanish language to them in order to lower illiteracy rates. It had only partial success. By 1940 illiteracy rates were still as high as 58 percent, and one-third of Peru's population did not speak Spanish. In terms of literacy efforts, indigenous populations included a varied set of Amazonian tribes who had been largely untouched by anything happening in the country throughout the 19th century, and they certainly did not speak Spanish.

Intellectuals of this generation sought to study Peru's society and history from a scientific point of view; they harbored anticlerical feelings, and they largely criticized the negative sides of Hispanic colonization and conquest. In their eyes Peruvians' aversion to manual labor and a culture inherited from Spain hampered ideas of equal opportunity and the development of science and industry. They believed economic progress could only be attained by political centralization.

10

THE TWENTIETH CENTURY: FIRST DECADES (1900–1929)

Between 1890 and 1930 Peru strengthened its ties to the international market. These four decades were fundamentally outward-looking, and Peru's economy was export-oriented especially exporting raw materials. In contrast to earlier decades, when guano and nitrate had been the most important export products, during these later decades Peru's exports diversified. New regions in the country became linked to the international market, and some old regions switched to new export products following international prices and demands. The need to look inside the country often came about only because the internal market eventually offered opportunities to diversify exports, to incorporate larger areas into commercial production, and to satisfy a need for food for Peru's growing urban and industrial population.

Socially and politically these decades were the golden years of Peru's export-based oligarchy. Only gradually, beginning in the early 1920s, was oligarchic power undermined by the emergence of a middle class made up of state employees, people in the armed forces, and commerce and education workers and by the growing numbers of salaried workers in rural and urban areas. Throughout the 1920s and 1930s these new social groups formed their own political parties and developed their own views about the country's present and future and the role they were to play in Peru's development.

Often, such views came into conflict with what had been in place for decades. New solutions for old concerns were debated through the pages of a proliferating press. Cultural identity, political participation, and the benefits or detriment of political decentralization were some of the main issues of debate. Another topic was a matter that had gone unresolved throughout the 19th century: Peru's boundaries with its neighbors—Bolivia, Ecuador, Colombia, Chile, and Brazil. In contrast to earlier centuries, the 20th century witnessed a rapidly accelerating population growth and an acceleration of the rural-to-urban migration, which fueled this shift in power and focus.

Demographic Changes

Between 1876 and 1940 Peru's population grew from 2.6 million to 6 million people. Population growth was largely urban and coastal, whereas population density in the highlands and the Amazon basin remained low. In 1906 Alejandro Garland, a distinguished member of the Geographical Society, calculated that population density in the highlands was higher (4.78 inhabitants per square kilometer) than on the coast (4.53 per square kilometer). The Amazon basin had the lowest urban concentration index at 0.39 per square kilometer. (One square kilometer equals 0.39 square mile.) But a massive rural-to-urban migration began in the 1920s causing a sharp regional shift. In 1940, 65 percent of Peru's population was rural; in 1970 this would drop to 30 percent.

Lima grew from 114,788 inhabitants in 1890 to 172,927 in 1908. By 1908, 58.5 percent of *limeños* had not been born in Lima. The population further increased to 223,807 in 1920, to 376,097 in 1931, and to 540,100 in 1940. Other cities also saw increases in population, especially Arequipa, Cuzco, and Trujillo. Most city dwellers, especially in the smaller cities, lacked electricity and running water, and a single telegraph often was the only connection to the outside world. Administrative changes—especially the expansion of the state bureaucracy and a higher commitment to hygiene—and, even more important, job opportunities in urban centers and political peace promoted not only the natural growth of the population but also an internal migration from Peru's rural areas. The 1940 census registered in Lima an even gender distribution (49.42 percent men, 50.58 percent women) and a predominantly young population (50 percent of the population was 19 years old or younger). The economically active population in the country numbered 2.5 million people, of whom 62 percent worked in agriculture or husbandry, 17.5 percent in industry, and 20.5 percent in services. By 1940, 65 percent of Peru's population spoke Spanish, and many were bilingual in Spanish and Quechua.

The 1940 national census was Peru's last census to register race. It counted 52.89 percent whites and mestizos, 45.86 percent Indians, 0.47 percent blacks, 0.68 percent "yellows" (that is, Chinese or Japanese), and a 0.10 percent of "undeclared" race. This racial count was a surprise to many contemporaries. Only 10 years earlier Peru's intellectuals

A street scene in Lima, around 1900. The capital city's population grew rapidly during the first decades of the 20th century. (Christine Hunefeldt)

were firmly convinced that Indians amounted to four-fifths of Peru's population. When the census counted less than half of Peru's population as Indians, it reflected not a changed composition of Peru's racial mix but a dramatic change of racial perception and self-perception. The national debate about *indigenismo* had been based on the presumed existence of an Indian majority; however, by 1940 Peru had self-defined itself as an essentially mestizo country.

Traditionally the terms *Indian* and *peasant* were almost synonyms. Not all peasants were Indians, but most Indians were considered peasants. Population pressure had exceeded the availability of land in Peru's highland provinces, and peasants migrated to nearby cities and to Lima. With a declining rural population and an increasing urban population, more former "Indian" peasants were being counted as mestizos, a tendency that continues to this day.

In the decades between 1890 and 1940 Peru experienced what historians commonly call a "demographic transition"; that is, the growth of population created the conditions necessary for industrial development. However, as the Peruvian case shows, demographic growth is only one part of the story.

Japanese Immigrants

Japanese immigrants arrived in Peru under very different conditions than the earlier Chinese immigrants had experienced. In 1889 a few Japanese technicians opened a silver mine in the Cerro de San Francisco. Japan established diplomatic representation in Peru in 1897, and a year later, the Peruvian government invited Japanese immigrants to work on Peru's coastal plantations. Augusto B. Leguía enticed the Japanese Marioka Immigration Company to initiate the immigration process from Japan. Contracts, most for four-year terms, were signed with individual workers that specified the amount of salary and working hours. The first Japanese immigrants arrived in 1899. In spite of many difficulties, by 1909, there were 6,000 Japanese immigrants in Peru.

After their labor contracts elapsed, some Japanese immigrants resettled in the Amazon basin, especially in locations such as Madre de Dios and Tambopata, where rubber was produced for the international market. Some Japanese immigrants worked their way up and became landowners on the coast. Especially in the Chancay Valley, they proved to be very successful agrarian entrepreneurs producing cotton and fruit, and a few even held political positions as local mayors. A future president of Peru, Alberto Fujimori, was a descendant of Japanese immigrants and an agrarian engineer who owned land on the Peruvian northern coast.

Proletarians Unite, Industrialization Nears

The regional and economic changes of the late 19th century produced a new social structure, with new social actors, that had far-reaching consequences for Peru's development in the 20th century. Lima was the only Peruvian city where a process of industrialization had already begun by the end of the 19th century. Textile factories such as El Inca, Vitarte, and Progreso employed more than 500 salaried workers. Although few in number, these workers proved to have vital political importance, especially during labor strikes. By 1920 Lima counted 30,255 artisans and 7,492 salaried workers. The first strike efforts were led by Lima's artisans, most prominently the bakers. In 1905 Lima's bakers were the first guild to demand an eight-hour work day. They were followed by shoemakers, and the two unions joined efforts to help bring Guillermo Billinghurst, outsider to the oligarchy, to power in 1912. Callao's port workers, many of them Italians, also became actively involved in the workers' struggles for higher salaries and shorter work days. It was 1913 when President Billinghurst decreed the eight-hour work day to some segments of the labor force, and in 1917 the eight-hour work day was extended to all.

By then Peru's workers had established international contacts with other labor organizations whose predominant political doctrines were the radical creeds of anarchism and anarco-syndicalism. Both philosophies sought the destruction of existing governments and societies in order to bring about a new age of equality and justice. Both also advocated the indiscriminate use of violence to achieve their goals. Although anarco-syndicalists celebrated the heroism and success of the workers in the Russian Revolution of 1917, they criticized the Bolsheviks for betraying workers' political independence. As international winds changed and Peru's working class grew, workers gradually moved from anarco-syndicalism to party participation. The parties representing workers' interests in the 1920s were the Peruvian Socialist Party (Partido Socialista del Perú, or PSP), led by José Carlos Mariátegui (1898–1930), and the Alliance for Popular Revolution in America (Alianza Popular Revolucionaria Americana, or APRA), led by Víctor Raúl Haya de la Torre (1895–1979).

Anarco-syndicalism had laid the foundations for workers' initial organization and—perhaps just as important—for a workers' culture. Organization and culture within the Peruvian labor movement were widely influenced by immigrants from northern Italy, and several workers' unions produced newsletters between 1911 and 1926, among them *Plumadas de rebeldía* (Strokes of rebellion), *El hambriento* (The hungry), *Los parias* (The pariahs), *El oprimido* (The oppressed), and *La protesta* (The protest). Newspapers and newsletters were widely read and, in spite of irregular publication, had a strong bearing on the gradual consolidation of the labor movement. Theater and novels (sometimes published as serials in newspapers and newsletters) dealt with workers' issues, as well as workers' lives and other concerns. Literary-musical gatherings (*veladas*) were used to discuss the works of Bakunin, Kropotkin, or Malatesta. Many workers' initiatives counted on the support of renowned journalists and writers, among them César Falcón and Mariátegui, and the university student leader Haya de la Torre.

Increasingly, politicians and journalists voiced their opinions through the pages of newspapers and magazines, and there was also an increasing tendency to think and write about both the past and the future of the country. The number of publications grew, which indicated a wide audience for such ruminations. From a total of 167 publications registered in 1918, the number rose to 443 by 1930.

The majority of such developments took place in Lima; however, some minor initiatives emerged in other areas that counted at least some salaried workers, especially in locations where mines and coastal plantations were producing for the international market. In 1905 Peru counted 9,651 miners; their numbers rose to 19,515 in 1913, to 22,000 in 1922, and to 32,321 in 1929. Miners were concentrated in areas like La Oroya and Cerro de Pasco, but many scattered mines located at more than 12,000 feet of altitude employed fewer than 50 miners. The smaller the mine, the more random was the political organization associated with it. Besides mining, another industry in which rural laborers began to organize was oil production. Oil production involved 5,831 workers in 1928, of which 3,918 worked on the oil fields in Talara, owned by the International Petroleum Company (IPC). Another important contingent of salaried workers could be found on coastal plantations. About 16,000 workers produced rice around 1922. Twenty thousand workers produced cotton on 226 haciendas around 1915; this number rose to more than 40,000 around 1922 and more than 65,000 around 1932.

Many of these nonurban workers, however, were not full-fledged salaried workers but were still hired under noncapitalist, nonsalaried

A military parade past the Cathedral of Santa Catalina in Cajamarca in 1919 (Reproduced with permission of the General Secretariat of the Organization of American States)

conditions through the exploitative *enganche* debtor-enlistment system. The greatest numbers of salaried workers were engaged in sugarcane production, where the most efficient technology could be found. Between 1912 and 1922 the amount of land cultivated for sugarcane almost doubled (from 80,000 acres to around 145,000). This expansion came with a concentration of landed property in fewer and fewer hands. In 1910 there were 118 haciendas; in 1927 there remained only 70, and by 1932 the number of haciendas was down to 64. The number of workers increased steadily from 19,945 in 1912 to 30,159 in 1925. The number of workers then decreased in the wake of the 1929 stock market crash to around 25,000 but increased again to 28,294 in 1933. Whereas around 27,000 workers labored in rice fields on 674 haciendas, 20,000 workers worked on 80 sugarcane haciendas. Thus, labor was highly concentrated within sugarcane plantations. As a result of geographical distance between haciendas, mines, and textile factories, and because of different ownership and hiring patterns, little communication was possible or even allowed between workers in these different sites.

Although scattered, social protest was on the rise. In 1912 workers went on strike for several days in the Chicama valley, burning down the sugarcane. Some people died during the protest. It was put down with a strong military intervention from Lima.

An Emerging Professional and Intellectual Class

A new professional class, mainly employed in the service sector and in an expanding state apparatus, was part of a changing social structure. Peru needed to solve specific economic-export problems, and one result was the founding of the School of Engineering and the School of Agriculture. Consequently, Peru developed a larger and better qualified corps of professionals. Initiatives sprang up not only to plan Peru's future, but also—more concretely—to reform the educational system as a first step toward economic improvement. Many such plans hailed from the provinces, especially from provincial universities. The most notable efforts came from the Universidad San Antonio Abad in Cuzco, where the election as chancellor of Alberto Giesecke, a U.S. citizen, changed the educational outlook by focusing the college curricula on regional problems and their solutions instead of mimicking European models. Puno and Arequipa students read more newspapers from Buenos Aires and Europe than from Lima. In general, intellectuals from the provinces greatly influenced intellectual life and political debate in Lima.

Previously barred from universities by the Partido Civil, this emerging intellectual middle class now swelled the ranks of the schools. Students' own resentment at their earlier exclusion and the influence of the Mexican and Russian revolutions led to a radicalization of the student movement. In turn the spread of radical, liberal, and even socialist voices inspired a backlash that led to the formation in 1917 of the Pontifical Catholic University in Lima (Pontificia Universidad Católica del Perú, or PUC). The Catholic University became the conservative counterpart to an increasingly radical student movement engaged in reforms and based out of the San Marcos University (Universidad Nacional Mayor de San Marcos, or UNMSM). Students and workers closed ranks in a massive strike in 1919 that brought about substantial gains for both. President Augusto B. Leguía, on the other side, responded by co-opting intellectuals for his Patria Nueva policies, by deporting irritating critics such as Haya de la Torre, or by handing out official support, such as paying for the trips of Mariátegui and Falcón to Europe. Despite the political climate and repression, Peru witnessed an era of intellectual effervescence through its "generation of reformers." Intellectuals of the caliber of historians Jorge Basadre and Raúl Porras Barrenechea, archaeologist Julio C. Tello, and political analyst and writer Luis Alberto Sánchez were part of this socially committed generation.

EL FÚTBOL

Soccer, called *fútbol* in Spanish-speaking countries, was imported to Peru originally by British sailors in the 1880s, who began playing matches among themselves in Callao. The British merchant and business colony in Lima soon took up the sport and established it as part of their recreation sports clubs, such as the Lima Cricket and Football Club. In 1890 local Peruvians were allowed to join soccer clubs, and soon the sport began to spread. Working-class teams sprang up, first among the stevedores and sailors of Callao but soon in the poorer neighborhoods of Lima. By the first decades of the 20th century, soccer clubs were established parts of life in Lima and its environs, and workers used the clubs as centers for social organization. The National Stadium opened in the 1920s and hosted what became a continuing rivalry between two teams: Alianza Lima, made up mostly of black players from the working-class neighborhoods, and Universitario de Deportes, a club composed of university students from middle- and upper-class families.

Academic publications aimed to reach larger audiences, and many academic articles were first published in journals and newspapers that were more accessible to more people. Intellectuals founded public universities meant to study Peruvian reality and to actively think about changing it.

An interesting side product of the rapid urbanization, social mobility, and state concerns was the emergence of sports as a means to enhance public health and morale. Clubs and sport associations, many of which still exist today, proliferated. Some of these associations promoted several new sports, such as basketball, rowing, swimming, biking, and soccer, all of them of European origin. These sports gradually replaced or complemented prior colonial social activities, such as religious processions, bullfights, and cockfights.

Indigenismo

A current of thought that described Peru's Indians from a non-Indian perspective, *indigenismo* was a movement within this larger intellectual reformism. It also was part of a nascent regional nationalism and pride and a reaction to the viewpoint, that Indians were an inferior race good only for manual work, the army, and serfdom. *Indigenistas,* in contrast, set out to revalue Indians' history and culture and to ease their path into modernity.

There were, in fact, many *indigenismos.* The movement began as a literary endeavor but soon involved politics, painting, social sciences, archaeology, and even medicine. An oligarchic version of *indigenismo* promoted Indians' integration to Peruvian society through education, hygiene, and religion. Writer Manuel González Prada, in a more radical version, held that the main problems Indians had were not religious or cultural but social and economic. Mariátegui and Haya de la Torre took González Prada's argument still further. They argued that without a redistribution of land nothing could or should be done for Indians. The only way to redistribute land was by eliminating *latifundia* (the large property-holding system that included haciendas) in the highlands. Not all *indigenistas* proposed such radical measures. Many writers and artists portrayed how Indians lived: their daily sufferings at the hands of unscrupulous landowners, priests, and state bureaucrats, but also the rich traditions and culture that informed their living and social interaction. By focusing on these subjects academic *indigenistas* spread a higher sensibility toward indigenous issues in Peru and beyond.

The novel *Aves sin nido (Birds Without a Nest)* by Clorinda Matto de Turner was published in 1889. It gained Matto de Turner instant

179

Peruvian peasants became the focus of the intellectual movement known as indigenismo during the early decades of the 20th century. (Photofrenetic/Alamy)

celebrity, excommunication from the Catholic Church (because she questioned celibacy), and her exile until her death in Argentina in 1909. Along with Matto de Turner, Pedro Zulen, Dora Mayer, and Joaquín Capelo were the most important protagonists of the literary component within *indigenismo*. They attempted to organize Indians into action groups and wrote lengthy treatises on the miseries of Peru's Indians, compiled in a landmark publication, *El deber proindígena* (Our proindigenous duty). José Sabogal and Julia Codesido painted Indians and their daily lives, while others, such as Daniel Alomia in his opera *El condor pasa* (first presented in 1913, and with 3,000 performances in the following five years), sang about Indians. In the social writings of Hildebrando Castro Pozo, José Varallanos, José Luis Valcárcel, Uriel García, and Ernesto Reyna, Indians appeared as historical subjects rather than as objects of philanthropic and compassionate policies. *Tempestad en los Andes* (Tempest in the Andes) by Valcárcel and *El nuevo indio* (The new Indian) by García had long-lasting impacts. Political writer González Prada often met with this group of artists in the Lima Literary Circle (Círculo Literario), and it was González Prada, who through his strong critical voice against racial discrimination and violence, later awakened the thoughts of Mariátegui (founder of the PSP)

THE PLIGHT OF THE INDIAN

The following is an excerpt from a speech given by author Víctor Andrés Belaúnde in Arequipa in 1915 when he was running for deputy in a local election.

> *The colonial ties have not disappeared. Once I said that we all carry the souls of encomenderos and corregidores. The illusion that Indians could become individual property owners led us to abolish the peasant communities. These communities, lacking a legal status and not having the support of the state, have been continuously losing their lands. The enganche has replaced the mita. Indians are still tied to the land through serfdom, a situation that historically puts us in the heart of the Middle Ages. . . . However, our situation is even worse. The feudal lord in Europe lived on his estate and was there to defend it and provide protection. He was the first one on the battlefield and often the first one to die. . . . In our society, feudalism reigns, but without religion, poetry, and glory (Belaúnde 1883, 127; translated by Christine Hunefeldt).*

and Haya de la Torre (founder of APRA). Mariátegui opened the pages of his journal *Amauta* to the *indigenista* writers because he was convinced that without taking into account and perhaps even involving Indians, Peru could not realize a socialist political program. Although many of these intellectuals were sincerely committed to the "Indian cause," some did not see the contradiction between exalting Indians in print while keeping indebted Indians on their landed properties. Often intellectual discourse did not translate into reality.

Some *indigenistas* applied a hands-on strategy. Educator José Antonio Encinas, for example, directed a primary school in Puno between 1906 and 1911 in which Indian children learned in their native language. Some of Encinas's students later became teachers in their home communities. Encinas himself called this "a new school," and many of his ideas were published in his 1932 book, *Un ensayo de escuela nueva en el Perú*.

There also was an "official" *indigenismo*, promoted by and through the Peruvian state. President Leguía gave speeches in Quechua (a language he did not know), facilitated a congress of Indian leaders in Lima, introduced a holiday into the Peruvian calendar (Día del Indio, June 24, coinciding with the Incan ritual of Inti Raymi), established an agency devoted to indigenous issues, and promulgated laws to provide official recognition to Indian peasant communities, thus providing these communities with an organization to defend themselves against attacks from large landowners. However, whenever peasant unrest threatened local stability, Leguía sided with the landowners.

Peasant Unrest

During Leguía's first presidency, from 1908 to 1912, peasant insurgencies became more radical and more widespread. In fact, the first two decades of the 20th century in Peru were of continued peasant unrest, reaching a peak between 1919 and 1924 (during Leguía's second presidency), at a time when the end of World War I greatly reduced prices of raw materials on the international market. Previously a hike of these international prices had produced a massive attack on peasant communities' lands in Peru's highlands. Some signs of unrest were plainly visible in the first decade of the 20th century, but it was 1912 when peasant unrest expanded, radicalized, and began questioning governmental policies. In response, the new president, Guillermo Enrique Billinghurst, further opened political opportunities for peasants and provided them with a sense that matters could change for the better. In 1913 Billinghurst sent Major Teodomiro Gutiérrez Cuevas to Peru's southern highlands. His mission was to investigate several complaints by Indians in the region about their sufferings at the hands of local *gamonales*. Gutiérrez Cuevas had been *subprefecto* of Chucuito in 1903 and of Huancayo in 1907, and had since then been known for his sensitivity toward the plight of the Indian. He became known as Rumi Maki (Quechua for "stone hand") among Indians. With Billinghurst's loss of power in 1914, all official channels were closed, and Rumi Maki—as some Indian leaders before him—was forced to resort to direct action—that is, insurrection. Once again this peasant upheaval was brutally suffocated.

GUILLERMO E. BILLINGHURST

Guillermo Enrique Billinghurst was Peru's first non-*civilista* president since the mid-19th century. Born in Arica in 1851, he was a former nitrate field owner in southern Peru who lost his mines to Chile in the aftermath of the War of the Pacific. Like most other leaders from southern Peru, he supported Nicolás de Piérola's Democratic Party. Billinghurst would seem to have been a natural choice for the party's presidential candidate in the 1899 elections, but he was passed over and subsequently retired briefly from politics. In 1909 he became mayor of Lima, and three years later he became Peru's first populist president. Previously Peru's congress had annulled the election of Antero Aspíllaga, one of the sugar barons of the coast. The argument for annulment was that the elected candidate had not received the required one-third of the votes needed to legitimate his election. Democrats, however, knew that in a national election process they would be unable to defeat the *civilistas*, who had, over many decades, established vast electoral networks and thus controlled elections in the provinces. During elections, the Democrats sabotaged the electoral process by physically burning down the polling sites and by intimidating voters. The electoral tribunal, in turn, annulled many election lists, making the one-third voting participation impossible. All this was possible because the Democrats could count on the support of Lima's workers and more generally on Lima's urban working class, who had recently seen a significant hike in their living costs. Begun in 1912, Billinghurst's presidency lasted less than two years. A coup d'état by Colonel Oscar R. Benavides, a military hero from a border skirmish with Colombia over rubber fields, brought Billinghurst's presidency to an abrupt end in 1914. Once again, *civilistas* regained power. Billinghurst died one year later in Tarapacá.

For some time, Indians continued to believe that some changes could occur. When Leguía assumed the presidency again, in 1919, local (often corrupt) bureaucrats were replaced by members of Leguía's New Party. The main change during Leguía's regime was the official and legal recognition of Peru's peasant communities, which had a far-reaching impact when used by Indians and Indian communities to defend their land.

On June 16, 1920, the Central Committee for Indian Rights (Comisión Central Pro Derecho Indígena "Tahuantinsuyo") was established, and Indians paid a *rama*, a small amount of money (one sol), for the committee's representation in lawsuits on their behalf. This *rama* funded a significant infrastructure of representatives for Indians to the central government in Lima that brought governmental concerns and peasant grievances somewhat closer. In response delegates from the government often visited local communities to hear their complaints. By doing so, they created many expectations among peasants, particularly that of regaining their land lost to *gamonales,* powerful local officials. Expectations were further heightened when the first Indian congress was held in Lima in 1924. In this congress, delegates approved a declaration of the principles of the Comisión Central Tahuantinsuyo. Four more congresses followed over the next few years, all important landmarks in the struggle to uphold Indian peasants' rights.

Legislative changes spilled over into actions. Beginning in September 1920 Indian peasant communities began mobilizing to regain their lost land. Often, violent confrontations, ending sometimes with the killing of hacienda managers, were the result. Around 1922, workers at various levels in the haciendas joined the peasant communities in their mobilization. The peasant movement not only gained numbers of participants but also spread over a large region. Massive peasant unrest was recorded in Huancané (Puno, 1923), La Mar (Ayacucho, 1923) and Parcona (Ica, 1924).

Lima's government and even some earlier supporters of indigenous rights began turning their backs on peasants. The government abolished the *rama* and founded a parallel institution to the Comisión Central Tahuantinsuyo called the Patronato de la Raza Indígena, which reduced the Comisión's power. With the loss of the *rama* the Comisión lost its financial underpinnings. Not much later, in October 1922, the Comisión itself was declared illegal. After this pivotal moment Peru's government sided with the *gamonales* and engaged in severe repressive measures against Indian peasants. *Gamonales* began organizing their own paramilitary groups, which quite often consisted of hacienda workers led by *gamonales.* Moreover, *gamonales* and their followers did not hesitate to use the military and government-paid police forces. Although minor skirmishes continued, the big wave of Indian rebellion had come to an end.

Peru's Leaders: Oligarchs and *Gamonales*

Oligarchs held direct power until the 1930s and retained much influence until the late 1960s. A combination of extended family ties, nepotism, consensus, and violence helped to keep them in power while excluding, neutralizing, and controlling Peru's lower and middle classes. Peru's oligarchy was a conglomerate of 40 to 200 families (depending on where one draws the power line) that regarded themselves as the owners of the country. Their meeting place—where much of the business was done and alliances forged—was the Club Nacional, located in the heart of Lima.

These families owned the most important resources of the country, especially the sugarcane-, cotton-, and rice-producing plantations as well as the growing insurance companies, the banks, and the commercial enterprises. Marriage alliances helped these families consolidate their power and often extend their influence beyond Peru's boundaries. Daughters of Peru's oligarchic families who married European bankers not only extended their families' economic ventures but also maintained their whiteness (or according to them even "enhanced" it). As in many other Latin American countries, the practices of the oligarchy deepened the already existing social and racial gaps within Peruvian society. However, this class was not quite equivalent to the colonial nobility. They engaged in new economic endeavors, employed new ways of thinking, and developed far-reaching networks that reached down in society.

After Billinghurst's short, two-year Democratic presidency, the oligarchy and the Partido Civil, reinstalled their initial political agenda, with some important additions and reforms. Their economic policies continued to be outward looking—that is, promoting raw-material exports and seeking foreign investment. However, they reorganized the state apparatus. Peru's oligarchs understood that a mounting social unrest needed a state able and willing to mediate and integrate. Fiscal and administrative modernization, a more professional army under civilian control, and the development of the educational and health system were the means used to reform the state apparatus. Indians, the oligarchy argued, would benefit from enhanced education and health and would in the long run be better equipped to integrate into society.

The cathedral facing the Plaza de Armas in Lima (Library of Congress)

Municipalities, in charge of the educational system since 1876, had been stripped of this prerogative during José Pardo y Barreda's presidency back in 1905. From there on education was a state issue, and education became universal and free. Similarly the Board of Public Health (Dirección de Salubridad Pública) had been created within the Ministry of Public Works in 1903, largely in response to a plague epidemic in Lima that year. However, the board's responsibilities grew beyond its initial administrative boundaries, and in 1935 it became an independent ministry of health. Following this modernizing trend other important institutions came to life between 1895 and 1915: the National Industrial Society (Sociedad Nacional de Industrias), the National Mining Society (Sociedad Nacional de Minería), the Board of Lawyers in Lima (Colegio de Abogados de Lima), the Engineering Society (Sociedad de Ingeniería), the National Agrarian Society (Sociedad Nacional Agraria), and the Peruvian Husbandry Association (Asociación de Ganaderos del Perú).

Provincial caudillos and *gamonales* did not belong to the oligarchy and therefore could not command as much political power, but they did nevertheless have considerable power, especially in Peru's highlands. Earlier caudillos had lost much influence in the wake of the War of the Pacific, and new caudillo-like leaders generally assumed regional power—mostly through land ownership and by holding political positions—while Peru diversified its export economy and enacted military reforms. These *gamonales* tended to replace *prefectos* and *subprefectos*—the official, Lima-appointed political leaders in the departments and provinces—in their roles of military leaders, allowing the *gamonales* to expand their power in tandem with their control of the best agrarian production sites. Military, political, and economic power were thus in the hands of a few regional bosses. Using their position they extended their social and political networks to control largely everything in their respective provinces. However, their power was not stable; they could be removed by the central government in Lima, and fights among *gamonales* over provincial resources were frequent. These power struggles between *gamonales* often involved the region's Indians, too, as they chose sides. The result was that no real political predominance was established.

During the *civilista* period, Peru was highly dependent on foreign capital and investments but experienced an important diversification of exports, a limited industrialization, and a certain level of autonomous development. Exports grew from 3.073 billion Peruvian pounds in 1899, to 9.138 billion in 1913, and to 35.304 billion in 1920. Unlike the earlier guano camps, export sites were not enclaves but promoted links to national producers (Thorp and Bertram 1985, 113, 132, 220). Services and inputs for the export economy came from local producers. The addition of oil, copper, vanadium, and wool, diversified exports. Diversification was intimately related to the opening of the Panama Canal in 1914, World War I, and the continued efforts by the Peruvian Corporation to extend the railroad network to Cerro de Pasco,

Huancayo, and Cuzco. Overall, this period was marked by Peru's search for material progress, social integration, and political and institutional expansion, albeit with uneven results and varied repercussions for the social groups involved.

Leguía's Eleven Years

Augusto B. Leguía, initially committed to *civilista* principles, used general dissatisfaction with oligarchic rule to prepare his path to Peru's presidency. Leguía lived in London from 1913 to 1919, when he returned to Peru to present his candidacy against the *civilistas,* whose sitting president, Pardo, had lost all support from workers and the middle class. Leguía, in turn, enjoyed the support of college students, workers, and the middle class. Students of the San Marcos University hailed him as the *"maestro de la juventud"* (mentor of Peru's youth). Concomitantly Leguía believed the newly emerging social groups of entrepreneurs, bureaucrats, professionals, and students, not the export-oriented oligarchs, to be the modernizing elements of the country.

Antero Aspíllaga, a northern coast sugar baron, turned out to be a weak *civilista* candidate, and the other parties in the presidential campaign flagged: The Democratic Party was debilitated after its leader, Nicolás de Piérola, died in 1913; the Constitutional Party—whose candidate was Andrés Avelino Cáceres, the hero of the War of the Pacific—was basically a conglomerate of war veterans; and the new Liberal Party—did not have a social base or a defined political project. Leguía seized the moment under these conditions and became president in 1919.

During his electoral campaign, Leguía had promised to solve the pending territorial issues with Chile, recover the provinces of Tacna and Arica, lower the cost of living, increase public works, and boost national defense (that is, the military). Together these promises formed an anti-*civilista* program. Though the electorate seemed to favor him, Leguía did not await the scheduled elections. On July 4, 1919, he instigated a coup d'état, which he believed would increase his ultimate control of the state. Even if Leguía had won the elections, he certainly would have found much opposition in congress, where only two-thirds of its members were newly appointed every four years. The coup allowed Leguía to dissolve congress and put together another that would support his policies. The national assembly nominated Leguía as constitutional president and prepared a new constitution to replace the 1860 constitution. The main changes in the Constitution of 1920 were the cancellation of the one-third parliamentary renewal clause, the extension of the presidential mandate from four to five years, the introduction of a progressive income tax, and the formation of regional congresses in Peru's north, center, and south. These congresses were an attempt to decentralize Peru. However, soon after his initial decentralization effort, Leguía moved in the opposite direction, toward a heightened political and economic centralization in Lima. Municipalities were turned into Assemblies of Notables (Juntas de Notables), and the notables were hand-picked by the government.

By controlling elections such that he was the only presidential candidate, Leguía managed to stay in power for a second term from 1924 to 1929. His main electoral agenda was the consolidation of the "Patria Nueva" (New Country), a program geared toward social progress and the participation—mostly rhetorical—of the working class and Indians. To finance the state's course of modernization and growth, Leguía increased export taxes despite fierce opposition from export barons, resorted to foreign (especially U.S.) loans, and instituted income taxes, which actually represented only a very small portion of total state revenues. Incomes higher than 15,001 soles only paid 6 percent of income tax; nevertheless, total state income grew from 66 million soles in 1919 to 123 million in 1925 and to 149 million in 1930. Peru's foreign debt increased in tandem, from 25 million soles in 1919, to 221 million only 10 years later. In spite of fiscal deficit, in 10 years the Peruvian sol only lost about 15 percent of its exchange value against the U.S. dollar.

During his second term, Leguía continued in his efforts to undermine the *civilistas'* political power. He also followed a populist policy that affected *gamonales* in the south. Leguía officially recognized Peru's peasant communities, established the Patronato de la Raza Indígena to defend Indians and the Day of the Indian (Día del Indio), and organized agrarian and technical learning centers in rural areas.

Gradually Leguía's government put in place large-scale irrigation projects, in the Chira and Olmos Valleys in Peru's north and in the Imperial Valley in the south, to expand the cultivation of sugarcane and cotton. These projects were guided technically by U.S. expert Charles Sutton. Leguía's administration also added some new railroads to the existing lines. The railway between Huancayo and Huancavelica was inaugurated in 1926, and the railroad between Cuzco and Quillabamba was begun. In 1923, the beginning of the construction of the Pan-American Highway for the first time allowed travel by car between the cities of Lima, Ica, and Trujillo, and Huancayo became connected to Lima via the Central Highway. Regular airplane routes were established, and air travel between Lima and the outside world, as well as between Lima and other Peruvian cities, became an everyday experience. For

Principal Exports, circa 1910

ECUADOR

COLOMBIA

Napo R.

Putumayo R.

Amazon R.

Pastaza R.

LORETO

AMAZONAS

Marañón R.

PIURA

CAJAMARCA

SAN MARTÍN

Yavari R.

LAMBAYEQUE

BRAZIL

Huallaga R.

Ucayali R.

LA LIBERTAD

ANCASH

HUÁNUCO

UCAYALI

PASCO

Pacific Ocean

LIMA

JUNÍN

MADRE DE DIOS

Apurímac R.

Urubamba R.

HUANCAVELICA

CUZCO

ICA

APURÍMAC

PUNO

AYACUCHO

AREQUIPA

Lake Titicaca

Coffee

Sugar

Cotton

Guano

Wool

Minerals

Oil

Rubber

MOQUEGUA

BOLIVIA

Contemporary national boundary

TACNA

Contemporary provincial boundary

N

0   250 miles

0   250 kilometers

CHILE

international flights, Panagra airline opened its offices in Limatambo, and for national flights to the interior Faucett Airlines was in charge. In one of his many public speeches Leguía encapsulated his vision: "On the coast I water, in the highlands I connect, in the jungle I colonize" (Contreras and Cueto 2000, 223).

Leguía also improved Peru's cities with public health and hygiene efforts, such as building water and sewage systems, paving streets and sidewalks, and organizing trash collection and city lighting. During the centennial anniversary of Peru's independence from Spain, in 1921 and 1924, Lima saw the inauguration of the Hotel Bolívar, Hospital Arzobispo Loayza, and Plaza San Martín. Soon, a network of roads connected Lima's expanding outlying areas with its center and its port city, Callao. All such endeavors created new jobs (the number of business and state employees in Lima grew from 6,821 in 1908 to 37,588 in 1930), the development of industries such as cement and civil construction enterprises, and new business sites for local banks.

Another important product of governmental involvement was Peru's territorial boundaries. Colombia and Peru signed the Salomón Lozano Treaty in 1922 by which Colombia gained access to the Amazon basin through the Leticia Triangle. Treaty of Lima, with Chile, was signed in 1929, through which Peru recovered Tacna and Arica became part of

ELMER FAUCETT AND PERU'S FIRST AIRLINES

Lima's modern airport is named after the American Elmer "Slim" Faucett. Faucett, who was one of many pilots from the United States and Europe who flew in Peru between 1915 and 1930, came to Peru in June 1920 to attend flight school, graduating in 1921. In the same year, the Peruvian government offered a reward to anyone who could fly from Lima to Iquitos, crossing the country from west to east and surmounting the high Andean mountain peaks. Faucett took up the challenge in his 150-horsepower Oriole Wright, a two-engine biplane with an open cabin. Faucett did not reach Iquitos but landed only 40 miles away. He got the reward and went on to open an airline in 1928 to transport mail and passengers between Lima and the Talara oil fields. The first commercial flight of the new airline, between Lima and Chiclayo, was in September 1928, the same year that the first transatlantic flight from Paris to New York was undertaken. A few months earlier, the commercial firm Grace, following a proposal from U.S. pilot Harold Harris, who had been hired to fumigate cotton plantations in the north of Peru, established the Panamerican Airways company, which began its commercial flights between Lima and Buenos Aires. In 1929, Faucett built the first commercial airport in Peru.

Chile; both provinces had been under Chilean command since the War of the Pacific.

But not all that came from the presidential headquarters was so positive. A lack of labor was seen as the main obstacle to expanding Peru's internal road network, so in 1920 Leguía signed a law to conscript labor. State service (the *conscripción vial*) was imposed on all males between 18 and 60 years of age. In practice, however, it were essentially Indian peasants who had to work. Men between 18 and 21, and 50 and 60, had to work for the state for one week each year; all other age groups had to deliver two weeks a year. Quite frequently this law was used to force people to work for the state every Sunday. Although the law stipulated that workers should do their service no more than eight miles away from home, many peasants complained that they were forced to travel for more than 20 or 30 miles without receiving any compensation for traveling by foot or on mule-back. *Indigenistas* were alarmed by what they interpreted as a "republican *mita*" and a new form of the Indian tribute. Recruiting the laborers for state service was no minor task, and local political authorities and engineers in charge of road building often had to call on the Guardia Civil, a police force founded in 1923, to bring in laborers. As might be expected, the use of force led to extended abuse and complaints. Aside from the Guardia Civil, Leguía also established a secret police force, commonly referred to as the *soplones*. A Spanish group of experts invited by the Peruvian government gave technical and military advice to Leguía's secret police force.

Aside from internal unrest Leguía's government was pierced by unchecked corruption. Leguía's own son and a Peruvian diplomat Juan Leguía, faced severe criticism in 1932, when U.S. policy on foreign loans was debated in the U.S. Congress. In these sessions the younger Leguía was accused of obtaining illegal commissions, of hiding important information under the cover of diplomatic immunity, and soliciting loans at inflated prices for projects of little benefit to his country. Once more, at the end of President Leguía's second term, the Peruvian government was taking out loans whose repayment depended on the grant of future new loans to the government. In short, spending exceeded by far the revenues obtained from exports and taxes.

Diagnosing Peruvian Reality and History: Mariátegui and Haya de la Torre

The most severe critique of oligarchic rule came from the pens and voices of two influential members of the Peruvian intelligentsia: José

Carlos Mariátegui and Víctor Raúl Haya de la Torre. Their intellectual and political philosophies shaped and framed much of the political debate from the first decades of the 20th century to this day. Mariátegui and Haya de la Torre founded the Peruvian Socialist Party (PSP) and the Alliance for Popular Revolution in America (APRA) respectively.

Initially, at least, *mariateguistas* and *apristas* shared a common Marxist underpinning, and the two men worked together. Mariátegui gave lectures at the Manuel González Prada Popular University, and he welcomed Haya de la Torre's founding of the APRA party in Mexico in 1924 during his eight-year exile. Haya de la Torre conceived APRA as a pan-national political movement that could coalesce general dissatisfaction among several social groups throughout Latin America. Mariátegui's political journal *Amauta* opened its pages to *aprista* writers.

In 1927, however, Haya de la Torre entered into a prolonged debate with Eudocio Ravines, who at the time was an important agent of the Third Communist International and Mariátegui's designated successor as leader of the socialist-communist groups in Peru. (Mariátegui was sick with tuberculosis and did not have long to live.) In 1928 the APRA launched a new party in Peru called the Partido Nacionalista Libertador (Nationalist Liberation Party) and Haya de la Torre was the designated presidential candidate. Mariátegui severely criticized this move. In his view, the *aprista* effort to participate in elections negated his call for patience and long-term preparation. Mariátegui thought it necessary to engage in a long-term consciousness building and the organization of the working class as a prerequisite to taking power.

Disagreement between the leaders was on more than strategic grounds. Whereas Mariátegui made a socialist critique of the capitalist establishment, Haya de la Torre was convinced that capitalism was a necessary path to achieve development. In spite of his severe anti-imperialist stand, Haya de la Torre admitted that capitalism had a positive side. Imperialist money, he argued, brought needed investment and thus progress to the country. In Haya de la Torre's political view, an anti-imperialist state, based on private enterprise, state capitalism, and cooperativism, would negotiate with imperialist interests to save capitalism's positive aspects and dismiss its negative aspects. He conceived of the state as the assembly of all exploited classes: peasants, proletarians, small bourgeoisie, and what he called a nationally oriented bourgeoisie. The middle class, more educated, more numerous, and more affected by imperialism than the proletarians, would lead this political change. Imperialism—the last stage of capitalism in Europe—was, for him, the first stage of capitalism in Latin America.

Mariátegui thought otherwise. According to him, imperialism was the same stage of capitalist development for Europe and Latin America, and through it the capitalist centers of Europe became richer while the periphery of Latin America was doomed to become poorer. National liberation from the imperialist grip was impossible from within capitalism. In Mariátegui's eyes salaried workers and eventually peasants were the only ones who should and could offer an organized resistance to capitalism, in spite of their small number, whereas the middle class was

JOSÉ CARLOS MARIÁTEGUI: ON TRADITION

Tradition is alive and mobile, quite the opposite of what the traditionalists would like to imagine. It is created by those who renovate and enrich it precisely in their resistance to it. It is suffocated by those who want it dead and inert, who want to stretch the past into an exhausted present . . .

As long as the colonial mentality has dominated this country, we have been a people that imagined itself born of the Spanish conquest. Lazily, the Creole national consciousness obeyed this prejudiced conviction of Spanish descendance. The history of Peru, in this view, began with Pizarro, Lima's founder. The Inca empire was felt only to be a prehistory. Everything autochthonous was considered outside of our history and, by extension, outside our tradition. This traditionalism impoverished the nation, shrinking it to mestizos and Creoles.

More recently, the national tradition has been stretched to reincorporate a sense of the Inca past. But this should not swing to the other extreme of denying that other factors or values have also decisively shaped our being and personality as a nation. With the conquest, Spain's language and religion entered permanently into Peruvian history, connecting and joining it to Western civilization. The gospel, whether one takes it as a truth or as religious ideology, came to weigh more than indigenous mythology. And, later, with the Independence Wars, the concept of the Peruvian republic also entered forever into our tradition.

When told about the "national tradition," then, we must first establish which "tradition" is being talked about, because we have a triple tradition [Spanish, Indian, African]. And also because tradition always remolds itself before our eyes, which so frequently insist on imagining it as motionless and exhausted (Starn et al. 1995, 228–229).

too dispersed and had a weak nationalistic outlook. Furthermore Mariátegui was firmly convinced that any revolutionary process needed to involve Peru's peasant majority. Not only were peasants numerous; also, through communal landownership and culturally distinct social organization within the communities, peasants had developed an incipient form of socialism. Mariátegui saw this as a sound basis for the implementation of socialism throughout the country.

Such diverging views led to a deep split between the two anti-imperialist leaders and their parties. In 1928 Mariátegui founded the PSP and sent delegates to the first international socialist meeting in Hispanic America that took place in Buenos Aires in 1929. He transformed *Amauta* from a journal of the "new generation" or of "vanguardism" to simply a "socialist journal." Through *Amauta* socialism gradually moved away from the increasingly more conservative followers of Haya de la Torre. Mariátegui also began editing a journal (*Labor*) explicitly written for workers. After only 10 issues, President Leguía's government shut down *Labor.* Mariátegui also promoted a workers' organization, the General Confederation of Peruvian Workers (Confederación General de Trabajadores del Perú, CGTP), but it ended with his abrupt death in April 1930, at age 35. One month later, his handpicked successor, Ravines, renamed the PSP the Communist Party, and from there on *Amauta* became a "class journal." Only three editions later *Amauta* disappeared.

By then, the effects of the great stock market crash of 1929 had hit Peru, and Leguía's government was losing its earlier firm grip. Peru's popular classes became more radical, while political leadership—confronted with a severe economic crisis—dispersed and new splinter parties surfaced. Communists, intent on promoting a class confrontation (proletarians against bourgeoisie), soon found themselves politically isolated. Intellectuals and the middle class, who had been patiently won over by Mariátegui and his journal *Amauta,* withdrew their political support and doomed Peru's Communist Party to a marginal and sterile isolation. Thereafter all social discontent was channeled through APRA. It was in this context that Peru's popular classes became part of the political power struggle. They entered politics amid capitalism's most severe economic crisis, at a time when, in Europe, similar political struggles led to the emergence of fascism, the defeat and obliteration of communists in Germany, World War II, and, in its aftermath, the cold war.

11

DEPRESSION AND CONFLICT
(1929–1948)

During the 1930s and 1940s Peru's history was dominated by the effects of the global depression, which was signaled in autumn 1929 with the crash of the U.S. stock market, and then the economic and political influences exerted by World War II. At the outset, Leguía's presidency came to an end, and he was replaced by the first of several military figures who maintained steady control of the Peruvian government for decades thereafter. The military and the oligarchy, which formed an uneasy alliance, were challenged by Haya de la Torre and his *aprista* party, a challenge that often turned violent and was marked with government massacres, *aprista* uprising, and assassinations. Added to the mix was another outbreak of the ongoing conflict with Ecuador over borders. By the end of the World War II, however, Peru entered a period of economic recovery.

The Big Crash and Its Repercussions

In 1929 the U.S. stock market crashed, prompting worldwide economic crisis. One of the immediate consequences was the abrupt end of Leguía's presidency. One day in 1930, returning from watching his weekly horse race at the Santa Beatriz track, Leguía was confronted by hundreds of angry citizens on his way to the presidential palace. Using this demonstration as a pretext, a young colonel, Luis M. Sánchez Cerro (nicknamed "El Mocho"), took Leguía prisoner and put him in a cell in Lima's largest jail, the Penitenciaría. The ailing Leguía was transferred to the Bellavista Hospital, where he died in 1932. Sánchez Cerro shifted the headquarters of his coup to Arequipa and Puno, where he set up a military junta that governed Peru for six months. He became an instant national hero and was compared to Julius Caesar, Jupiter, and Christ.

After taking over, Sánchez Cerro persecuted corrupt Leguía followers and abolished the *conscripción vial,* the forced public work introduced by Leguía. Sánchez Cerro was a mestizo in a country where people had grown used to seeing white presidents. Many people, especially young people in the army, perceived his access to power as a watershed moment in Peru's history. Surprisingly Peru's oligarchy also saw Sánchez Cerro as the right man for the difficult economic situation Peru was facing. According to their view Sánchez Cerro would keep popular unrest in check and would also—given his popularity—prevent the Socialists and Communists from taking advantage of the situation.

But maintaining control was not so easy in practice. The new government was greatly challenged by the severity of the world crisis. The international depression brought a steep drop of Peruvian exports. Between 1929 and 1932 copper exports dropped by 69 percent, wool exports by 50 percent, cotton by 42 percent, and sugar by 22 percent. During these same three years 18,000 mine workers out of 32,000 lost their jobs. A virtual halt in construction resulted in 73 percent unemployment among Lima's painters. Masons recorded 70 percent unemployment, carpenters 60 percent, plumbers 58 percent, and electricians 52 percent. The textile industry and agrarian enterprises did somewhat better, with unemployment in the range of 12 percent. Simultaneously, British and U.S. investments languished, as did foreign loans. Banks went bankrupt. The state budget was cut from $50 million to $16 million between 1929 and 1932. Devaluation, emission of state bonds, and moratorium on payments followed.

Given this situation Sánchez Cerro lost control. Salary cuts and unemployment led to violent protests in the streets, especially among those who had been employed in the more modernized sectors of the Peruvian economy. Many mine workers in Cerro de Pasco led by the Communist Party were killed during a protest in 1930 when troops were sent from Lima to repress the growing unrest. The leaders were persecuted and jailed, and the Communist Party was banned.

Between February and December 1931, there were 18 military mini coups all over the country, some of them led by sergeants and soldiers. Street fights were part of daily life in the cities, and former president Leguía's properties were looted. Strikes continued in the textile factories, on the northern sugar plantations, among oil workers in Talara, and even among bus drivers and telephone operators (most of them women) in Lima. In the mines workers destroyed the machinery and imprisoned firm employees. Mining enterprises responded to these attacks with lockouts and massacres. Soon the fiscal disaster hit education. For several months the San Marcos University was closed, professors did not receive their salaries, and in April 1931 teachers in public schools also stopped receiving their monthly payments. As in many other countries around the world in 1930, the global fallout of the 1929 crash left Peru in complete economic, social, and political disarray.

Turbulent Elections and Civil War

In 1931 Haya de la Torre returned from eight years' exile to run for president. The Communist Party had been completely dismantled since the crash, providing ample ground for APRA to grow. Haya de la Torre's political agenda sounded less radical than in 1928; in fact, the U.S. ambassador in Lima reported to Washington that there was nothing to fear from Haya de la Torre's candidacy. Such mellowness enhanced APRA's chances to increase its following, and Haya de la Torre began organizing the Partido Nacional Libertador along almost military lines.

VÍCTOR RAÚL
HAYA DE LA TORRE

Haya de la Torre was born in Trujillo in 1895 into a middle-class family that had suffered from the rapid modernization in Peru's northern coast sugar plantations. His father, the son of schoolteachers, was born in Cajamarca. His mother was a daughter of small hacienda owners. Haya de la Torre went to law school in Trujillo but in 1917 left for Lima where he became a student leader at the San Marcos University. He participated in workers' strikes and in student movements that led to university reform in 1919. Eventually he became chancellor of Manuel González Prada Popular University, where he came into close contact with the student body, Lima's workers. In 1923, the same year that Mariátegui returned to Lima, Haya de la Torre was exiled. He founded the Alliance for Popular Revolution in America in 1924 in Mexico. He also visited other Latin American countries, as well as Europe; in Russia he attended the Fifth International Communist Congress and read Marxist literature. Initially his political agenda included social justice, resistance to U.S. imperialism, political unity of Latin America, nationalization of land and industries, and the internationalization of the Panama Canal.

Upon his return to Peru in 1931, Haya de la Torre traveled extensively throughout the country and organized a massive rally in Lima's bullfight arena, the Plaza de Acho. During his electoral campaign he

Then, and in later years, the APRA and its organization was often compared to fascist parties in Europe. APRA provided its followers with a new political identity as they saw that their opinions mattered. This empowerment involved whole families and sustained an almost religious relationship between Haya de la Torre and his supporters. The combination of politics and popular religiosity provided APRA with the strength to survive much political turbulence over the many decades until it would finally come to power (with Alán García in 1985).

Sánchez Cerro defeated Haya de la Torre by a small margin of 50,000 votes in the December 1931 election, although the *apristas* challenged the results, alleging fraud. Soon after the election, social unrest forced Sánchez Cerro to declare a law whereby the state in an emergency situation could shut down mass media, incarcerate people, and prohibit public meetings. *Apristas* were the targets of these dictatorial measures.

developed a governmental plan for immediate action, but it was less radical than his earlier positions. He proposed to reform the state by making it stronger and more redistributive and by engaging in reasonable bargaining with international sources of capital, progressive nationalization, development of capitalism, tributary reform by abolishing indirect taxes, universal and free education for all, social security, the vote for women, and the economic integration of Latin America.

Victor Raúl Haya de la Torre (Photo by Caretas/Andes y Mares)

In early 1931 a young *aprista* attempted to kill Sánchez Cerro during one of his public addresses. Haya de la Torre retreated to Trujillo and proclaimed himself Peru's "moral president."

A civil war resulted from these confrontations as *apristas* mobilized on the northern coast and in the central highlands, centering on Callao, Arequipa, Chiclayo, and Piura. Haya de la Torre was arrested, and 21 *aprista* congress members were exiled. On July 7 Trujillo took up arms. In response the national government sent out troops and planes to quell the rebellion, then summarily executed 5,000 *apristas* by a firing squad at the pre-Inca ruins of Chan Chan after condemning them in military trials. In revenge *apristas* killed a group of officials in Trujillo. These events became the basis for a long-lasting, hate-filled, bitter fight between *apristas* and Peru's military that lasted the next 50 years. The immediate conflict culminated on April 30, 1933, when Sánchez Cerro was assassinated by Abelardo Mendoza Leyva, an *aprista*, during a military parade.

In the wake of the disturbances Vice President David Samanez Ocampo called for presidential elections and gathered a group of intellectuals and politicians to draft a new electoral law. Among these intellectuals were the historian Jorge Basadre, educator José Antonio Encinas, anthropologist Luis E. Valcárcel, demographer Alberto Arca Parró, and *aprista* writer Luis Alberto Sánchez. Under the statute they drafted, the departments were to become the basic electoral unit, the vote was to be obligatory and secret, minorities were to gain parliamentary representation, and a national electoral jury was to provide some neutral and independent ground for elections. Women and illiterate people were still to be excluded from participating in elections.

The statute, however, was not implemented. Instead, in 1933, the Constitutional Assembly nominated Oscar R. Benavides, the commander in chief of the army, as president. Benavides stayed in power until 1939. With Benavides began another chapter of Peru's political history featuring violence and political confrontation, the absence of democratic parties, and the predominance of the military.

Militarism Anew

Peru, like other countries in Latin America, has had more military than civilian heads of government throughout its republican life. Whenever there were signs of a national crisis, the military stepped forward to seize power, usually claiming the need to keep order and repress popular protest. In contrast to Europe, where soldiers defended one country against another country, in Latin America soldiers have mainly fought internal wars, and Peru is no exception.

A period of uninterrupted military rule first occurred after Peru achieved political independence from Spain, between 1821 and 1872, and a second came in the aftermath of the War of the Pacific, from 1883 to 1895. A third era of military rule (called the "third militarism" by historian Jorge Basadre) began in 1930 with Sánchez Cerro, continued with Benavides between 1933 and 1939, and reappeared between 1948 and 1956 with Manuel A. Odría as president and in the early 1960s with Generals Ricardo Pérez Godoy (1961–62) and Nicolás López Lindley (1962–63). With General Juan Velasco Alvarado (1968–75) and General Francisco Morales Bermúdez (1975–80) the military cycles came to an end, but the involvement of the military in national issues did not. A more indirect involvement in politics surfaced in the 1980s, during the long-term fight against the guerrilla group the Shining Path, and again in 1995 during President Alberto Fujimori's (1990–2000) "self-coup" with support from the military.

The successive military governments were far from uniform. They espoused differing political and economic policies that ran the gamut from repressing labor to organizing labor and moved from market-oriented economic strategies to state capitalism and cooperativism, and back again.

The Military and the Oligarchy, 1933–1945

A distinctive feature of the third wave of militarism was that it coexisted with a ruling elite, whereas the two prior military eras had been responses to the temporary collapse of Peru's governing elites. In this new period of militarism Peru's oligarchy used the military to achieve what they themselves could no longer do, namely govern the country as their sole property. With Sánchez Cerro assassinated and Benavides in command, the oligarchy recovered some of its lost power. From here on, the sugar and cotton barons withdrew from congress as Peru's oligarchy began controlling the country from behind the scenes, using the military to implement whatever it saw fit. Consensus was replaced by violence and political strategies to avoid the dangers from below.

At the beginning of his presidency, Benavides attempted to negotiate with *apristas,* and a general amnesty allowed Haya de la Torre out of jail and into exile, after which popular protests subsided. Oligarchic reaction to these initial negotiations was to stifle any government acquiescence to popular demands. APRA resorted to conspiracy and secrecy as its main political weapons, but the party lacked the will to stage serious revolution. While they still organized workers and called for mass mobilization, APRA leaders always pulled back at the key moments. This lack of resolve had high political costs, because the government was able to crack down on the more radical union leaders and some members in the army who sympathized with *aprista* demands.

In the 1936 presidential election Lima's former mayor, Luis Antonio Eguiguren, won with the support of APRA, but Benavides annulled the electoral results because APRA was considered an international party, and according to the constitution, international parties could not participate in national elections. Benavides stayed in power for three more years governing the country through decrees in the absence of a congress. To exclude the voices of the workers, peasants, and the middle class, the military sought to persecute and dismantle the APRA and whatever was left of the Communist Party, a task which came easily in the aftermath of the government-run massacre of 5,000 Apristas at Chan Chan in 1932. The San Marcos University was closed between 1931 and 1935.

The continued bargaining and fight between APRA and the government deepened political rifts. The oligarchs no longer believed in democratic ideals and became more conservative. They dismissed liberal ideas, and some of their representatives openly and enthusiastically applauded the fascist European leaders Adolf Hitler and Benito Mussolini. Some conservatives admired the fascist states and considered them worthy of emulation. Peru's oligarchs sided with Francisco Franco against republicans during the Spanish civil war (1936–39), receiving *falangistas* from Spain with open arms. When exiled Spanish republicans had to flee their country, they could not come to Peru but immigrated to Mexico and Argentina and became part of the intelligentsia there. Peru's oligarchy harbored a fascist attitude rather than a fascist doctrine, but this became an obstacle for any Communist or *aprista* claims. Benavides himself used all avenues to profit from fascism (for instance, he frequently threatened to seek support from fascist Europe if the United States was not willing to concede to his demands) but stifled any fascist attempts to organize in Peru that could question or jeopardize his control of social matters.

At the beginning of World War II (1939–45) in Europe, Peru remained neutral, but in 1941 Manuel Prado Ugarteche (1889–1967), president from 1939 to 1945, sided with the Allies after the Japanese bombing of Pearl Harbor and withdrew Peruvian diplomats from Rome, Berlin, and Tokyo. In 1943 Peru denounced the collaborationist French Vichy government and its puppet president General Pétain and recognized General Charles de Gaulle as France's president in exile. A few months before the war ended, Peru declared war siding with the Allied forces.

The Peruvian government publicly echoed the ideals of the Allies on democracy and liberty, but at home the government ruled by authoritarianism and repression. World War II brought the United States and Peru closer. The United States bought more Peruvian produce, built a military base in Talara, and provided loans and technical assistance in education and public health, and Peru accepted U.S. price controls on its exported raw materials in exchange for lower U.S. import tariffs. During the war more than 1,800 Japanese immigrants to Peru were unjustly accused of siding with the enemy and were deported to internment in the United States, and the Peruvian government expropriated several commercial and industrial businesses belonging to German and Japanese citizens. The Banco Italiano was saved from expropriation but forced to change its name to Banco de Crédito del Perú.

Economic Recovery

After weathering the effect's of the worldwide economic downturn of the late 1920s and early 1930s, the Peruvian economy began to recover by the time Oscar Benavides became president in 1933, following the assassination of Sánchez Cerro. Between then and the end of World War II, Peru's economy prospered, even though Lima's government managed to continue excluding workers, Indians, and women from political participation, while co-opting willing intellectuals and exiling those who insisted on criticizing the government. Demands from below were partially and only grudgingly turned into state policies. In the 1930s and 1940s, the middle class kept expanding, literacy rates increased, and more indigenous people learned to speak Spanish. A new industry geared toward the internal market emerged, and the first social policies (such as labor legislation), an improved health system, and building schools were approved. Overall, state intervention in economic matters increased.

The Great Depression and World War II worked to diminish Peru's dependency on the international market. Earlier attempts promoted by President Leguía to restrain imports through protectionist tariffs were expanded by Benavides and Prado. Gradually Peru's exports began to grow and diversify in the hands of small and medium-sized Peruvian landowners, whereas the large sugar and copper enterprises shrank. Cotton produced on the Peruvian coast became the main export product during the 1930s, while—in response to governmental decrees—the sugar-growing land was reduced by 10 percent. Many haciendas located on the central and southern coast changed from sugar to cotton production. By 1940 around 15 percent of the economically active population on the coast worked on cotton fields. Former *yanaconas* (indentured peasants who labored on haciendas) became salaried workers, and many smaller producers either owned the land or were able to rent it.

A similar process of nationalization occurred in the mines. Reduced foreign investment permitted smaller mining enterprises to operate. The formerly all-powerful Cerro de Pasco Corporation reduced its capital and its activities and engaged only in refining metals. New mining sites were found and worked, increasing the kinds of minerals extracted. Zinc, mercury, tin, and lead now complemented the traditional silver and copper exports. A new product—fish—became one of Peru's most important exports after World War II, when no fish from Europe or Asia reached the U.S. market. Although it was a U.S. entrepreneur, Wilbur Ellis, who first opened the Peruvian market to U.S. consumers, domestic Peruvian investments promptly followed suit. Mining exports decreased in quantity and importance, whereas agrarian production and exports were on the rise. By 1945, 56 percent of Peru's total exports were of agrarian origin; however, Peruvian exports still had not recovered to the level of their 1929 value.

The Peruvian government promoted industrialization by creating new projects, financing industrial ventures, and opening new banks. For instance, the Banco Agrícola opened its doors in 1931 and the Banco Industrial in 1936. Devaluation of the Peruvian sol (from 2.50 soles to 6.50 soles per dollar) between 1929 and 1940 and higher import tariffs increased the prices for imported goods and consequently made domestic products more competitive. These macroeconomic policies stimulated new factories producing tires, shoes, glass, fertilizer, milk, and construction materials.

To keep the cost of living low for a growing industrial labor force, the government imposed a price control policy on agrarian producers, starting around 1935.

Heightened governmental involvement also resulted in a set of new laws. A new civil code came into being in 1936, for the first time regulating divorce. Until then divorce had been the exclusive realm of the Catholic Church. Based on earlier pressures from APRA, Benavides's government also founded the Ministry of Education and the Ministry of Public Health, Labor, and Social Well-being in 1936. That same year a social security system was inaugurated to help factory workers cover the health costs relating to disease, maternity, invalidity, and old age. A few years later the social security was extended to all salaried workers. The Ministry of Agriculture was put in place in 1943. The state employed between 60,000 and 80,000 workers to build roads, especially in Peru's southern highlands, thus helping to reduce unemployment among Peru's working class. Benavides also opened the first public shelters (*comedores*) where indigent people could get a meal and a temporary place to sleep. Concomitantly public expenditures rose from 91 million soles in 1932 to 221 million by 1938. The state could not finance these higher expenditures through foreign loans since a moratorium on loans to Peru had been in place since 1931, so internal credit and higher taxes were the only alternatives available.

Both Benavides and Prado came from the high ranks of Peruvian finance and were the owners of large cattle-raising haciendas in the central highlands and textile factories in Lima. Between their governments there was a line of continuity in terms of the state's economic involvement. Prado had been exiled in 1921 by Leguía, and upon his return in 1932 he worked at the Central Bank and became its president. Deemed a representative of the "national bourgeoisie," Prado won the 1939 elections with the support of the Communists, the silence of *apristas,* and a collective forgetfulness of his father Mariano I. Prado's cowardly abandonment of the country during the War of the Pacific. The brief and successful 1941 war with Ecuador on border issues cemented his recognition.

Prado and his Frente Patriótico, which was an umbrella party for many different political and social interest groups, won with 262,971 votes. His opponent, José Quesada, the leader of the profascist Unión Revolucionaria got only 76,000 votes. The transition from Benavides's government to Prado's was smooth, in spite of a strong earthquake that shook Lima and other Peruvian cities on May 24, 1940. Prado promoted-General Benavides to the rank of marshal and appointed him to the most desired foreign diplomatic posting, the embassy in Madrid.

Prado's government adopted an agenda of popular policies, especially concerning urban workers. He established a minimum wage and decreed an increase in workers' salaries while keeping strict price controls on urban rents and subsistence goods through the Superintendency of Social Welfare (Superintendencia de Bienestar Social, founded in 1939). Overall—and for the first time in Peru's history—direct taxes increased their relative weight within the state's total income. This was also one of the very few moments in Peruvian history when there were no foreign loans.

THE PERU-ECUADOR BORDER DISPUTE

Ecuador became an independent country in 1830 after it separated from Simón Bolívar's Gran Colombia. Ecuador and Peru had several border conflicts during the 19th century, including a war in 1860. That year Ecuador laid claim to three provinces in northern Peru—Tumbes, Jaén, and Maynas. Peru argued the boundaries should be set as they had been under Spanish colonial administration, or by self-determination of the inhabitants in the case of Jaén.

In 1910 the Peruvian embassy in Quito and the Peruvian consulate in Guayaquil were attacked. Peru mobilized 20,000 men to its side but, thanks to the mediation of other American states, war was avoided. Since Ecuador declared that it would not follow the advice of the Spanish king, the Spanish mediator never provided a verdict on this border issue. The border issue was latent until July 1941, when Ecuadorean troops stationed in the Provincia del Oro occupied Peruvian border posts in Aguas Verdes, La Palma, and Lechugal. This was the beginning of a one-month war. Peru won the most important battle at Zarumilla and occupied the Provincia del Oro, forcing Ecuador to surrender.

In January 1942 representatives of both countries signed a peace treaty in Rio de Janeiro, Brazil, and the Peruvian army withdrew from Provincia del Oro. The Protocol of Rio de Janeiro drew the borders and entrusted its execution to a mixed commission. Guarantors of this treaty were the United States, Argentina, Chile, and Brazil. However, 35 miles of the borderline in the Andean Cordillera del Cóndor could not be physically marked because the region was inaccessible. This small stretch of the border became the cause of more tensions between both countries, and in 1960 Ecuador annulled the Rio protocol because it could not be executed. Problems on the border resurfaced in 1981, when Ecuadorean troops invaded the Cordillera del Cóndor once again, and a few border skirmishes followed in 1992.

In 1942 Prado created development agencies aimed at promoting economic growth in areas untouched by private investors. These agencies were the initial pillars of what later became public enterprises. Prado's initiatives, and some pressure from the United States, slowly reopened political activities. He authorized unions and relegalized the APRA and the Communist Party. The Peruvian Workers' Confederation

Fiscal Income Between 1923 and 1949 (Percentage of Total Income)						
Source of Income	1923–24	1925–29	1930–34	1935–39	1940–44	1945–49
Customs	32.5	21.8	26.0	33.2	40.4	46.8
Indirect taxes	27.1	23.4	38.3	40.6	33.5	27.4
Direct taxes	5.9	6.1	9.5	11.4	11.1	11.2
Public services	2.7	2.6	5.5	5.0	4.4	3.0
External loans	22.9	38.7	3.4	0.0	0.0	0.0
Other	8.9	7.4	17.3	9.8	10.6	11.6
Total	100.0	100.0	100.0	100.0	100.0	100.0

Source: Boloña (1994, 103, 120)

(Confederación de Trabajadores del Perú, or CTP) was founded in 1944, and very soon afterward several federations representing the varied labor groups (workers in mines, oil, sugar, and cotton, employees, and *yanaconas*) sent delegates to the confederation's meetings and political debates. Communist leader Juan P. Luna became the CTP's first president. Eudocio Ravines, previously the Communist Party's leader, was expelled from the party during its first congress in 1942. Between 1940 and 1944 the Peruvian government officially recognized 118 unions, four times as many as between 1936 and 1939. Initially *apristas* and Communists shared their political leadership in the unions. Gradually, however, *apristas* took over, and Luis Negreros became APRA's most visible union leader.

Despite these positive developments the economy took a turn for the worse in the 1940. National defense expenditures before and after the war with Ecuador and redistributive policies, including food subsidies, drained the state budget. By 1942 Prado's government resorted to loans from Peru's Central Bank to pay for the 536 million soles of state expenditures. In contrast to a similar situation during Benavides's presidency, inflation resulted, albeit quite moderate by contemporary standards. Between 1939 and 1944 the amount of circulating money tripled; inflation

Peruvian president Manuel Prado Ugarteche, second from right, at an inspection at the U.S. Naval Academy at Annapolis in the summer of 1942. Prado supported the Allied side during World War II. (Library of Congress)

reached a low of 8.2 percent in 1941 and a high of 14.3 percent in 1944. Inflation did not result solely from the loans, however; it was also driven by sugar exporters. Beginning in 1938 the sugar barons drove down the value of Peruvian currency against the U.S. dollar. If the sugar producers maintained low production costs, they received higher profits from sugar exports. In 1940 banks and sugar producers reached a "gentlemen's agreement" by fixing the exchange rate at 6.50 soles to the dollar. When sugar producers tried to play at currency speculation again in 1944, Prado, for the first time in the 20th century, resorted to a fixed exchange rate to curtail the barons' manipulations. However, between 1939 and 1945, the cost of living had already increased by 190 percent.

Changes in the Amazon

Border skirmishes with Ecuador and Colombia stimulated Peru's interest in the Amazon, where large stretches of the border with these two countries (and Brazil) are located. Cultivation and colonization had been almost absent after the sporadic rubber boom. Aside from a few cotton, coffee, coca, tobacco, and rice plantations and many different Indian tribes, not much could be found in this region, in spite of its natural riches. In the central Amazon area, more closely linked to the central highlands and thus to Lima markets, some European colonies developed during the 19th century. In Oxapampa and Pozuzo, Germans in 1891 and Austrians in 1857, respectively, found homes, albeit in almost complete isolation until the railroad was expanded to Cerro de Pasco. Italian and Asian immigrants came to Chanchamayo. These settlers fared somewhat better because they had the city of Tarma as a link to the coast. In Perene, the Peruvian Corporation began a colonization project after the Grace Contract was signed in 1889. From it a bountiful coffee production emerged and gradually expanded, leading to the formation of another colony in Satipo in 1927.

A 1909 general law on Amazon lands and an Amazon settlement program spearheaded by Leguía were meant to open the Amazon to free colonization. The new laws completely disregarded the region's indigenous inhabitants, and Ashaninka, Matsiguenga, and Yanesha Indians (among others) were drawn into coffee plantations, mostly by force, and used to build roads.

The southern Amazon remained much more isolated from urban centers and markets. With the discovery at the end of the 19th century of the Fitzcarraldo isthmus (a heavily forested piece of land between two jungle rivers), the Manu area (nowadays a large natural reserve) became connected with Cuzco, which led to the opening of Puerto Maldonado in 1902. In Puerto Maldonado two of the largest Amazon rivers converge: the Madre de Dios and the Tambopata. The Department of Madre de Dios was created in 1912 on an area formerly included in the Department of Cuzco. Still, by 1940 the national census only recorded 1,032 inhabitants in Puerto Maldonado, the departmental capital. The whole Department of Madre de Dios, a stretch of 35,000 square miles, barely counted 5,000 people, most of them at a subsistence level, some of them searching for gold on riverbeds. The first roads were not opened in this southern part of the Amazon until 1960.

In the 1940s the Amazon witnessed a heightened interest from Peru's government and army and from national and foreign entrepreneurs. These groups wanted variously to exploit Amazonian natural resources (including medical herbs and plants), "civilize" natives, improve military posts, tighten links with Lima, and—last but not least—fight leprosy, a disease that had spread in the region in the aftermath of the rubber boom. Some religious orders joined in such efforts, especially Augustinians and Dominicans. In 1948 a U.S. religious organization, the Summer Linguistic Institute (Instituto Lingüístico de Verano, known as ILV) established itself in the town of Pucallpa. This institute combined Protestant religious preaching and linguistic study. Over the years the ILV has been repeatedly attacked by the Peruvian press and accused of proselytizing and even practicing eugenics.

The 1940s also saw the advent of the U.S. government–owned North American Rubber Reserve Company. The company's goal was to find new sources of rubber because Japan, at the beginning of World War II, had occupied the rubber-producing Southeast Asian islands. (As a side benefit Americans also collected quinine, a substance used to cure malaria that was available in the Amazon, to save U.S. soldiers stationed in Asia.) Goodyear, a private enterprise, opened a factory in Lima and exported tires to the United States. The Peruvian government joined this venture and founded in 1942 the Peruvian Corporation of the Amazon (Corporación Peruana del Amazonas). Rubber production increased

Stilt-supported houses at a settlement in the Amazon region of Peru. There was intense but short-lived commercial interest in the area during the 1940s. (© Philip Baird, www.anthroarcheart.org)

dramatically as a result of all these efforts, from 130,000 pounds in 1941 to 2.84 million pounds in 1944. With the end of World War II, however, interest in the Amazon and its natural resources declined and the Amazon returned to official oblivion, at least for a while.

The 1945 Threshhold

The end of World War II marked the beginning of pressure from the United States for democracy in Latin America. Leaders like Haya de la Torre took the United States at its word and requested active political support to end dictatorships in Latin America while still in exile. Claiming democracy also meant that Peru could no longer marginalize or ignore APRA, which had become the most important political voice in the country. The National Democratic Front (Frente Democrático Nacional, FDN) under President José Luis Bustamante y Rivero, an executive, lawyer, and law professor at the University in Arequipa, provided APRA with a political venue. Bustamante had written Sánchez Cerro's takeover proclamation and briefly served as Sánchez Cerro's minister of justice. Until 1945 Bustamante was Peru's ambassador in Bolivia. Bustamante believed in the need for greater morality in government, the reduction of state bureaucracy, balanced budgets, and decentralization. Prado made several attempts to win Bustamante for his cause. Prado represented the right wing; Bustamante was an independent intellectual with strong socially oriented political convictions and this is why he decided to listen to Haya de la Torre's propositions. Thus, instead of siding with Prado, Bustamante allied himself with the now legalized APRA. APRA became the "party of the people and for the people," and its goal, in Haya de la Torre's expressed wish, was to create ownership for those who owned nothing without taking ownership away from those who had it. In the end Bustamante's intellectual prestige, his defense of national sovereignty, and his deeply rooted Catholicism made him an acceptable candidate among the oligarchy, APRA, the army, and the church. The FDN won the elections against the official candidate, Marshall Eloy Ureta, victorious commander in the war with Ecuador, with 300,000 (67 percent) against 150,000 votes. APRA gained a parliamentary majority.

In spite of a happy beginning, a rift between APRA and President Bustamante soon appeared. Bustamante meant to demonstrate that by cooperating with APRA the movement had gained responsibility and had shed its early Marxist extremism. Bustamante, however, was determined to go his own way. He appointed Rafael Belaúnde (brother of Víctor Andrés Belaúnde) as his prime minister, passing over Haya de la

Torre, the APRA party leader. Elected *aprista* congressmen swore loyalty to their leader and proved this loyalty by systematically blocking changes proposed by the executive branch, thereby following partisan rather than national interests.

Violence broke out again when *Apristas* set bombs, burned down buildings, and even assassinated their enemies, including the *prefecto* of Cerro de Pasco. Lima's two main newspapers, *El Comercio* and *La Prensa,* denounced this reign of terror and requested governmental intervention. In parliament the *aprista* majority instead asked for press censorship. When San Marcos students protested against censorship, APRA strongarm squads (known as the *búfalos*) attacked them.

These incidents illustrate APRA inconsistencies. While assuring the oligarchy that properties would be respected, APRA also promised to give more to the poor. All attempts to balance the fiscal budget were systematically opposed in congress. APRA promoted salary increases by simply increasing export taxes or regulating exchange rates. Without a redistribution of wealth, higher salaries increased inflationary pressures. In response, APRA demanded price controls, which led to scarcity, corruption, and smuggling. In the end only those holding an *aprista* membership card could get food without standing in long lines.

Economic circumstances, however, did not favor Bustamante. His initial plan included the reinforcing of the state, creating a stronger internal market, promoting industrialization, attracting foreign investment, and recognizing the rights of workers. He did enact measures to realize some of these goals. Pay for a day off on Sunday was introduced, rents were frozen, the numbers of bureaucrats and the amount of their salaries was increased, and secondary school was made free. A new law in 1947 prohibited the use of free Indian labor, a measure geared toward forcing sugar and cotton planters to pay adequate salaries to their workers and to free these workers from the requirement to sell their produce to the hacendado at below-market prices.

But Bustamante's economic policies led to many distortions in Peru's economy. His attempts to control the exchange rate, to regulate food prices, and to direct imports met a dead end and provoked growing resistance. The oligarchy responded by drumming up the *aprista*-Communist threat through their guild, the National Agrarian Society (Sociedad Nacional Agraria), and the newspaper *La Prensa,* edited by Luis Beltrán, a prominent entrepreneur and economist who graduated from the London School of Economics and was the Peruvian ambassador to the United States. In January 1947 Francisco Graña Garland, one of the directors of *La Prensa,* was killed, and APRA was the suspect.

In response Bustamante dismissed his three APRA ministers and rebuilt his cabinet with five military and five civilian ministers. Manuel A. Odría became the minister of government. Pedro Beltrán called for an anti-APRA alliance, and most parties responded to his invitation, including Eudocio Ravines's Socialist Party. At this point in his political career Ravines proposed to defend the sugar and cotton barons for the sake of capitalist development. In July 1947 the congress was unable to reopen its doors due to a boycott from its independent representatives and the legal manipulations of Héctor Boza, the leader of the Senate. Negotiations to establish a congress failed, so APRA could no longer govern the country through congress. With no congress Bustamante continued his term using ad hoc decrees to govern the country.

In a last attempt at survival APRA sponsored an unsuccessful strike, which was followed by governmental repression, the abolition

AN EPISODE IN THE PRESIDENTIAL PALACE

Historian Frederick Pike in his 1967 history of Peru recounted what happened when senate leader Héctor Boza went to the presidential palace one day in 1947 in the midst of a terrible national crisis. Boza's faction in the senate had effectively shut down the National Assembly by absenting themselves, a series of *aprista*-inspired strikes had crippled the economy, and killings and violence were increasing rapidly. The nation was suffering and the government seemed paralyzed, so Boza wanted to consult with President José Bustamante.

When he arrived, Boza was told the president was too busy with important duties to see the senate leader and could not be disturbed. Summoning all his authority Boza insisted and was finally admitted to Bustamante's private office, where he found the president seated before a typewriter, busily typing in two-finger style what appeared to be a long document. When asked what he was doing, President Bustamante explained he was in the middle of an important project that had consumed all his time and attention for the previous two weeks: He was preparing a scholarly paper on legal theory that he was scheduled to deliver to a legal convention.

Bustamante told Boza he did not have time to spare to discuss the nation's problems (Pike 1967, 287).

of constitutional guarantees, and the jailing of 57 union leaders. In November 1947 Haya de la Torre ordered Major Víctor Villanueva to organize APRA brigades to bring down Bustamante's "dictatorship." Rumors spread of an impending bloody insurrection. In February 1948 Bustamante appointed an entirely military cabinet, only to find out later that his ministers had conspired with conservatives to overthrow his government. In October 1948 APRA civil and military followers in Callao began an uprising. Bustamante responded with force and declared APRA illegal, a step that allowed him to hound *aprista* leaders and followers. Bustamante's uneasy coexistence with his *aprista* and oligarchic tormentors was coming to an end.

Political conflicts had reached insurmountable hurdles. Peru's problems were exacerbated by a U.S. withdrawal of support for democratic governments because of its cold war fears of communism and by economic crisis. Shortly after World War II, the United States cut back its purchase of Peruvian goods, and revenues from export taxes dropped sharply. To bring in revenue Bustamante tried to increase oil production. Accordingly the government of Peru prepared a contract with the International Petroleum Company to open for exploration the oil fields of Sechura, a site that had become a national reserve during the Benavides administration. APRA warmly supported this project, whereas in business circles Peru's wealthiest denounced it as a giveaway to foreigners. The contract was not signed.

Oligarchic voices were heard elsewhere as well. In April 1947 the Gildemeisters, the owners of the largest sugar plantation on Peru's coast, refused to deliver the U.S. dollars earned by their hacienda. Instead, the plantation attempted to pay its taxes and export revenues in soles. The owners wanted to force Bustamante's government to unfreeze the exchange rate. On September 6, 1947, Bustamante agreed to allow for a free dollar market conversion of 35 percent of the revenues obtained from exports. Exporters, however, wanted all.

Only a few weeks after the *aprista* uprising in Callao and closely following the increasing pressures from coastal exporters, Odría, Bustamante's minister of government, staged a coup in Arequipa. This new movement was christened the "Restorative Revolution" (*revolución restauradora*). Bustamante realized he had to resign when Lima's commander, General Zenón Noriega, refused to march to Arequipa, fearing it would plunge the country into a bloodbath. An uninhibited persecution of *apristas* followed, and on January 3, 1949, Haya de la Torre sought asylum in the Colombian embassy, where he stayed for the next five years.

12

DICTATORSHIPS AND REFORM (1948–1968)

The first years of the second half of the 20th century witnessed some continuities from the earlier decades. Between 1948 and 1968 successive governments expanded the role of the state and its bureaucracy and attempted to achieve social integration and cohesiveness. The early decades of the second half of the century also saw some marked differences. Peru's population tripled from around 7 million to 22 million people; massive migration from rural to urban areas began with the first shantytown settlements around 1945, especially in Lima; and the government engaged in a dramatic expansion of educational efforts.

In the two decades between 1948 and 1968 Peru resumed an export-oriented economic growth pattern. Initially the economy expanded as a result of Europe's reconstruction after World War II and the war in Korea. During this period, Peru's exports grew and reached pre-1929 heights. Foreign investment also increased. Acting as bookends to these 20 years were two military dictatorships, one led by Manuel Odría (1897–1974) from 1948 to 1956 and the other by Juan Velasco Alvarado (1910–77) from 1968 to 1975.

Eight Years of Odría

Odría, born in Tarma, was 51 years old and a brigadier general when he became Peru's dictator. A worldwide economic recession was just coming to an end. During the Korean War (1950–53), prices for Peru's exports skyrocketed, and foreign investments had reached $800 million by the end of Odría's eight-year presidency—twice as much as at the beginning of his tenure. Mining production and oil exports, in the hands of foreign investors, increased state revenues from export taxes. The drawback was an increased exchange rate: From 9.20 soles per dollar in 1942, at the end of Bustamante's presidency, to 20.40 soles per dollar in

215

1949. In large measure this hike was the result of financial speculation by two foreign enterprises, W. Grace and the Cerro de Pasco Corporation, and of economic recommendations dating from 1931 by the Kemmerer Mission. The latter an expert group of U.S. economists invited to assess Peru's economy, designed a plan that included an adjustment and reform program for the country's central financial and fiscal system. The Kemmerer plan also called for stringent credit and monetary policies, high central bank reserves, closure of several large banks, and altered tax and customs codes. In addition it recommended cancellation of official exchange rate parity, free price fluctuation, and a modest increase of salaries. All these measures followed the exact wishes of exporters and were implemented in late 1949. These economic adjustments—along with strong assertions of control over dissidents by Odría—resulted in a period of relative national well-being, political stability, and social peace, and exporters were held in check when they once again tried to directly control the state.

Odría and his military junta did not see any need to reopen the adjourned congress. Constitutional guarantees were suspended, and the 1949 Law of Internal Security gave the government free rein to do as it pleased. The judicial system was also shut down. By 1950 all *apristas* and Communists had been forced underground and often when their hiding places were found, the government did not hesitate to shoot them. Odría's only opponent, General Ernesto Montagne, soon found himself in prison as well. Having cleared the political grounds Odría decided to run as sole candidate for election in 1950 to a regular six-year term. Not surprisingly he gathered 500,000 votes. Protests from students were bloodily suppressed by the police, and a general strike in Arequipa in June did not hamper Odría from becoming a duly installed constitutional president, based on support from Lima's growing shantytowns.

Odría's political theme was "Health, Education, and Work." His policies and public statements were much influenced by his contemporary in Argentina, Juan Domingo Perón. According to historian Frederick Pike Odría groomed his wife, María Delgado de Odría to play a role in Peru similar to Evita Perón's in Argentina by appearing to be a patroness of the poor. She handed out Christmas gifts to poor children and provided large amounts of government-financed charity through the María Delgado de Odría Center of Social Assistance (1967, 291). Odría also expanded the social security system.

In spite of such public displays of charity a survey at the end of Odría's presidency showed that almost half of primary-school children in the country did not have a desk in their school building. Such token bows toward social concerns were nevertheless needed to respond to growing demands from Peru's popular classes. Odría, while making some concessions to these demands, was more interested in building projects, especially in Lima. Monumental buildings, such as the Ministries of Education, Commerce, and Labor on the Abancay Avenue were begun, as were the Employee Hospital on Salaverry Avenue, the Public Health Cooperative Service, and Lima's barracks-like large public schools. In Peru's 1949 budget public spending increased by 45 percent from the year before, and between 1950 and 1955 public spending amounted to 13 percent of Peru's annual gross national product.

All this cost more money than Odría had in his state coffers, and he resorted to printing paper money. This brought on inflation, and by 1956 the cost of living was twice as high as in 1948 and per-capita food consumption declined. Arequipa soon was up in arms again demanding guarantees for free 1956 elections. Odría's promises to remove his hated minister of government, Alejandro Esparza Zañartu, and to suspend the Law of Internal Security calmed *arequipeños*.

Former presidents Prado and Bustamante returned to Peru and aligned under a new party, the National Coalition. APRA was reorganized after Haya de la Torre won a lawsuit at the Hague International Court. The coalition gained rapid and widespread support, and Odría lost ground. Another candidate, Fernando Belaúnde Terry, 44 years old and an architect trained at the University of Texas, formed the National Front of Democratic Youth, basing his support on Peru's predominantly young population. Belaúnde Terry had been elected to the Chamber of Deputies in 1945, his first public political office. He was a nephew of Víctor Andrés Belaúnde and the son of Rafael Belaúnde, the first prime minister during the short-lived Bustamante regime.

The Odría regime saw Belaúnde Terry as a threat to its continued hold on power even before his party had been officially registered. To forestall its registration Odría and his advisers exerted great pressure on the National Electoral Jury (Jurado Nacional de Elecciones). Belaúnde Terry hastily returned to Lima and called for a mass rally in the Plaza San Martín. Thousands of people followed his call, and after delivering a powerful speech Belaúnde Terry led a procession to the nearby headquarters of the National Electoral Jury. The police were ready and fired tear gas and water from fire hoses into the marching crowd in an attempt to halt the procession. Even though most of his supporters were scattered by the attack, Belaúnde Terry seized a Peruvian flag and marched forward to confront the members of the national jury with an ultimatum: If he was not officially inscribed on the electoral list as a candidate, Odría would have to face the consequences (Pike 1967, 294–295). Soon afterward, the dictator backed off, the National Electoral Jury followed suit, and Belaúnde's National Front of Democratic Youth became a legal political party.

Prado's Second Presidency

Nonetheless it was Manuel Prado who won the election in 1956, with support from APRA. The official candidate, Hernando de Lavalle, had no chance, and Belaúnde Terry could not overcome the popular combination of APRA and Prado. Those who objected to APRA's support of Prado called the alliance *"la convivencia"* or *"super-convivencia,"* implying an illegal and immoral relationship. In 1956 three times as many people voted as in 1950, a result of heightened literacy; still, the numbers represented only about one-third of eligible voters. As a result of the election Prado not only became president again; he was also the owner of what some have called the "Prado Empire." He and his family owned the Banco Popular, the Popular and Porvenir Insurance Companies, the textile factories Santa Catalina and Manufacturas del Centro, and large urbanization projects.

Politically Prado opened democratic avenues. His government allowed for the organization of unions and a return of the Communists and *apristas*. In response to the growing demographic pressure in Peru's highlands Prado created the Institute for Agrarian Reform and Colonization. This institute did not engage directly in agrarian reform, but it conducted research that was used by later governments to begin an agrarian reform in the country.

Prado's minister of the treasury, José Pardo y Barreda, attempted to peg the sol artificially at the level of 19 to the dollar. Between 1950 and 1955 Peru's export tonnage had tripled, but the value of exports had only increased from $200 million to $330 million. Imports had doubled; Peru was importing one-fourth of its consumer goods and half of its capital goods. As a consequence, dollar reserves at the Central Bank dwindled. Pedro Beltrán, in the meantime, wrote severe editorial attacks against the government in his newspaper, *La Prensa*, and in a bid to co-opt him, Prado invited Beltrán to become his prime minister and minister of the treasury. Though hesitant, Beltrán accepted.

With Beltrán's appointment as minister for economic affairs in 1958, economic policies under Prado became market oriented, marking, perhaps, Peru's first attempt at neoliberalism. True to his beliefs Beltrán was eager to cancel all consumer food subsidies, adjust Peruvian oil prices to international prices, and in general diminish the state's intervention in economic issues. As a result of these policies, Prado did not pursue the intensive industrialization project he had hoped to undertake. He still opened a steel factory in Chimbote, however, and together with increasingly better fishing on Peru's coast it turned Chimbote from a fishing village into a city. Despite economic reforms oligarchs continued to dominate agrarian exports on Peru's northern coast, and oil, copper, and iron mines remained in foreign hands. During Beltrán's tenure at the economic ministry, Peru experienced a 4.5 percent annual increase in its gross national product, and the state began to replenish its foreign currency reserves. The rich became richer, the landless still had no land, and agrarian per-capita production continued to decrease.

By 1950 agrarian exports represented approximately 50 percent of all Peruvian exports. Although agrarian production kept rising in the following years, it accounted for a decreasing proportion of total exports, and toward 1960 mining and fishing exports became relatively more important. In 1969 agrarian exports amounted to 16.3 percent of all exports, mining made up 55.0 percent, and fish and fishmeal exports amounted to 25.6 percent. Fishmeal, initially produced as a fertilizer to replace guano, found a high demand in European and U.S. markets to feed pigs and chicken. Rising to meet this demand, Peru expanded its fishing fleet and became ever more profitable. Peru even began to build its own ships. In the early 1960s the fish industry employed approximately 30,000 people, and in 1964 Peru was the world's largest fish exporter. Growing exports, however, led to overexploitation of fish, and in 1973, when the Peruvian government nationalized the fishing industry, the industry was in crisis. Thanks to the efficiency of modern fishing technology, there were no more fish left to feed European and U.S. pigs and chicken.

Peru's balance of trade was in deep trouble in 1962, when Beltrán made a run at the presidency. Faced with an open rebuff during a political rally, he withdrew and instead watched the electoral process from the sidelines.

Changing Leadership

The 1962 elections had seven presidential candidates; however, only three had any chance of winning the elections: Haya de la Torre, polled 558,000 votes; Belaúnde Terry received 544,000 votes; and Odría, 481,000. No single candidate had obtained the absolute majority

PERUVIAN WRITERS: JOSÉ MARÍA ARGUEDAS AND MARIO VARGAS LLOSA

Political changes and social conditions during the 1950s and 1960s were captured by two of Peru's most renowned writers, José María Arguedas (1911–69) and Mario Vargas Llosa (1936–   ).

Arguedas was a mestizo from Andahuaylas in Peru's highlands. During the Prado (1939–45) and Odría (1948–56) regimes he was working at the San Marcos University in Lima. In his novel *Yawar Fiesta* (1941) he documented the deep-seated antagonism between modernity and Andean Indian culture from the perspective of an Indian community. In *Los ríos profundos* (1958) Arguedas portrayed people and their social relations in Peru's southern Andes. He paralleled his literary endeavors with anthropological research and published several works on ethnology and folklore meant to reassess Peru's indigenous cultures. His last novel before he committed suicide was *El zorro de arriba y el zorro de abajo*. This unfinished novel deals with Chimbote's migrant workers.

Vargas Llosa was born in Arequipa. His novels, *La ciudad y los perros* (1962), *La casa verde* (1966), and *Conversaciones en la catedral* (1969), created a new national literary genre by dealing with nonindigenous themes. Vargas Llosa was interested in exploring Peru's cities, the middle class and the poor in the city, and their moral and religious makeup. His depiction of the military and life in the barracks is unparalleled.

required, which forced these parties to negotiate agreements among themselves. Amid accusations of fraud, Haya de la Torre struck a deal with his former enemy Odría, who had once said that Haya de la Torre was not morally worthy of Peruvian citizenship and who had shed more *aprista* blood than any other Peruvian leader. Beltrán, who had sworn unrelenting opposition to APRA, soon joined the Odría-Haya alliance. Ten days before congress had to take a final decision on who would become president, the military took over and exiled Prado to Paris. APRA had gained control of the country as a result of their majority in congress, but Peru's military was determined not to allow APRA to command the country, even if this meant unseating Odría, who would have been the nominated president based on the earlier deal with Haya de la Torre.

The head of the joint chiefs of staff, General Ricardo Pérez Godoy, became the president of a ruling military junta. New elections were planned within a year, and Pérez Godoy refrained from pursuing vindictive policies. *Apristas* and Communists were left unhindered, a free press continued, and individual liberties were respected, at least until January 1963, when the military junta staged a roundup and imprisonment of some 1,000 people accused of being Communists or having communist affiliations. Pérez Godoy believed in the need for deep changes in Peru, changes he could not see happening either under Odría's or Haya de la Torre's command.

In an article published in the U.S. magazine *Life,* Haya de la Torre wrote that "democracy and capitalism were the solution to the world's problems." His views were indeed far removed from what he had thought and said in the 1930s. In response many younger and more radical *apristas* left the party, and some even became guerrilla leaders and joined radical left groups. Such was the case of Luis de la Puente Uceda, who led the most important guerrilla movement in the 1960s.

Victor Raúl Haya de la Torre became the leading candidate for the presidency in 1962 after he forged an alliance with former enemies Manuel Odría and Pedro Beltrán, but a military coup canceled the election. (Photo by Caretas/Andes y Mares)

In only one year, Pérez Godoy established an institute to plan development (Instituto de Planificación), a bank to extend low-interest credits to purchase inexpensive homes (Banco de la Vivienda), and a housing agency to carry out slum-clearance projects (Junta Nacional de la Vivienda). In addition several pilot land-reform projects began, new regions were opened for colonization, and peasants and colonizers were given credit facilities.

Belaúnde Terry's Presidency

For some Pérez Godoy was too reform oriented; for others he exhibited too much ego. Such criticisms led to a reshuffling within the junta. Pérez Godoy was demoted in 1963, and General Nicolás Lindley replaced him as president. The new junta abided by the free election pledge, and in the same year Belaúnde Terry became president with 39 percent of the votes. *Apristas* and supporters of Odría got 34 and 26 percent, respectively, and in parliament, the congressional coalition APRA-UNO (Alliance for Popular Revolution in America–National Union of Odría) made Belaúnde Terry's attempts at reform almost impossible. The constitution Peru had in the 1960s did not provide a mechanism to reconcile and to mediate between the executive and legislative branches. The president designated his ministers, but they could be deposed by the National Assembly. Thus, opposition in congress could prevent any action for an entire presidential term of six years.

Belaúnde Terry, however, had big plans and found increasing popular support. With moderation and compromise, and without respite, he had campaigned throughout the country between July 1962 and June 1963. In the wake of his campaign he gained adherents from members of the lower middle class who were dissatisfied with APRA's turn to the right, from *apristas* who criticized the pact with Odría, from Peru's disenfranchised, and from many of the more enlightened members of the well-to-do. Last but not least Belaúnde Terry could also count on a discreet military junta and a willing Catholic clergy.

One of his first steps was to call for municipal elections. Municipal authorities, following a pattern established by Leguía (1919–30), had been arbitrarily designated. In the first municipal elections in 1963 and 1966, most mayors came from the ranks of Belaúnde Terry's renamed party, the governing Acción Popular (AP), and the Democracia Cristiana (DC), led by Héctor Cornejo Chávez. To the chagrin of the APRA-UNO, which had hoped to score a victory with

María Delgado de Odría as their candidate for Lima's mayoralty, Luis Bedoya Reyes, a close friend of Belaúnde Terry, won overwhelmingly.

Neither of the two winning parties had a well-defined government plan. The DC denounced social injustices and labeled capitalism as cruelly exploitative in its very essence. Capitalism, in the party's view, should be replaced by a somewhat undefined kind of communitarianism following socialist principles. The AP was more of an assembly of important personalities following the call of a charismatic leader, or, as some put it, a dreamer.

Anticipating Alejandro Toledo (who became president in 2001), Belaúnde Terry announced that his economic policies would follow those of Pachacútec, and he described such policies as "the conquest of Peru by Peruvians." He visited "every corner" of the country on muleback. To some he sounded much like a socialist *indigenista* of the Mariátegui tradition. His most grandiose project—also following Incan design—was the construction of the Marginal, a highway along the edges of the jungle in the eastern Andes, connecting Perú with Buenos Aires, Argentina, and Asunción, Paraguay, to the south and Caracas, Venezuela, to the north. Besides improving travel, this move was also meant to alleviate migrant pressure on Lima by resettling highland Indians into the eastern slopes of the Andes to produce food for coastal and city-based laborers. Construction, however, was never finished.

In the meantime problems attendant upon land distribution and use had staggering proportions. Less than 2 percent of Peru's territory was under cultivation. Only half an acre per capita of land produced domestic food, a number woefully inadequate for a decent diet for a growing population.

Response to Belaúnde Terry's attempts at agrarian reform was lukewarm, and he confronted solid opposition from Peru's large coastal landowners. During his presidency coastal plantations were left intact. Only a little more than 400,000 acres (out of a total of 11 million acres of cultivable land) were subjected to expropriation, mainly "idle" land of sierra estates, for which the owners received government-designated compensation. More important perhaps was Belaúnde Terry's effort to develop peasant communities. By the end of 1965 more than 2,000 of the estimated 5,000 Indian communities had been surveyed and their leaders engaged in building roads, clinics, and schools with modest financial support from the government. Often these development projects were staffed with volunteers, young and usually urban Peruvians, mostly university students from medicine, engineering, veterinary, and agronomy programs.

President Fernando Belaúnde Terry, center foreground (Joachim Hunefeldt)

Such well-intended projects came to an end when the majority bloc in congress drastically reduced the funds for the agrarian reform program.

More important in its long-term repercussions was Belaúnde Terry's commitment to education. Between 1960 and 1965 Peru's spending on education increased by 85 percent, representing fully 5.1 percent of gross national income and 33 percent of the budget, percentages much higher than the average spending among underdeveloped countries and close to amounts spent in developed countries. The number of students increased by 50 percent and the number of teachers by 67 percent; however, educational content deteriorated. More Peruvians earning a university degree found no outlet for what they had learned because there were no jobs, and soon education stopped being an avenue for social mobility. Graduating students became "learned

LAND DISTRIBUTION IN THE 1960S

In the 1960s land distribution in Peru was more skewed than ever. Most concentrated land holdings were devoted to producing agrarian exports, whereas the appallingly small amount of land available to produce food for Peruvians was dispersed. On the coast there were approximately 40,000 landholders who owned plots of less than 25 acres and 27,000 landholders who had less than five acres. Quite in contrast there were 181 landholders who held estates of more than 1,250 acres each.

In the highlands around 1960, there were 33,000 landowners. More than 27,000 of these held farms of 75 acres or less, in an often arid landscape subject to only seasonal rains and without irrigation systems. Within this category one-third, or nearly 10,000 landowners, held less than five acres of land. In addition there was an entirely landless peasant population, the *yanaconas*. They were serfs, allowed to use small tracts of lands within established haciendas, often no more than a furrow or two, in exchange for working a certain number of days throughout the year on the hacienda lands. Differentiation in terms of land ownership in the highlands was not as marked as on the coast, but it was dramatic nevertheless. The 1,233 highland landowners who owned properties of 2,500 acres or more controlled nearly 80 percent of land under cultivation or used for pasture. From this it seems quite clear that there was basically no middle ground in Peru's agrarian sector. In a different historical setting—France in the late 18th century—such a dramatic inequality of land distribution had produced nothing less than the French Revolution (Pike 1967, 312; based on the 1961 Peruvian census).

unemployed"; they were the future leaders of an increasingly more radical left.

The international context during these years appeared to be promising for the Belaúnde Terry government. The end results of the Cuban revolution (1956–59) had awakened nightmares about communism in the United States, which offered help to American countries through the recently founded Alliance for Progress, the Salvation Army, and the International Development Agency. The United States, however, was relatively hostile toward Belaúnde Terry, and the U.S. State Department intended to wring guarantees to maintain the favored treatment accorded to the International Petroleum Company (IPC). IPC held one of the most favorable concession contracts in the world, a 50-50 profit-sharing agreement with Peru, at a time when other governments received 70 percent from foreign oil concerns. Internal pressure in Peru to renegotiate the terms of the IPC concession—or proceed to expropriation—mounted. The Lyndon Johnson administration declined to cooperate, and the Alliance for Progress funds that Belaúnde Terry's government had been expecting never materialized.

During these years the Catholic Church shifted gears. Liberation theology, which emphasized ministry to the downtrodden and dispossessed, replaced conservative clerical stands, and the lower clergy installed hundreds of *comunidades de base* (base communities) among Peru's poorest. As late as 1937 Lima's archbishop had been heard to say, "poverty is the most certain road to eternal felicity. Only the state which succeeds in making the poor appreciate the spiritual treasures of poverty can solve its social problems" (Pike 1967, 313). In contrast Lima's archbishop in 1959, Juan Landázuri Ricketts, had this to say about poverty: "The Church sees that the present economic and social order must be reformed and improved. . . . A living wage must be paid to workers and there must be a better distribution of wealth; private selfishness must be curbed, for there is no longer an excuse of the miserable conditions in which rural labourers and the urban proletariat live" (Pike 1967, 313).

Actions followed these words. Cuzco's archdiocese had by 1956 divested itself of much land and sold it at below-market value to rural laborers. U.S. Maryknoll priests and nuns in Peru's southern highlands helped establish credit and consumer cooperatives. By the beginning of 1964 a total of 365 credit cooperatives with 130,000 members from the poverty-stricken rural regions boasted total savings of approximately $35 million. Soon bicycles replaced horses and mules in the highlands, and bike riders held transistor radios to their ears listening to church-sponsored lessons in reading and writing and culture, hygiene, sanitation, or agricultural methods in Spanish, Aymara, and Quechua.

During these years Peru's military redefined its role in society. Instead of being the repressive arm of the state, it now aspired to help the country achieve social and economic betterment, a goal that met wide applause. The Center of High Military Studies (Centro de Altos Estudios Militares, CAEM) had been established under the Odría administration (1950–56). Military and civilian professors taught a large variety of subjects but concentrated on identifying Peru's problems and suggesting solutions. The CAEM produced some of the most expert plans for future development. At the same time the military was somewhat "democratized," and army officers and soldiers were engaged in dozens of development projects, advising with technological expertise. Belaúnde Terry greatly contributed in redesigning the mission of Peru's military, and he sent many military officers, at government expense, to study abroad and learn what they needed to participate in the agrarian reform program.

In some regions agrarian reform was preceded by guerrilla movements rumored to have had support from Cuba and the Soviet Union. Guerrillas, operating on rugged terrain, had considerable nuisance potential and managed to occupy some of the larger haciendas in the regions where they operated. In Cuzco, *aprista* militant Luis de la Puente Uceda and Trotskyist Hugo Blanco organized a guerrilla group, the Movement of the Revolutionary Left (MIR) in 1965, and Guillermo Lobatón did something similar in the central highlands, founding the Tupac Amaru group. For the first time in Peru's history peasant unrest encompassed the whole country. Peasants invaded haciendas, often preceded by a music band and holding a Peruvian flag, and began a well-organized strike. As a result peasants came to control hundreds of thousands of acres of land. For the time being the Peruvian government was powerless to stop the popular movements. By the 1960s many people in Peru, as well as some observers in the United States after the Cuban revolution, understood that social structures needed to change to prevent violent explosions. Notwithstanding these changing perceptions it was with U.S. help, bombardments of napalm, and the hesitant intervention of Peru's military, that the guerrilla movement was subdued between 1965 and 1966.

In spite of growing internal unrest the Peruvian state continued economic policies first implemented by Odría, and macroeconomic indicators showed progress. Between 1950 and 1965 direct U.S. investments in mining grew 379 percent; in nonmining ventures U.S. investment grew 180 percent, whereas in the rest of Latin America it grew only 111 percent. Only Mexico experienced higher direct U.S. investment. Foreign investors owned 100 percent of Peruvian oil and iron production, and foreign ownership of other industries was likewise significant: copper up to 80 percent, zinc to 67 percent, fishing 30 percent, and sugar 23 percent. In 1968 the U.S. Anderson Clayton firm controlled 83 percent of cotton exports. That same year 12 of the most important U.S. corporations held 54 percent of Peru's 10 most important export products. A similar situation existed in banking. By 1966 money held by foreign capital amounted to 62 percent. It has been calculated that the Peruvian state subsidized foreign investments with about 10,000 million soles, or 75 percent of public spending, in 1963.

A severe economic crisis in 1967 was the beginning of the end. The coast suffered from a persistent drought, dollar reserves were close to nothing after several years of external commerce deficits, foreign investments had diminished, and the sol was devalued from 27 per dollar to 39 per dollar. Fiscal crisis translated into increased taxes, the cessation of public works, and—once again—increasing unemployment rates. Peru's external debt had grown from $237 million to $685 million between 1963 and 1967.

Opposition parties, which were increasingly more divergent, used the crisis to anticipate the 1969 elections by further discrediting Belaúnde Terry's government. However, this often senseless and unfounded opposition had another effect: It completely discredited the entire political system. A page (*"escándalo de la página once"*) from a new contract with IPC was literally lost. Allegedly, because it contained clauses that transferred national wealth to a foreign firm, and the acute political crisis resulting from the ongoing confrontations between the legislative and executive branches brought the military back to power in 1968 with General Juan Velasco Alvarado.

This time around, reforms would not be directed at isolated peasant communities or untouched regions. A national awareness had grown, and it was multiplied by technology. In the late 1960s transistor radios had reached the hands of peasants in villages and rural migrants working in domestic service in Lima. Bicycles had replaced mules, and trucks connected a vast and varied territory, despite insufficient roads. More newspapers circulated with more ease within and among towns, cities, and regions. Technology brought people closer and made the exchange of ideas more fluid. More information led to a heightened sense of shared problems, creating a political consciousness and a nationalization of Peruvian culture.

13

AGRARIAN REFORM AND THE SHINING PATH (1968–1990)

The military dictatorship under General Juan Velasco Alvarado (1968–75) launched a large-scale agrarian reform movement that would have wide and long-lasting effects on modern Peru. Despite what might have been expected of military rule, Velasco's government embraced left-leaning policies and took over or expropriated nearly all major segments of the Peruvian economy. It attempted to redistribute the land, thereby hoping to break Peru's traditionally inequitable pattern of land holding and thus the hold of the traditional oligarchy. The 1968 coup was in a sense the continuation of the self-redefined role of the military. National strategy rather than military strategy was the theme of the day, and what Peru's military leadership envisaged was a "socialism from above" in order to prevent "socialism from below."

Unfortunately the nation again went bankrupt, this time due to the costs of agrarian reform. Moreover, parcelization and the process of expropriating and redistributing land led to a series of unexpected consequences. Renewed attempts at land reform under APRA's first elected president, Alan García, only exacerbated conditions, stimulating violent response in the form of the Shining Path guerrilla movement.

The Corporatist State and Populism

Velasco encountered a dismal situation when he took over in 1968. Between 1940 and 1961 Peru's urban population had grown three times as much as the rural population. During the following decade the urban population grew 10 times as much as the rural population. Rural population growth almost came to a standstill. The reasons for this stagnation were twofold. On one side the Peruvian government fostered industrialization, and in doing so it tried to create a cheap industrial labor force. To reduce the cost of labor meant to decrease food prices so the labor force could survive despite low wages. On the other side technological changes and state subsidies to food production in the United States and Europe had turned these countries into exporters of food after World War II, and Peru readily imported from them. Peru's highland agriculture, with its rudimentary technology and vulnerability to international market prices, could not compete with these increasingly cheaper food imports. Some statistics document this process. Between 1954 and 1959 per-capita income on Peru's coast grew 4 percent; in Peru's highlands it decreased by 7 percent. Between 1960 and 1969 gross national income grew by 350 percent, but agriculture in the highlands decreased its participation in the gross national income from 14 to 11 percent (Cotler 1978, 284–286). These circumstances forced thousands of peasants to migrate to the cities, especially Lima, and made Peru thereafter dependent on food imports.

During the preceding decades Peru had lagged behind other Latin American countries with populist governments that had implemented industrialization substitution policies and agrarian reform projects. Lázaro Cárdenas in Mexico, Getúlio Vargas in Brazil, the Popular Front party in Chile, and even Víctor Paz Estenssoro in Bolivia had been active. In a sense Velasco wanted to catch up with history by engaging in long-overdue reforms: a radical agrarian reform; a reform of Peru's enterprises by which he meant to turn over 50 percent of firm shares to its workers; the nationalization of mining, fishing, and banking; educational reform; designation of Quechua as Peru's second official lan-

LIMA'S UNBRIDLED GROWTH

Whereas in the early 1940s about one-fourth of Peru's population lived in Lima, by 1970 half of Peru's population lived in Lima, and most of its inhabitants came from Peru's most economically devastated rural provinces. Lima became "Andeanized," or as some put it "Indianized." There were few jobs for this massive influx of migrants, and low-level self-employment and the often violent occupation of land in Lima's outskirts were the migrants' solutions. Lima's dramatic radial growth was not guided by urban planning, and most newcomers to the city had no water, no sewage, no electricity, and no roads.

guage; and organization of folklore festivals (Inkarri) together with a reevaluation of Peru's historic Andean figures, such as Tupac Amaru II. Changes were undertaken from above and guided by the military maxim that orders were to be obeyed, not discussed.

Velasco's military government, self-labeled the Revolutionary Government of the Armed Forces (Gobierno Revolucionario de la Fuerza Armada), designed a government program called the Plan Inca. By it the government intended to find a route of development for the country that would be neither communist nor capitalist, a sort of state capitalism with social redistribution to benefit the poorest in the country. The military was very much aware of who these poor were, both because they had been engaged in development projects and because soldiers for the army were drafted from all over the country. The sons and daughters of rich people could pay to excuse themselves from obligatory military service, but few sons and daughters from lower income groups could do the same. Velasco himself was born in Piura in 1910 to a lower middle-class family, and he attended public school and joined the army as a simple soldier.

To gain popular support Velasco created new union organizations for peasants, students, workers, and professionals, such as the Central Bureau of the Peruvian Workers Confederation (Confederación de Trabajadores del Perú, CTP), the National Agrarian Confederation (Confederación Nacional Agraria, CNA), and a state-sponsored entity designed to mobilize popular groups referred to by the initials SINAMOS. SINAMOS was short for Sistema Nacional de Apoyo a la Movilización Social (National System of Social Mobilization) but some also read it as *sin amos*, that is, "without masters," underlining the relative independence of this entity. While mobilizing the masses Velasco also silenced opposition voices. Congress remained closed; the Supreme Court was supplanted by the Council of Justice (Consejo Nacional de Justicia); and political parties and the free press were suppressed. In spite of his dictatorial measures, Velasco counted on the support of many prominent intellectuals and social scientists, many of whom had been students at Lima's San Marcos University during the reform-oriented 1950s. Velasco's policies were soon labeled in the United States as the "Peruvian experiment" and in the Soviet Union as "Peruvian socialism."

Following his economic plan Velasco began extensive expropriations of what the government considered strategic resources, beginning with the oil fields in Talara; then the Cerro de Pasco Mining Corporation and the Southern Peru Copper Corporation, with a total of 21,000 workers;

and next the fishing industry. Huge public enterprises replaced these privately owned enterprises, and all had mammoth administrative headquarters in Lima.

A similar pattern applied to the distribution of what was produced. The state became involved in the marketing and distribution of the products coming from these new public enterprises. More state-appointed administrators had to be put in place to control the distribution of goods. Moreover, maritime transport, the airlines, communications, energy, telephones, and rail lines now became the property of the state or state-controlled corporations. Only one bank, the Banco de Crédito, escaped expropriation. Smaller industrial enterprises, not deemed to be strategic, were reorganized.

According to Velasco's plan, these enterprises were to become "industrial communities," in which workers became shareholders and participated in the enterprise's management and profits, or they might directly become a "social property enterprise," owned by the workers. Surprisingly, public enterprises showed higher levels of efficiency than the private enterprises did. By 1977 the public sector produced 50 percent of the gross national income.

The overarching move toward industrialization was implemented through import substitution policies, begun belatedly (compared with other Latin American countries) in 1969 and meant to gradually replace imports by national produce. Some imports were subjected to high taxes; other imports were forbidden. The success of these policies was uneven. Whereas, for instance, industrial production of stoves and refrigerators prospered, domestic car assembly proved to be a disaster.

Internationally Velasco's regime aligned with a pattern of leftist regimes in Latin America: Salvador Allende was Chile's president; the Peronist Héctor Cámpora governed in Argentina; and Fidel Castro was leader of Cuba. This leftward tilt brought Latin American countries closer to the Soviet Union and the Eastern European countries. Soviet tanks and planes, Romanian buses, motorcycles from Czechoslovakia, and medical equipment from Hungary and Cuba reached Peru. Peru became one of the strongest voices for nonaligned countries in the world.

Possibly Velasco's most important success was the opening of political opportunity for all Peruvians by expanding political participation. In 1968–73, Peru ceased to be a country ruled by a powerful and backward-looking minority. The agrarian reform programs, backed by the reform of the educational system, nourished this heightened level of political participation.

Agrarian Reform

Peru, as seen earlier, has a very diverse and heterogeneous countryside. No simple reform model could encompass traditional haciendas, large coastal plantations, peasant communities and communal property, and small landholdings in the highlands. Even within each region (coast, highland, Amazon basin) the rural landscape showed striking differences. What most rural sites had in common, though, was a process of land concentration, resulting in an uneven land distribution. Three-quarters of the cultivable land was controlled by one-half of 1 percent of Peru's population. Many peasants did not have enough land to feed their families. For a long time Peru's complex land patterns and the power of large landowners frustrated reform. By the early 1970s, however, the government could no longer close its eyes to the plight of a vast majority. Conditions seemed ripe for change.

The model used to unleash change was the associative enterprise, in which former salaried rural workers and independent peasant families would become members of different kinds of cooperatives. The military government was ready and willing to invest huge amounts of money to transform Peru's agriculture to socialized ownership and management. These state expenditures explain in some measure the enormous increase of Peru's external debt at the beginning of the 1970s. State bankruptcy was partly caused by the cheap credit the government extended to promote agrarian development, state subsidies, and administration expenditures to carry out the agrarian reform during a period

---

REFORM SUCCESSES

Critics abounded when the agrarian reform was first implemented. Statistics show that the agrarian reform had some success, however, not only in creating a wider political consciousness but also in economic terms. A total of 2,889 units of production, involving 429,384 beneficiaries (roughly 30 percent of all peasants and agrarian producers), were allocated almost 4 million acres of land (out of a total of 9.3 million acres). About 40 percent of the economically active population was directly or indirectly affected by the agrarian reform. In no other country in Latin America and in few countries anywhere in the world was land distribution so far reaching, not even in those places—such as Castro's Cuba and Allende's Chile—where socialist governments were in power.

233

when prices for export crops were declining and much of Latin America was pursuing industrialization to replace imports.

In 1972 Velasco dissolved the National Agrarian Society (Sociedad Nacional Agraria, or SNA), which for decades had been the bastion of oligarchic political organization, and founded the Peruvian Peasant Confederation (Confederación Campesina del Perú, CCP) and the National Agrarian Confederation (Confederación Nacional Agraria, CNA). The CCP and CNA were top-down organizations designed to rebuild state–rural sector relations.

General Velasco regarded agrarian reform as a necessary first step toward more sweeping reforms throughout society, very closely following the ideas of Manuel González Prada and José Carlos Mariátegui. From the beginning the agrarian reform was part of a more ambitious plan of national development in which agriculture would assume its traditional role of producing cheap food and labor. In the initial stages of the agrarian reform in the early 1970s extreme optimists speculated

President Juan Velasco Alvarado, leaning on the sign in the center of the railcar, addresses a crowd of peasants during his agrarian reform campaign in 1972. (Reproduced with the permission of the General Secretariat of the Organization of American States)

that export-oriented agrarian production would generate profits high enough to repay the so-called agrarian debt, thus fueling other investments, particularly in industry. The 1971–75 plan was based on the assumption of a 4.2 percent increase of agrarian production. Debt payments would go to former hacendados, who would then invest at least half of their revenues in industrial development. Another portion of the expected profits were meant to repay credits to the state.

As a result of their agrarian reform program the military expected to gain popular support, destroy oligarchic domination, control conflict and rural discontent, improve income distribution, stop massive migration to the cities, and create a stable supply for an expanding internal market. This was quite in contrast to what actually happened. Very few of the newly created cooperatives were able to repay accumulated debts. In most cases debts skyrocketed, production stagnated, and exports declined. Shortly after implementing the agrarian reform (and following a historical pattern) Peru was forced to spend 25 percent of its annual budget on food imports, in spite of the fact that peasants, small landholders, and medium-sized entrepreneurs were still producing cheap food for urban, industrial consumption. Industrial investments, on the other hand, were utterly nonexistent since the 1960s.

Once again, invoking a glorious indigenous past Velasco sought peasant support for his agrarian reform program. On June 24, 1969, he expropriated the large modern sugar haciendas on Peru's northern and central coast. Previously observed as the holiday Día del Indio (Day of the Indian), June 24 became known from then on as Día del Campesino (Day of the Peasant). Large landowners were allowed to retain a maximum of 20 acres of their irrigated land, or 60 acres if the land did not have irrigation. By 1979, 3.68 million acres of land had been expropriated, about 30 percent of Peru's total cultivable land, and expropriation affected about 16,000 property owners. Expropriation not only included land, but also machinery, livestock, and industrial installations.

Expropriation went hand in hand with accusations against former owners, especially if they were known to have mistreated their workers. Such owners were brought to popular courts presided over by the government. In a few cases former owners were compensated for their lost properties. If the state recognized a debt toward former owners, it was often repaid with state bonds at very low interest rates. The government expected these bonds to be invested in industrial ventures by former landowners. This never happened, thus the government's attempts to expand Peru's industrialization in tandem with the agrarian reform failed. Moreover debts to former owners were calculated based on their own tax reports; since most landowners either did not pay taxes at all or had extremely undervalued their properties to evade tax payments, they received little from the state.

"Land for those who work it" ("*la tierra para quien la trabaja*") was the general goal of the reform, consequently the expropriated land went to some 369,000 peasant families. However, the *yanaconas,* landless rural laborers, especially in the highlands, who had been laboring on haciendas on a temporary basis, were excluded even though they were most in need of land. The management of the new workers' cooperatives was in the hands of state-appointed engineers and administrators.

In spite of its initial success, corruption, lack of foresight, and lack of technological innovations eventually led to the partial dismantlement of the agrarian reform. To a great extent discontent in the agrarian sector emerged as a result of the unfulfilled promises and expectations agrarian reform had generated. The flaws of the agrarian reform and the rural discontent it brought about led to privatization of land ownership within state-sponsored cooperatives, peasant invasion of cooperatively managed enterprises, and the emergence of the radical Maoist Shining Path terrorists. Privatization (basically on the coast) and the violent confrontations between cooperatives and peasant communities (basically in the highlands) were the outcome.

State control was meant to increase grassroots support; however, it also had negative consequences, such as corruption, misuse of funds, regional distortions, and managerial inconsistencies. As production faltered, real and artificial scarcities of basic consumption products for the urban population became commonplace, and some groups acquired preferential treatment based on their links to the power structure. Rage on the part of those left out or whose expectations were raised by the reforms created a willingness to listen to radicals who promoted terrorism and from those who demanded privatization. Response to either one of these alternatives greatly depended on who and where the listener was.

Each government following the Velasco regime since 1975 has adopted differing policies toward the agrarian issue, each in turn tinged by differing political ideologies and priorities.

Politics and Economics after 1975

In February 1975, amid a strike of the capital's police forces, Lima was ransacked. Violence was rampant, and the army was called into action to stop massive looting. A few months later Velasco was replaced as president by General Francisco Morales Bermúdez (1975–1980), a former minister of economics. The leaders of the ruling military faction were divided: Some generals wanted to deepen reforms and lead the country into socialism; others thought that the reforms had gone too far and that the time had come to return to the barracks. Economic crisis, social protests, two national strikes in 1976 and 1977, and a generalized sentiment of the need to return to democracy led Morales Bermúdez to establish the Constituent Assembly in 1978, charged with writing a new constitution that would lead Peru back to democracy and remove the military from government. The octogenarian Haya de la Torre became president of the assembly. As such he signed the new constitution a few days before dying, in August 1979.

New presidential elections followed in April 1980, and for the first time—and without any resistance—illiterate Peruvians (who made up 20 percent of the population) were allowed to vote. A second round of elections was to take place if none of the candidates obtained a large majority in the first round of elections. It came as a shock to many to learn that former president Fernando Belaúnde Terry once again won the presidency with 42 percent of the votes, in spite of a long campaign of defamation directed against him after Velasco had literally dragged him out of the presidency. APRA's candidate only got 28 percent of the votes, and Luis Bedoya Reyes, former mayor of Lima, received 11 percent.

After his reelection, Belaúnde Terry led a country that was very different from 1968, the year he was ousted. Immediately after taking office, Belaúnde Terry decreed the reestablishment of the free press. All journals and newspapers that had been expropriated by Velasco were returned to their former owners. In 1980 Belaúnde once again held municipal elections in order to expand his power into local communities. His party, the AP (Acción Popular), won the municipal elections, and for the first time the United Left (Izquierda Unida) came in second place, ahead of APRA and Bedoya's party, the Popular Christian Party (Partido Popular Cristiano, or PPC). The United Left was a conglomerate of various marxist and non-marxist splinter groups under the leadership of Alfonso Barrantes Lingán, a Cajamarca native who was elected Lima's first marxist mayor in 1983.

In his second term as president Belaúnde Terry did little to reverse the reforms implemented by the military, nor did he move them much further along. He began urban building projects in a lukewarm fashion, but he had no funds to do more because interest on Peru's huge external debt was eating up revenues. He was faced also with a devastating agrarian crisis (made worse by a strong El Niño weather pattern in 1983) and the drain on the economy of the gigantic, wasteful government bureaucracy. Moreover, during his second term, two militant guerrilla movements emerged that were to play huge roles in Peruvian history during the coming years: the Maoist-inspired Shining Path (Sendero Luminoso) and the Marxist-Leninist Tupac Amaru Revolutionary Movement (Movimiento Revolucionario Tupac Amaru, or MRTA).

Added to these problems was the effect of Belaúnde Terry's policy of easing import restrictions, which resulted in rapidly diminishing Peru's money reserves as spending on import goods shot up. The results were devaluation of the Peruvian currency on the international exchange market and severe price inflation at home. When Belaúnde Terry took office in 1980, the exchange rate was 200 soles to the dollar. When he finished his second term in 1985, the rate was 1,200 soles to the dollar.

Belaúnde Terry's principal attempt at reform between 1980 and 1985 involved the dismantling of the associative enterprises. A new liberal political policy of monetarism prevailed during Belaúnde Terry's second presidency. Liberal technocrats believed that the only way to increase productivity was through private ownership. This meant a shift in focus, from widespread political change and land distribution to a more narrow concern with better and higher yields. Efficiency, not social justice, was on policymakers' minds, and consequently, state subsidies were eliminated.

In order to incorporate more beneficiaries into the process of agrarian transformation—and thus ease social and political pressure—new agrarian options were created. Traditionally held communal rights within peasant communities in the highlands were made more flexible; that is, land could be sold and/or mortgaged, a move that benefited richer peasants within the peasant communities and alienated those who did not have the money to purchase land. Through costly colonization projects a narrow agrarian frontier was expanded into the Amazon basin. However, this move exacerbated ethnic conflicts. Once again, attempts to colonize the Amazon basin touched upon traditional land rights of several Amazonian Indian groups.

In 1981 and 1982 statistics registered an increase in food production. This was more a result of good weather, however, than of the policies implemented. A decrease in output followed in the third year of Belaúnde Terry's term. Opposition to the government and ongoing processes in the cooperatives resulted in the first national agrarian strike and the formation of the United National Agrarian Congress (Congreso Unitario Nacional Agrario, CUNA). The entire cabinet of ministers resigned, and new ministers were appointed to office.

In 1982 Peru had been hit by several natural disasters, and food production declined dramatically by 9.3 percent in 1983. In 1984 and 1985 agrarian production increased again, in part because international development agencies opened new avenues for private capital, especially on the coast and in the jungle region. Growth came hand in hand with claims from former landowners to regain the land they had lost in the early stages of the agrarian reform.

As a result of this turn of events privatization (or parcelization) of the associative enterprises began—in spite of widespread resistance from members of the cooperatives and from the defenders of socialist development. The government countered this resistance with "agrarian developmentalism," an approach based on higher productivity, increased participation of producers, and broader consensus. Similarly more private initiatives to commercialize agrarian production challenged existing state monopolies.

The Shining Path and Alan García

Belaúnde Terry failed to recognize the potential danger of the Shining Path terrorist group that rapidly expanded its influence in the face of official neglect. The group took its name from Mariátegui's party, which had changed to the Communist Party of Peru for the Shining Path of José Carlos Mariátegui. The Shining Path leaders were the children of highland landowners who had lost their land in the wake of the agrarian reform in the early 1970s, most of them university students and teachers in provincial universities, mainly in Ayacucho/Huamanga, where the movement originated. The principal leader, Abimael Guzmán Reynoso, later known as Presidente Gonzalo, was a philosophy professor from Arequipa. He and his followers split from the mainline Peruvian Communist Party and took Maoism as their ideological guide.

The Shining Path's first violent action was the burning of ballot boxes in the little town of Chuschi in 1980. Between 1980 and 1984 the group operated only in the Department of Ayacucho, where it managed to get a toehold among peasants, some of the poorest in the country. After 1984 it extended its activity to Lima with bombings and blackouts. In 1983 the military launched serious antiterrorist warfare against the group. In Ayacucho alone it has been estimated that 10,561 people died between 1980 and 1993, and more than 20,000 in the country overall. More recent reports estimate about 60,000 in total.

Meanwhile APRA won the 1985 elections, and Alan García Pérez, only 36 years old, became president with 46 percent of the votes. He became the first elected *aprista* president and the youngest president in Peru's history. His closest opponent, Alfonso Barrantes Lingán of the United Left (Izquierda Unida), renounced his right to a second round, and Luis Bedoya Reyes only received 10 percent of the votes.

President García was an indefatigable orator—some Peruvians said that he continued to sound more like a candidate than a president—but rhetoric alone did not make for a good government. He managed to keep the military out of the direct political game, and he also obtained support from many leftist groups seeking to distance themselves from the radicalism of the Shining Path. Heterodoxy characterized his economic measures. At one time, in an attempt to deal with inflation, his administration promulgated half a dozen different exchange rates for differing monetary transactions. Through his monetary reform the Peruvian sol became the inti (meaning "sun" in Quechua) and 1,000 soles became one inti. García and his prime minister and minister for economics, Luis Alva Castro, were very successful at managing the economy during the first two years of his term. Inflation dropped 60 percent per year; growth rates resembled those of the 1950s; and the Shell Company found a huge gas deposit in Cuzco.

However, the ongoing price controls and fixed exchange rates that the García administration kept in place led to fiscal deficit. García uni-

President Alan García Pérez, the first elected aprista presidential candidate and the youngest president in Peruvian history, is shown here reviewing Peruvian troops. (Alejandro Balaguer photo)

laterally fixed the repayment of Peru's external debt at 10 percent of Peru's exports, an arrangement that came close to a moratorium on repayment. Creditor reprisals followed, and Peru was left without lines of international credit. Both the Interamerican Development Bank and the World Bank stopped sending money. Peru's external debt had doubled since the end of Velasco's regime, up to $20 billion.

In his presidential address in 1987 García announced the expropriation of the banks, claiming that it was the banks that had restrained Peru's development by constricting the money supply and limiting credit. The measure proved largely ineffective, in some cases because banks sold their shares to their employees. At that point the Peruvian economy entered a stage of utter confusion; the money needed to buy a large house in 1985 would only buy a toothbrush in 1990. In 1990, daily inflation was 2 percent; monthly inflation amounted to 60 percent. The exchange rate soared from 13 intis per dollar to 175,000 intis per dollar in 1990. Recession, poverty, and the collapse of public services followed. Annual per capita income dropped to $997, and the central bank reserves were down to $105 million.

Amid this economic chaos the Shining Path launched what its leadership considered the final attack against the "fascist state." By then the Shining Path had increased not only the number of its followers from the ranks of public universities, national schools, factories, and shantytowns but also its connections with drug dealers in the Amazon basin. The Maoist guerrillas cashed in money from the drug dealers and also from factory owners, who were forced to pay protection money in monthly installments to avoid the bombing of their factories. Factory owners hired guards to protect their properties, the so-called *huachiman,* a sort of a Spanish phonetic conversion of "watching man." Scornfully but not without humor, some analysts said that in Peru at that time there were three kinds of Peruvians: those who had a job, those who were looking for a job, and those who watched over those who had a job. The Shining Path was literally in charge of several regions of the country, and it also controlled vast areas within the city of Lima. Selective trials, judgments, and killings were its chosen strategy to intimidate a whole population.

The Shining Path's increasingly radical strategy led to its gradual decline. It lost support from peasants in an array of efforts: when it tried to forbid commercial activities in order to "starve the city," when it attempted to expel the church from the countryside, and when it began to execute local authorities and to confront international aid organizations. And in a moment of miscalculation the Shining Path lost support among urban shantytown dwellers when its terrorists publicly dynamited a beloved leader, Elena Moyano. Likewise many people in more middle-class residential areas had given the Shining Path silent support, but in 1988–90 when the terrorists began attacking the residences in these areas, such people finally gathered in demonstrations against the Shining Path.

The government—that is, the military—reacted with increasing violence. Since around 1985, thousands of peasants were killed simply because the day before a couple of terrorists had stopped in a community to extort food. In June 1986 when an international socialist congress was taking place in Lima, terrorist prisoners in three Lima jails staged a mutiny. Following the president's orders the army entered the jails and slaughtered inmates, even after the terrorists had surrendered. Yet this was still not the end of terrorism. Peru seemed on the edge of an abyss. The police had registered 219 "subversive actions" in 1980; in 1989 the number rose to 3,149. Between 1988 and 1994 about 1 million Peruvians—mainly from the middle class—emigrated, heading especially to the United States. Those who remained took precautions in case the Shining Path was taking over the country, as did Peru's neighboring countries. A national strike called by the Shining Path in 1990 paralyzed the nation.

Privatization and Parcelization

The specific problems of peasant communities were not addressed in either the first or second periods of agrarian reform. These peasant communities, approximately 5,000 of them, encompassed more than 1 million *minifundistas,* or small landholders, most of them with less than two acres of land. Cooperatives called social interest agrarian associations (*sociedades agrícolas de interés social,* or SAISs) were intended to incorporate peasant communities, but they did so in very limited ways. And it was particularly in these communities where appalling demographic conditions were recorded: Life expectancy averaged 46.6 years, and infant mortality was 145 for every 1,000 births.

In a third phase of agrarian developments, privatization became more intense when in 1985 APRA's leader, Alan García, was elected president. As Velasco had done before him, García put agriculture at the forefront of his economic policy of national self-reliance. He intended to provide new stimulation to food production and to incorporate the so-called Indian regions in the highlands in his policies to reduce Peru's dependency on food imports. His plan included a new round of land distribution, particularly for peasant communities, and economic policies designed to strengthen small-scale producers. His economic policy package included price controls, state subsidies, credits (in some cases with negative interest rates), and privileged exchange rates to allow for the purchase of capital goods in order to improve peasants' access to modern technology.

Initially the García government supported and promoted associative enterprises; however, between 1986 and 1990 it also sponsored privatization both within the agrarian production cooperatives (*cooperativas agrarias de producción*, CAPs) and the SAISs. In 1985 *parceleros* (owners of small private plots of land within the cooperatives) formed the National Association of Parcel Holders (Asociacion Nacional de Parceleros, ANAPA), which from its inception defended private property within the cooperatives and opposed state interference altogether. It probably was the first time in Peruvian history that organized sectors of rural workers directly imposed their will on a government.

Notwithstanding policy vagaries under García, relative prices tended to favor agrarian production. Food supply increased and better technologies became available; however, optimism and progress were short lived. A decline in agricultural production came in 1987. Budget deficits reached appalling heights and fueled desperate printing of new money. Inflation followed, and no more money from abroad entered the Peruvian economy. Social discontent, delayed payments to producers, and price increases finally led to strikes in several provinces, including Puno, Cuzco, Huaraz, and Ucayali. A once-promising interaction between producers and government came to a standstill. In 1990 a renewed drought further worsened political conditions.

In 1989 the Board of Agrarian Reform (Dirección General de Reforma Agraria) claimed that 430 out of 609 associative enterprises had been subdivided to *parceleros*. In 234 of the cases, mostly on Peru's coast, official recognition had already been granted; 69 were still being processed; and 127 had proceeded to divide land with no consultation whatsoever.

Land privatization within the cooperatives had far-reaching consequences. It diminished the associative enterprises' capacity to produce enough for urban and industrial needs, for exports, and for the smaller internal market. Particularly in cotton and sugar production, *parceleros'* smaller holdings were not competitive in the international market. The former members of the cooperatives also lost some of the social benefits formerly guaranteed by the larger enterprises. The loss of social benefits has been calculated at approximately 25 percent of their real income. Recreation, infrastructure, health, and education tended to be

THE DISRUPTION OF RURAL LIFE

Policy shifts—from the socializing efforts of Juan Velasco Alvarado to the market-oriented efficiency criteria of Fernando Belaúnde Terry and the heterodox approaches of Alan García Pérez—deeply disrupted rural processes, leading to growing distrust of the government by the rural population. Over the years the state lost control. Governmental policies had moved from strict state intervention to a complete absence of the state in rural affairs. Two different processes, which caused and at the same time were a consequence of state action, intensely marked the rural landscape throughout these years. The first was the privatization process in the big associative enterprises, concentrated but not exclusively located on the coast. The second was the invasions of the social interest agrarian associations (SAIS) by peasant communities in the highlands. Both processes reflect the state's incompetence and laissez-faire attitude, the result of which were the emergence of the Shining Path guerrilla movement and the increasing mobilization of rural interest groups, including peasants.

neglected, unless some other forms of cooperation replaced privatization tendencies.

Another important consequence of parcelization was the narrowing of the labor market. Prior to parcelization, cooperatives provided temporary and even permanent jobs to migrants from the cities and the highlands. Migrants sold their labor much as they had done while the haciendas still existed. The cooperatives employed a huge pool of temporary, landless workers. But *parceleros* tended to prefer family labor in order to reduce labor costs.

Overall *parceleros* suffered from the same economic situation the associative enterprises had to face but at an earlier stage: fluctuating international prices, controlled internal prices, credit problems (both with state banks and private capital), inefficient systems of distribution resulting from an overabundance of intermediaries, delay in payments coming from state agencies, and the lack of storage facilities.

Around 30 percent of the *parceleros* were concentrated in the coastal provinces of Lima, Cañete, Huaral, Chillón, and Huaura. The Departments of La Libertad, Cajamarca, Piura, and Lambayeque—also with large coastal areas—constituted a second region with important levels of parcelization. In these areas the average property size per family was 2.67 acres of highly fertile land. Thus, in terms of land redistribution, the process of parcelization may have been even more important than agrarian reform itself.

Many peasants in rural Peru still rely on llamas for both transportation and for their wool.
(Reproduced with the permission of the General Secretariat of the Organization of American States)

245

Yet even optimists recognized that there were limits to the capacity of *parceleros* to expand production. As demographic pressure increased, land fragmentation seemed to be unavoidable, given the limitations of alternative means of subsistence. As soon as a *parcelero's* property was legalized—meaning that the state recognized his or her property and extended property rights—the *parcelero* was entitled to sell and divide land. Without official recognition property rights remain blurred, hampering transactions to transfer landed property. The land market remained restricted and state credit was not available without official recognition. Control over official recognition and credit gave the state some say in the viability of associative enterprises and the emerging new patterns of land distribution.

In spite of the drawbacks of parcelization in Peru's rural landscape, there were some positive developments born out of this process. Having experienced the benefits of cooperation, coastal peasants and small landholders knew that there were social services and tasks that could not be obtained through individual efforts. As a result many *parceleros* began new cooperative efforts aimed at joining forces to achieve better schooling, health services, and infrastructure, and the active agent was the individual agrarian producer, not the state. This movement brought the practices of coastal *parceleros* close to what peasant communities in the highlands had been doing for centuries.

In several provinces cooperatives were diversified. The formation of loosely defined organizations such as users' agrarian cooperatives (*cooperativas agrarias de usuarios,* CAUs), workers' agrarian cooperatives (*cooperativas agrarias de trabajadores,* CATs), permanent agrarian workers' enterprises (*empresas de trabajadores agrarios permanentes,* ETAPs), and even new peasant communities suggested a willingness to solve problems that reached beyond the organizing capacity of smaller units of production or of individual producers. More than 200 CAUs were founded throughout the country, and 80 percent of these even had communal lands, which served for the payment of common services and sometimes included land that could not be subdivided. Each new entity defined its own commitments. Thus, after subdividing land, new and original processes of cooperative reorganization were visible. In some cases these new processes demonstrated great success in solving managerial problems.

On the political front, though, parcelization produced polarization. Although initially the National Agrarian Organization (Organización Nacional Agraria, or ONA), the organization that included both medium-sized and large landowners, favored the formation in 1985 of

ANAPA for small landowners as a means to strengthen privatization efforts, over the years the organizations came to stand for two distinct ideas of desirable agrarian development: a rural sector populated with small producers or a countryside in which market forces determined the size of landed property. Although many seemed to believe the answer was in small producers, in many places a new process of land concentration had begun.

Conflicts in the Highlands

Parcelization basically occurred within CAPs located in the coastal region. This agrarian reform was less significant in the highlands, where the most heterogeneous rural landscapes were found, as opposed to on the coast, where it intervened on behalf of salaried laborers by giving them first access to production decisions and later control of land itself. In the highlands agrarian reform was basically a result of ongoing fights between community peasants (*comuneros*) and hacendados. Peasant communities and agrarian workers, many of them laboring under sharecropping arrangements, had been struggling for control of land with hacendados and the big agro-industrial owners for decades. The solution proposed by the government was to create SAIS agrarian cooperatives. These were aimed at consolidating enterprises on expropriated haciendas by incorporating their labor force and the surrounding peasant communities.

But in some highland regions agrarian and other progress, if any, became impossible to track systematically. Peru's central-southern departments (such as Ayacucho, Apurímac, and Andahuaylas) became closed to outside scrutiny because of the presence of the Shining Path. Beyond general indicators and anecdotes little was known about the region, and peasants there were victims both of the Shining Path and military repression. Where the Shining Path controlled production no links to the market existed, and links to the state were more tenuous than ever. The only outside force present was the military. Many people fled, or were killed—although no one knows for sure how many. The peasant communities and small landholders of the highlands were not only neglected by the agrarian reform but had never had political rights in preceding centuries. It was among these producers and in their name that the Shining Path started its terrorist activities. Only then did these regions move to the center of political attention.

The diversity of change in the highlands and its results may be illustrated by looking at three quite distinct regions of Peru's rural highlands:

247

Cajamarca (in the northern highlands), Puno (in the southern highlands on the frontier to Bolivia), and Junín (located in the central highlands).

Cajamarca was modernized before the advent of agrarian reform through links to sugar production in the coastal departments of La Libertad and Lambayeque. By 1972 Cajamarca had one of the highest average plot sizes per household in the highlands: 0.64 acres—about five times more than in Ayacucho and other highland regions. Between 1940 and 1981 the rural population decreased only from 86 percent to 79.8 percent. Nearly 3 percent of all the communities incorporated into the new SAISs were located in Cajamarca. By 1988, 70 percent of the agrarian enterprises had undergone parcelization in Cajamarca, following the existing trend toward small holdings with high levels of productivity. With a predominantly mestizo population and few peasant communities, conflicts in this region were almost nonexistent.

In contrast to Cajamarca, Puno and Junín accounted for 25 percent of all peasant communities in Peru. Internal organization of Puno's haciendas varied depending on market proximity and labor availability. In general the haciendas had undergone a very slow process of modernization. Only a few were successfully integrated into expanding wool export markets. Generations of hacendados had divided land among many heirs or had sold it to other landowners and even peasants before the agrarian reform. Thus the hacienda system in Puno and Junín—quite in contrast to coastal haciendas and Cajamarca's haciendas—had already been weakened. Under agrarian reform the larger remaining haciendas were merged into new administrative units.

Puno had the highest percent of family beneficiaries through the formation of SAISs between 1971 and 1988. There, 76 peasant communities received 18,800 acres, which represented 11.7 percent of all the land given to peasant communities in Peru. In Puno, prior to the agrarian reform, peasant communities and smaller communities called *parcialidades* controlled 19.5 percent of the department's land. After agrarian reform this percentage jumped to 30 percent. The large associative enterprises controlled 49 percent of the land, and medium-sized properties accounted for the remainder. Inside the peasant communities land was divided among families. Thus, in spite of the increase of available land, a tacit and rapid parcelization occurred. Annually 13.3 percent of peasant families left the region. This was the highest outmigration rate nationwide. Average plot size in Puno's peasant communities was less than one-sixth of an acre. Natural disasters periodically accentuated poverty so that even those peasant communities that were part of associative enterprises suffered.

The result was an ever-escalating conflict with SAISs over land. Even before the government intervened to solve the land problem, SAISs had already given away 7.8 percent of their lands to peasant communities by 1982. García's government recognized the tensions between SAISs and peasant communities, and engaged in a thorough restructuring process. When the restructuring process began between 1986 and 1987, 44 agrarian enterprises came under scrutiny, and anticipating government intervention, peasant communities invaded SAISs without official permission.

On a national level only 6 percent of all legally recognized peasant communities participated as members in SAISs. Given the low participation of peasant communities in SAIS and CAPs, many demands for hacienda lands (which were typically the most fertile in the respective areas) forwarded by peasant communities remained dormant. Given these patterns it is not surprising that conflicts arose between new associative enterprises and peasant communities.

The few peasant communities in Puno and Junín that gained access to land in the new SAISs soon encountered problems in their relationships with SAIS management. Typical of Puno was the *vía huacchillera*, a traditional cattle-raising pattern by which workers on former haciendas, sometimes linked to surrounding communities, would graze their own cattle on the haciendas' pasture lands. The incorporation of more community members into the SAISs meant that more cattle had to be fed than the meager pasture lands could supply. Soon the new SAISs found themselves confronted with excess labor and declining salaries, thus provoking conflicts between ex-hacienda laborers and community peasants. Similar longstanding disputes over land between the former haciendas and peasant communities had not been solved prior to the creation of the SAIS. These quarrels made concerted action in the SAIS practically impossible. Furthermore these disruptive forces acted as an invitation to the Shining Path. In siding with one of the contending parties, the Shining Path elicited new political loyalties.

Long-term changes in Junín were less dramatic. The reform created cooperatives in which much of the haciendas' former internal organization was retained, and even administrative personnel continued in charge after 1969. This provided a line of continuity in management going back to the 1920s. In contrast to conditions in Puno haciendas in Junín were prosperous and intensely linked to coastal markets. Nevertheless, even in Junín demographic pressure steadily increased. In some peasant communities annual population growth was 2.69 percent; average size of plots was less than one acre and sometimes less than one-half acre. Junín peasants were doomed to look for alternative sources of income: commerce, artisanry, labor in Huancayo and Lima, or work in the cooperatives.

In Junín pressure was exerted by peasant communities in SAISs searching for changes in entrepreneurial leadership. The state proposed that communal and multicommunal enterprises should be constituted on the lands of the SAISs, thus strongly linking peasant communities to the associative enterprises. In Puno pressure originated in peasant communities that were not part of the agrarian enterprises, and changes were forced through invasion.

Reactions in the three highland regions, thus, very much depended on the kind of relationships that had developed between small producers and haciendas and among small producers, haciendas, and peasant communities. In Cajamarca the hacienda system was firmly consolidated, small producers had reasonable portions of land, and peasant communities were almost absent. Parcelization thus followed a long-term pattern of small landholding in the region. In Puno the haciendas were in decay, and peasant communities were strong but had few resources and many open litigations with former haciendas over boundaries and land. The result was violent conflicts between the associative enterprises and surrounding peasant communities. In Junín modern haciendas and peasant communities had found ways to coexist. Coinciding interests made the peasant communities' incorporation into SAIS a relatively smooth process. This was further facilitated by the fact that associative enterprises in this region were—at least in their initial stage—economically successful. Conflicts in Junín resulted from mismanagement. These very broadly described regional disparities had their origins in disparate regional histories and would in the following decades lead to different political options and viewpoints.

14

NEW STRUCTURES AND FUJIMORI (1990–2003)

grarian reform had long term effects on many of the basic power relationships and political structures in Peru. Recent years have witnessed widespread and fundamental shifts, although the nature and ultimate direction of these shifts have seldom been clear to observers. The emergence of ultraviolent groups, such as the Shining Path and MRTA, had a dramatic impact on the nation, as did the election of Alberto Fujimori (1938–   ) in 1990 and his 10 years of increasingly dictatorial rule.

Drift Toward New Structures

Agrarian reform, political violence, and government macroeconomic policies radically changed rural Peru between 1990 and 2003. New political and economic pressures were brought to bear on rural areas, and many of the traditional political structures changed in response. In the past workers on the big coastal plantations were organized either by APRA or by parties of the Left. In the wake of agrarian reform of the 1980s, workers had learned patterns of cooperative entrepreneurial and labor organization from state-created institutions such as the associative enterprises. They had become *parceleros* with their own political organization, ANAPA, whose goals were improvement and progress for the *parcelero,* not just growth. In spite of all its internal disagreements and sometime chaotic behavior, ANAPA aimed to facilitate alliances between industry, agriculture, and ranching. The importance of this small and medium-sized peasants' organization grew to the extent that 1990 presidential candidate Mario Vargas Llosa optimistically believed that *parceleros* could be a significant source of support for his campaign.

The 1990 elections proved otherwise. The election of ANAPA's founder and leader, Germán Gutiérrez Linares, as a deputy for Lima's provinces on the leftist coalition ticket of Izquierda Unida demonstrated that political manipulation in the countryside was no longer easy.

CAPs, SAISs, and ETAPs continuously reexamined their internal organization and, as a result, changed the ways in which their members were represented and their interests defended against external pressures. Mixed cooperatives that tended to combine the advantages of individual effort and associative administration were able to reassess levels of economic efficiency. Other CAPs completely changed their legal composition by becoming joint stock companies whose members not only had a new legal status but in some cases changed political affiliation, joining the political organizations of Peru's large landowners.

New rifts were also visible in other areas. Regional agrarian federations began to compete successfully with long-standing power groups. After 1984 the Regional Agrarian Federation of Piura and Tumbes (Federación Regional Agraria de Piura y Tumbes, FRADEPT)—composed of small and medium-sized producers, communal units of production, peasant communities, and agrarian cooperatives—successfully challenged one of Peru's most important power groups, the Grupo Romero. Although the federation controlled only 30 percent of cotton production, the FRADEPT managed to establish cotton prices to the benefit of many producers. This success propelled the emergence of new associative models and redistributive patterns in several sectors of the agricultural economy.

In the highlands the picture was more confusing. Until 1990 only 4 percent of the peasant communities benefited from land distribution after peasants had invaded SAISs lands and organized communal enterprises. Elsewhere some invaded land was eventually abandoned resulting in much disorder. In part this was a result of the long-standing boundary disputes between haciendas and peasant communities, among peasant communities, between associative enterprises and peasant communities, and between peasant communities and small landholders both within and outside peasant communities.

In Junín the Shining Path completely devastated the existing infrastructure and then reorganized peasant production without addressing conflicts over land or the distribution of land. Peasants reacted by trying to reorganize their communities to confront the Shining Path, even amid profound political unrest.

The Shining Path at its peak controlled about one-third of the country. In the face of this rural dominance the government organized poorly equipped peasant militias, called *rondas campesinas*. *Rondas* first appeared in Cuyumalca (Cajamarca) in 1976 as a peasant response to increasing cattle theft. The *rondas* suffered persecution from local state authorities and the police until 1986, when they were officially recognized. In 1989, the Roman Catholic bishop José Antonio Dammert of Cajamarca helped organize the first regional *ronda* organization, many of whose leaders were evangelical Protestants. *Rondas* had an air of popular justice or "direct democracy" because their anger was often directed against corrupt local judges and political authorities. They represented a new political culture, which in the eyes of some analysts and peasant communities aided the government in resisting the spread of the Shining Path. By 1991 there were 3,435 *ronda* committees covering an area of 50,000 square miles on the coast and the northern highlands, where few peasant communities existed. Imitating the *ronda campesina* model, the government tried to institute similar self-defense organizations (sometimes called the *rondas falsas*) in other parts of the country, and some *ronda* leaders received much journalistic coverage decrying the threat of an imminent civil war between the *rondas* and the Shining Path.

SAISs no longer seemed to represent a viable alternative for peasant communities. Peasant communities still organized within the Peruvian Peasant Confederation (Confederación Campesina del Perú, known as CCP), and the National Agrarian Confederation (Confederación Nacional Agrania, known as CNA) turned its attention back to the state. This was reinforced by the promise of President Alberto Fujimori, who had defeated Vargas Llosa in 1990, to support and defend peasant communities. However, due to the experience of the agrarian reform, in the course of the last two decades peasant communities' expectations have increased, and so has their capacity to exert pressure on the government. If the government does not listen, peasant communities are now more ready to act in defense of their interests, either militarily by forming militias and invading lands they have long been asking for, or politically by seeking to participate in the government's decisions about fiscal and monetary policies. At the end of 1991, president Fujimori issued a decree that ultimately dismantled the initial social character of the agrarian reform. This decree removed all restrictions on the sale of land and agrarian enterprises. It was the beginning of a long and thorough privatization program that ultimately also included all previously state-owned public enterprises.

At the other end of the social spectrum the agrarian middle class survived the agrarian reform and reorganized itself. It moved into export crops on the coast and in the jungle region, obtained access to cheap credit and export subsidies, and successfully joined the regional trade organization the Acuerdo de Cartagena. An alliance with cooperatives partially solved the disputes over land ownership and tenure between the agrarian middle class and the peasants. As a result, the government continued to support industry in rural areas in spite of the prevailing rhetoric about liberalization and privatization.

In the highlands former hacendados (and their heirs) regained access to portions of their haciendas and became—with state aid—a part of a new and more dynamic landed elite. The reduction of the landed estates and hacendados' own distrust of Indian and mestizo laborers succeeded where centuries of sporadic uprisings and national trade policies had failed: It forced hacendados to improve the technology of production. Some worked in close connection with international agencies and development projects. In some areas a complete new spectrum of modernizing owners—some of foreign origin—developed new agrarian-based projects, such as trout, shrimp, and cheese.

New trends also appeared in the jungle, a region often overlooked as part of the rural landscape. The jungle region has never been a priority for agrarian reform for any government since 1969, but colonization projects were started to ameliorate through relocation the pressure on land in the highlands. In the "lower jungle" (selva baja), seven special developmental projects carried out one of the most ambitious colonization projects ever initiated, but the major development in the jungle region was the emergence of a massive coca growing industry.

A mildly narcotic leaf used by the Inca for divination and ritual and today, following custom, chewed by Indians and mestizos alike for its stimulative effects, coca can be chemically altered to make cocaine. In recent decades coca became one of Peru's most important export crops with a boom in cultivation and trade dating from the 1970s. Colombian narcotraffickers moved into the regions bordering the Huallaga River, from which they organized production and export of cocaine. In 1982 coca exports produced $850 million, which represented approximately 25 percent of Peru's total agrarian production. Coca transactions carried out in Peru in 1988 amounted to between $1.5 billion and $2 billion, from which around $600 million to $800 million remained in Peru. In that year half of the world's supply of coca paste came from Peru.

The growing number of coca producers were outside any kind of government control and immune to government-structured incentives. The Shining Path, the military, and drug lords competed for control, and from very early on the United States exerted pressure on Peruvian governments to deal with the massive growth of coca production. The first attempts to curtail the production of coca had come under the presidency of Morales Bermúdez in the 1970s. Many control and eradication efforts followed, mostly funded by the United States. While the Peruvian military was engaged in suppressing coca production, the Shining Path managed to organize small coca producers, providing them protection against drug traffickers and the military. The Shining Path also exacted taxes from drug traffickers and allowed contacts between peasants and drug traffickers only after they paid the imposed taxes. The revenues obtained allowed the Shining Path to expand its recruitment efforts by paying salaries to its members that were higher than the official salaries of a general in the Peruvian army.

Open confrontations among the Shining Path, the military, and the drug traffickers followed and reached a peak in 1986 with the takeover by the Shining Path of the town of Tocache, the coca capital of the jungle. Then in 1987 the competing marxist guerrilla group MRTA attempted to oust the Shining Path from Tocache but was defeated. It was calculated that at the time more than 100,000 acres were cultivated with coca in the Peruvian Amazon, employing approximately a quarter million people. In large measure because of the connections among drug traffickers, coca producers, and terrorists, much of the money provided by the United States to eradicate coca production and dealers was spent on fighting domestic terrorism rather than on alternative development projects in the agrarian sector.

In tandem with this process native groups in the Amazon began to organize politically. For the first time they had gained status as a social force through organized action under the political leadership of leftist-inspired organizations (the CUNA and the CCP). Violent struggles between the state and Indian organizations, as well as among the military, the police, and drug lords, became a vivid part of the redefinition of political boundaries and actions.

Political Fallout of Agrarian Reform

Although rapid changes in Peru's rural landscape over the past two decades make it difficult to identify an overarching direction for political development, there have been several trends.

In the past, immediate economic considerations and political pressures often defined policy making. The urgency of change left little room for anything but improvisation. Under numerous differing governmental policies and bureaucratic inefficiency, patterns of land tenure and rural organization irrevocably changed. An underlying feature of these changes has been the overwhelming trend toward privatization of the associative enterprises created in the wake of the agrarian reform. Nevertheless, privatization did not imply the dismissal of cooperative efforts. In some cases cooperative initiatives represented a successful answer to organizing distribution and transportation and to providing better public services.

Another, more social, solution to agrarian questions was based on the continued existence of peasant communities. In fact, the agrarian reform and its varied consequences reinforced peasant communities: In Puno peasant communities organized land invasions to assert their rights on disputed lands from haciendas and associative enterprises; in Junín peasant communities resorted to their traditional communal organization to confront the Shining Path; and in Cajamarca and Junín peasant communities developed and expanded entrepreneurship to successfully manage their associative enterprises.

Along with patterns of land holding Peru's political landscape changed dramatically. It became obvious that there was no single state-guided transformation of the agrarian sector but several quite distinct initiatives brought to the political forefront by Indians, peasants, small producers, and rural enterprises. The initiative shifted from the government to society's organized social groups. Peasants and rural workers took the lead in asserting social projects that they hoped would reach beyond the government and beyond the Shining Path. Emerging rural options offered visions of a country very different from that encountered at the end of the 1960s.

It is likely that the Shining Path understood the meaning of this shift much better than the Peruvian government did. To gain power and exert influence the Shining Path not only took part in rural conflicts but also tried to disrupt Peruvian society at several levels of civil organization. The Shining Path encountered extensive resistance in those areas with strong self-organization (the *rondas* in Cajamarca, the peasant communities in Puno), and moved its headquarters to Lima, funding itself by deals with the drug lords in the Amazon.

The Unexpected Fujimori

When one of Peru's most brilliant writers and novelists, Mario Vargas Llosa, ran for president in 1990, his most visible opponents were APRA and some leftist groups. Vargas Llosa, who in his early writings showed a leftist, *aprista* leaning, in 1990 became the chosen candidate of a rightist alliance known as the FREDEMO (Frente Democrático, or Democratic Front). A kind of cultural revolution and a radical liberalism character-

Internationally renowned novelist Mario Vargas Llosas gives a speech at a campaign stop during his unsuccessful run for president in 1990. (Alejandro Balaguer photo)

ized his electoral campaign. Vargas Llosa's announcement of an austere economic neoliberal adjustment policy, which called for a movement toward a free-market economy and the elimination of most government subsidies, estranged him from Peru's popular classes, who feared the possible consequences of his economic plan: an even lower standard of living, higher prices for essential goods, and unemployment.

Out of these fears stoked by APRA and the Left emerged Alberto Fujimori, who until then was practically unknown in political circles. He was an agrarian engineer, the son of Japanese immigrants, partially educated in the United States, and a former chancellor of the National Agrarian University. His campaign theme was straightforward and simple: "Technology, honesty, and jobs." Identified as part of a successful Japanese colony in Lima whose members were known for their efficiency, discipline, and honesty, Fujimori won the presidential elections with his Cambio '90 party. In the first voting round Vargas Llosa received 28 percent of the votes and Fujimori only 25 percent. A second round was called for, and APRA and the Left endorsed Fujimori's candidacy. He polled 57 percent of the votes. No one could even guess what Fujimori would do.

Fujimori first moved to open Peru's economy to the world. Once again a market economy was given free rein, and the state retreated into minimal administrative business and public services. Businesses became privatized, and efficiency ranked high in the presidential rhetoric. Very closely following a concept that Vargas Llosa had espoused during his presidential campaign, Fujimori engaged in a "shock treatment" of the Peruvian economy, an austerity program he considered necessary to reduce inflation and fiscal deficit, and thus, to align internal prices with international prices. As expected, prices increased. To make things worse, a cholera outbreak struck Lima, and 320,000 people were infected in 1991 alone.

Fujimori met increasing opposition in parliament, and twice he had to change his minister of economics. In April 1992 he staged what has been called an auto-coup by aligning with the military. He suspended the constitution and shut down congress, the judiciary, and regional governments. Mostly as a result of international pressures Fujimori had to announce elections for a new congress with a new constitution (the 12th in Peru's republican history) that allowed presidents to be reelected. In September 1992 the national police captured Shining Path leader Abimael Guzmán and some of his closest followers. Although domestic terrorist activities did not completely subside after this, the country suffered much less from terrorist attacks and the fears they inspired.

With this political capital in his hands Fujimori began to fiercely privatize public enterprises. Between 1991 and 1998 the sale of state-owned

Alberto Fujimori, while campaigning for the presidency (Alejandro Balaguer photo)

Abimael Guzmán, the leader of the Shining Path terrorist organization, was captured and put on public display in September 1992. The activities of Shining Path declined following Guzmán's and other leaders' capture. (Alejandro Balaguer photo)

enterprises and bonds to private buyers amounted to $8.65 billion. Capital from the United States, Spain, Chile, and China was most prominent among these purchases. The most spectacular amount paid was from Spain, when it purchased all Peruvian telephone services for more than $2 billion. A Lima newspaper commented ironically that this was the return of Atahualpa's ransom. As a result, however, the number of telephone lines increased from 643,000 to 1.92 million, and service reached for the first time poor urban dwellers and small towns that had never before seen a telephone.

Privatization also reached peasant communities. Farm cooperatives, which carried an enormous debt on their shoulders, had to either become shareholding enterprises or disappear. Still, in 1996 only 971,000 plots of land out of a total of 5.718 million were properly registered by their owners. By 1995, there were 6,872 highland and Amazon native communities, who possessed 32.5 percent of the cultivable land, when a new law allowed peasant communities to sell their land. Export's held steady throughout the 1990s, both in terms of what was exported and the value of exports, which lent stability to the economy overall and reduced inflationary pressures on the middle and lower classes.

In December 1996, a year after Fujimori's reelection, MRTA guerrillas captured and occupied the official residence of the Japanese ambassador in Lima, taking hostage 452 people who were attending a celebration in honor of the Japanese emperor's birthday. Fujimori had left the building shortly before the attack and escaped capture, but his

Exports, 1990–1999 (Percentage of Total Exports)			
	1990	1997	1999
Sea produce	12.3	16.5	9.8
Agrarian products	4.9	6.9	4.6
Minerals	41.9	39.9	49.2
Petroleum	7.3	5.5	4.0
Nontraditional exports	28.0	30.0	30.6
Others	5.6	1.2	1.8
Total in billions of U.S. dollars	$3.321	$6.814	$6.114

Source: Contreras and Cueto (2000, 358)

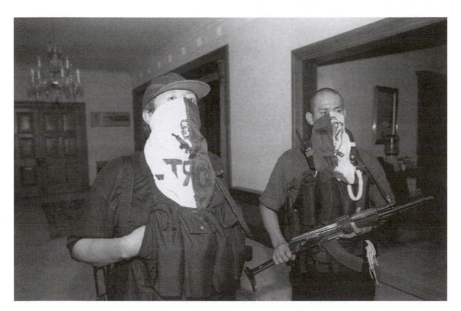

In December 1996 members of the marxist guerrilla group MRTA captured the residence of the Japanese ambassador in Peru and seized hostages. The MRTA negotiated with authorities for several months and held frequent news conferences. Two of the terrorist leaders, Cerpa (left) and Árabe (right), are shown here at one of the conferences with the media. All the occupiers were subsequently killed in a government assault. (Alejandro Balaguer photo)

brother, several of Peru's highest-ranking officials, and the Japanese ambassador were there when the guerrillas occupied the compound. The MRTA terrorists demanded the release of several hundred political prisoners in return for the freedom of the hostages (they released most of the women early on). After several months of fruitless negotiations, followed closely around the world, Fujimori ordered an attack on the embassy in April 1997. All terrorists were killed and all the hostages rescued, save for one man who died of a heart attack. The triumph over MRTA reaffirmed Fujimori's popularity.

The Fall of Fujimori

After successfully sidestepping the single-term limit to the presidency by having the constitution rewritten, Fujimori, now prepared for his campaign for a third term as president. Despite the apparent successes of his presidency, however, he faced increasing opposition, particularly since the economic situation was worsening. El Niño hit again in 1997–98, setting off another round of agricultural crises, and the financial collapse of the Asian countries at the same time meant that anticipated new investments from that source were cut off. The internal growth rate in Peru moved close to zero, credit became tight, and unemployment rose.

Fujimori's response was to tighten his control of the country, acting in tandem with the military to consolidate power. To continue the fight against terrorism, he declared several regions "emergency zones" and placed army generals in command. The former *rondas* that had fought against the Shining Path were now invited—with much publicity—to deliver social services. These maneuvers were labeled as "Fujipopulism" or as Fujimori's "Chinochet" policy, playing on his Asian heritage and his adoption of an outlook similar to Chile's general Augusto Pinochet, who came to power by a coup d'état. Fujimori also moved to silence his political opposition and exerted an increased control on mass media.

Fujimori's chief opponent for election in 2000 was Alejandro Toledo (1946–), an Indian from a poor family with 15 brothers and sisters. Toledo overcame the handicaps of his ethnic and economic background with academic brilliance, winning a scholarship to the University of San Francisco and eventually earning a Ph.D. in economics from Stanford University in California. He had served as minister of labor under Belaúnde Terry and as an adviser to the World Bank. During the campaign, he was known as "El Cholo" (a denigrating term to refer to acculturated Indians) in reference to his ethnic background. Fujimori won more votes than Toledo, but he was just short of the 50 percent needed to win outright. Although he alleged the vote had been fixed, Toledo conceded the election and withdrew from the projected runoff.

Just when Fujimori seemed on the brink of a third term and appeared to be in firm control, his hold on power and office began to crumble in a hail of complicated scandals and public disgraces. Most of the difficulty revolved around Vladimiro Montesinos, a rather shadowy figure who served as the head of the notorious National Intelligence Service (Servicio de Inteligencia Nacional, or SIN). A former army officer, Montesinos had for years been a power behind the scenes in Peru, often manipulating politicians and office holders through the power of his secret information and dossiers. During Fujimori's administration, he also headed many of the efforts to suppress the coca traffic between Peruvian growers and Colombian drug lords.

However, in September 2000, the Peruvian public was treated to the broadcast of a stolen video tape that showed Montesinos bribing a congressman in a move that was designed to help cover up the sale of arms to Colombian guerrillas. As the revelations began to pile up, it became apparent that Montesinos had been playing the role of double agent for several years and had siphoned off millions upon millions of dollars into Swiss bank accounts. He was also accused of sanctioning the worst of the repressive measures taken by the military against innocent peasants during the war against the Shining Path. Montesinos's relationships with drug lords, the U.S. Central Intelligence Agency, arms dealers, and politicians appeared to be a labyrinth of manipulation and corruption, and Fujimori was closely tied to his chief of intelligence.

Montesinos tried to flee to Panama but went into hiding in Peru when his requests for asylum were refused. He eventually escaped to temporary sanctuary in Venezuela. His disgrace, however, brought Fujimori's reign to an end: In November 2000, while in Asia for a meeting of national leaders, Fujimori diverted his trip to Japan, where he claimed residence based on his parents' Japanese citizenship and faxed to congress his resignation as president of Peru. The following June Montesinos was arrested in Venezuela and returned to Peru for trial. Eventually he was convicted of embezzlement (on relatively minor counts) and sentenced to prison. Fujimori remained in Japan, which refused to extradite him, despite his being placed on the most-wanted

The corrupt former head of Peruvian intelligence, Vladimiro Montesinos, at his arraignment before a Peruvian judge in June 2001 after his capture in Venezuela (Alejandro Balaguer photo)

263

list by Interpol, the international police agency, and indicted by the Peruvian congress on charges of treason in 2003.

Alejandro Toledo: First Indian President

In the wake of Fujimori's defection and resignation, the Peruvian congress set up an interim government and scheduled a new presidential election for May 2001. Previous presidential candidate Alejandro Toledo immediately declared candidacy under the banner of his Perú Posible party. His principal opponents were Lourdes Flores, who had been a congressional deputy and was the first woman to make a serious run at the presidency, and former president Alan García, who had only recently returned from nine years of self-imposed exile in Colombia. García had ended his presidency in 1990 in disgrace and defeat with the nation suffering from raging inflation, a huge national debt, and devastating internal warfare between the government and the Shining Path guerrillas. In 2001, however, García reinvigorated the electoral machinery of his *aprista* party and attempted to brush aside the baggage of his past failures by appealing to younger voters who had only vague knowledge of his first term of office.

Under the 1993 constitution, a presidential candidate needed more than 50 percent of the vote in order to win outright. After the first round of balloting, which international observers declared to be honest and fair, Toledo was in the lead but had only 36 percent of the vote. García and Flores finished in nearly a dead heat with around 25 percent each (splinter party candidates got the balance), but García's slight edge moved him on into a run-off against Toledo in early June. The campaign was vicious, with García accusing Toledo of cocaine use, fathering an illegitimate daughter, visiting prostitutes, and misappropriation of campaign funds. Nevertheless, the presidency was decided when Toledo won 53.1 percent of the ballots; García finished with 46.9 percent.

Alejandro Toledo thus became the first Indian president of Peru, and he opened his term of office with a burst of rhetoric that celebrated Peru's native people and their heritage, promising that he would reform government corruption and, most important, deliver jobs and prosperity to the disadvantaged and poverty stricken. As an academically trained economist and former adviser to the World Bank, Toledo believed in the neoliberal doctrine that called for a free-market economic policy coupled with a program of domestic economic austerity, privatization, and an avoidance of further national debt, which he hoped, would lead eventually, to deep-reaching prosperity and high employment. He agreed to follow a macroeconomic plan along these lines, laid out for Peru by the International Monetary Fund (IMF), and he surrounded himself during his first months in office with experts and academics.*

While Toledo's economic program had success insofar as the Peruvian economy as a whole grew during his first two years in office at an annual rate of around 5 percent, surpassing most other South American countries, the jobs he had promised at his inauguration failed to materialize, and everyday Peruvians saw little or no improvement in their lives. Many Peruvians also were opposed to the Toledo government's neoliberal, free-market policies and IMF agreement. The first major sign of unrest came in June 2002, when strikes and riots broke out in Arequipa over a proposal to privatize two local power stations. Toledo declared a temporary state of emergency in the city and tried to stifle the protest, but in the end, the government had to rescind the privatization plans.

Throughout the balance of 2002 and into the first months of 2003, protests and anger over several economic and political issues continued to grow, reaching a boiling point in March 2003. During the 1990s, the Peruvian government had succeeded in curtailing coca production, but when the government of neighboring Colombia launched a U.S.-financed campaign against coca growers in 2000 and 2001, the pressure forced producers back into Peru. Peruvian farmers began to assert themselves politically, and in the spring of 2003, they brought pressure on Toledo's government with demonstrations and protest marches. Coca farmers challenged the long-standing U.S.-supported government program to suppress coca growing in the eastern jungle provinces. The farmers argued they were not involved in producing illegal drugs but rather were only following centuries-old indigenous traditions by raising the mildly narcotic coca, even though the plants indeed provided the raw material for the manufacture of cocaine. Toledo's popularity continued to plummet, and by May 2003 his approval ratings in national polls had fallen to 15 percent.

A widespread crisis developed late in the same month, when teachers, public employees, farmers, and health workers went on strike, shutting down transportation, public service, and health care in several regions. The strikers demanded salary increases from the government,

---

*Author's note: Many of my former colleagues at the Catholic University in Lima and the Institute of Peruvian Studies, the largest private research institute in the country, served from 2001 to 2002 at the side of President Alejandro Toledo, governing the country and hoping to build a better future for Peru. In 2003, they were replaced by more "loyal" political cadres.

but Toledo responded that there was no money in the national treasury to pay for significant raises for the workers without violating the policies laid down by the IMF. The workers response was to organize large-scale protests. They staged marches in Lima, shut down public schools all over the country, occupied public office buildings in several provincial capitals, and blocked key highways.

In June, Toledo declared a state of emergency and sent troops to put down the protests. In the city of Puno, troops fired on rock-throwing student protesters, killing one and wounding several more. Elsewhere, troops fired tear gas and turned fire hoses on protesters. The strikers responded by staging a 20,000-person march in Lima to protest the state of emergency. By mid-year, an uneasy peace had been reestablished after Toledo reshuffled his cabinet and promised the nation a renewed effort to improve the lives of average workers. His approval ratings, however, had fallen to an all-time low of 11 percent. Toledo's presidency, which had begun with such high expectations, was damaged, perhaps fatally, and no one was willing to predict the political future. Few people today believe that there will be anything noticeable for which Alejandro Toledo will enter future history books.

Appendix 1

Basic Facts About Peru

Official Name
República del Perú (Republic of Peru)

Government
The 1993 constitution makes the president (currently Alejandro Toledo, elected in 2001) both chief of state and head of the government. The president is elected by a plurality of the popular vote for a five-year term. Run-off elections are held between the two top vote getters in the event no single candidate receives a plurality in the first election. There are also two vice presidents and a prime minister, but the president exercises all executive powers. The national legislative body is the unicameral 120-member Congress of the Republic of Peru, whose members are elected by popular vote for five-year terms. The members of the Supreme Court of Justice are appointed by a National Council of the Judiciary. The Peruvian Aprista Party (Alliance for Popular Revolution in America) is the longest-standing national party, founded in the 1920s, and has elected one president, Alan García (1985–90), who also finished second in the 2001 presidential elections. Other parties form around specific presidential candidates: President Toledo was elected as leader of his Perú Posible party; his predecessor, Alberto Fujimori (1990–2000), ran under the banner of the Cambio '90 Party. Other recent major parties that fielded presidential candidates or elected members to Congress are Acción Popular, Frente Moralizador Independiente, Unidad Nacional, Solución Popular, Somos Perú, and Unión para el Perú.

Political Divisions

Capital
Lima was founded in 1535 by Francisco Pizarro.

Departments

Peru is divided into 24 departments and one constitutional province (Callao). These are subdivided into 194 provinces, 1,828 districts, and 69,951 towns.

Geography

Area

Peru covers an area of approximately 496,223 square miles (1.28 million square kilometers) and comprises extremely diverse regions, including the Pacific coast, the towering mountains of the Andes, high plains known as the altiplano or *puna*, eastern mountain slopes called the *montaña*, and the rain forests *(selva)* of the Amazon basin that take up almost 60 percent of the nation's land mass. Peru is slightly larger in area than neighboring Bolivia and four and a half times the size of Ecuador. It is roughly one-seventh the size of the United States.

Boundaries

Peru is bordered on the west by the Pacific Ocean, by Ecuador and Colombia to the north, Brazil and Bolivia in the east, and Chile to the south.

Topography

The western coast *(costa),* is mountainous and arid, from 10 to 100 miles inland. The Andes in the center (sierra), which cover 27 percent of the land area, are among the world's highest and most rugged mountains. High-altitude grasslands *(puna)* cover about a quarter of the sierra, widening to an extensive plateau (altiplano) in the south and into Bolivia. Eastern lowlands include semitropical forests on the mountain slopes *(montaña)* and thick jungles *(selva)*. About 3 percent of the land is arable, 21 percent meadows and pastureland, and 55 percent forested. About 1 percent is irrigated.

Climate

The climate is extremely dry along the coast but temperate in the highland valleys. Temperatures in the *puna* and on the western slopes of the mountains are harsh and chilly. It is semitropical in the *montaña* and tropical in the *selva*. In the higher mountains the climate is arctic. The rainy season runs from October through April, and it is dry the rest of the year.

Highest Elevation

The highest peak is Huascarán at 22,205 feet in the Andes.

Demographics

Population

The population of Peru was estimated in July 2003 as 28.4 million people, making it twice as populous as Chile and nearly three and a half times larger than Bolivia. Only Brazil, Argentina, and Colombia in South America have larger populations than Peru.

Largest Cities

Lima, the capital of Peru, is by far the largest city, estimated to have more than 7.5 million residents. It has grown extremely rapidly over the last two decades due to a large internal migration of population from the highlands to Lima. The nation's second largest city is Arequipa in the south with a population of 710,000. Callao, the port city for Lima, is third largest at 424,295.

Language

A majority of the population speaks Spanish. It and Quechua, the language of the descendants of the Incas, are the official languages. There is a relatively small minority of native Aymara speakers and several native languages survive in the Amazon basin.

Ethnic Groups

Forty-five percent of the population are Native Americans, and of these, 47 percent are Quechua, 5.4 percent Aymara, and the rest various Amazon tribes. Mestizos comprise 37 percent of the general population. Whites, blacks, Asians, and other ethnic groups make up the balance.

Population Distribution

The overall population density is 56 persons per square mile, but the population is distributed very unevenly, with a high concentration in the coastal region and Lima, where more than a quarter of the population lives. Only about 25 percent of the population lives outside the cities. Slightly more than a third of the population is under the age of 14 years, and only 5 percent older than 65 years. Life expectancy is 68 years for men and more than 73 years for women.

Religion

More than 90 percent of the Peruvian population is Roman Catholic, with a small minority of Protestants and Mormons.

Economy

Gross Domestic Product (GDP)

$132 billion (2002 estimate)
Per capita GDP, $4,800 (2002 estimate)

Currency
Nuevo sol = 100 céntimos (3.477 = US$1 [October 2003])

Imports
$7.3 billion (2002)—from United States, 23.9 percent; from Chile, 8.2 percent

Exports
$7.6 billion (2002)—to United States, 25.2 percent; Switzerland, 8 percent; to China, 6.3 percent; to Japan, 5.6 percent

Tourism
$913 million (1999)

Business

Industrial
Fishing, mining, food processing, textiles

Minerals
Copper, silver, gold, iron

Crude Oil Reserves
614.7 million barrels (2002 estimate)

Agricultural
Coffee, cotton, sugar, rice

Livestock
4.9 million cattle, 81.3 million chickens, 2.07 million goats, 2.79 million pigs, 14.4 million sheep

Transportation
Railroads, 1,318 miles
Passenger cars, 500,000
Commercial vehicles, 275,000
Aviation, 1.8 billion passenger miles (27 airports)
Ports, Callao, Chimbote, Matarani, Salaverry

Communications
Television, 85 per 1,000 population (140 stations)
Radios, 221 per 1,000 population
Daily newspapers, 87 per 1,000 population

Appendix 2

CHRONOLOGY

Prehistoric and Inca

10,000 B.C.	First identifiable cultures in area of modern-day Peru
500	Chavín culture flourishes
	Nazca and Mochica cultures flourish
A.D. 500	Tiwanaku culture emerges
750	Huari culture develops
c. 1200	Chimor Kingdom and Inca dynasty are established
1438–71	Inca conquest begins under Pachacútec; Chimor is absorbed
1471–93	Topa Inca Yupanqui extends conquests
1493–1525	Huayna Capac consolidates the Inca Empire
1526–32	Civil war between Huáscar and Atahualpa

Conquest

1531	Francisco Pizarro lands on Peruvian coast
1532–33	Francisco Pizarro captures and executes Atahualpa and takes Cuzco; Inca Empire falls
1535	City of Lima is founded by Pizarro
1536	Manco Inca leads his people in a failed attempt to drive out the Spaniards
1537	Diego de Almagro seizes Cuzco
1538	Hernando Pizarro defeats and executes Almagro
1541	Francisco Pizarro is assassinated by Almagro partisans
1546	Gonzalo Pizarro instigates coup; Viceroy Blasco Núñez Vela is killed
1548	Pedro de La Gasca restores Spanish authority and executes Gonzalo Pizarro

Colonial Period

1551	Antonio de Mendoza, the second viceroy, arrives
1572	Fifth viceroy, Francisco Toledo, executes Inca leader Tupac Amaru after second failed Inca uprising
1700	Last Spanish Hapsburg king Charles II dies and is succeeded by Philip V, a Bourbon and grandson of Louis XIV of France
1701–14	War of Spanish Succession
1739	Philip V creates the Viceroyalty of New Granada
1767	Jesuits are expelled from Spanish territories
1776	Viceroyalty of Río de la Plata is created
1780	José Gabriel Condorcanqui, calling himself Tupac Amaru II, leads another Inca revolt. He is defeated and executed the following year
1782	Intendancy system is established; Peru is divided into seven intendancies
1808	Napoleon Bonaparte makes his brother Joseph king of Spain
1809	Spaniards crush rebellions in Quito, La Paz, and Chuquisaca
1810	Buenos Aires declares independence

Liberation

1818	General José de San Martín defeats royalists in Chile
1820	Rebel forces under San Martín land in Peru
1821	San Martín declares Peruvian independence
1822	San Martín meets with Simón Bolívar and abandons efforts in Peru
1823	Bolívar arrives in Peru and assumes power
1824	Peruvian royalists are defeated in Battles of Junín and Ayacucho

Independent Peru

1827	José de La Mar is named president by Peruvian congress
1829	Agustín Gamarra seizes presidency in a coup d'état
1839	First contract signed to export guano
1863	Congress makes the sol Peru's currency
1864–66	Spanish-Peruvian war

1872	Manuel Pardo becomes Peru's first civilian president
1879–83	War of the Pacific against Chile
1881	Chile occupies Lima
1883	Peace treaty frees Peru from foreign occupation
1886	Andrés Cáceres elected president
1889	President Cáceres signs Grace Contract with British creditors
1895	Nicolás Piérola takes presidential office as a result of civil War
1899	Eduardo López de Romaña elected president
1908	Augusto B. Leguía becomes president
1912	Augusto Billinghurst becomes president as result of workers strike
1915	Military deposes Billinghurst and installs Oscar Benavides

Modern Peru

1919–30	Augusto Leguía begins second presidency
1924	Alliance for Popular Revolution in America (APRA) is founded by exiled Víctor Raúl Haya de la Torre
1932	Government puts down *aprista* uprising in Trujillo and executes 5,000
1941	Peru takes Amazon territory from Ecuador after brief war
1945	Civilian government of José Luis Bustamante, backed by APRA, is installed
1948	General Manuel Odría takes power in military coup
1963	Return to civilian rule with Fernando Belaúnde Terry
1968	Leftist military coup by General Juan Velasco Alvarado
1968–75	Wide-scale agrarian reform under military government
1975	Velasco ousted in coup by General Francisco Morales Bermúdez
1980	Civilian rule returns with reelection of Belaúnde Terry; Shining Path guerrillas begin campaign against the "fascist state"

273

1981	War with Ecuador over borders
1980s	Three-way war in Peru among government troops, Shining Path guerrillas, and drug traffickers
1985	Alan García becomes first elected *aprista* president
1990	Alberto Fujimori wins presidency in surprise victory
1992	Fujimori suspends constitution with military support
2000	Fujimori wins third term but later in year seeks asylum in Japan, resigning as president amid scandal
2001	Alejandro Toledo is elected as Peru's first president of Indian background
2002	Riots and strikes force Toledo to declare state of emergency and to reorganize cabinet
2003	Beatriz Merino is named Peru's first woman prime minister; strikes, widespread protests, and violence lead to second state-of-emergency declaration by Toledo; state-appointed "Truth Commission" reports more than 60,000 deaths caused by military and Shining Path between 1980 and 1991
2004	Corruption scandals force Toledo to replace cabinet members, vice president, and prime minister; Fujimori campaigns for scheduled 2006 presidential election from exile in Japan

Appendix 3

Bibliography

Adorno, Rolena. *Guaman Poma: Writing and Resistance in Colonial Peru*. Austin: University of Texas Press, 1986.

Aguirre, Carlos. *Agentes de su propia libertad: Los esclavos de Lima y la desintegración de la esclavitud, 1821–1854*. Lima: Pontificia Universidad Católica del Perú, 1993.

Aguirre, Carlos, and Charles Walker, eds. *Bandoleros, abigeos y montoneros en el Perú republicano*. Lima: Instituto de Apoyo Agrario, 1990.

Amayo, Enrique. *La política británica en la guerra del Pacífico*. Lima: Editorial Horizonte, 1988.

Anna, Timothy E. *The Fall of the Royal Government in Peru*. Lincoln: University of Nebraska Press, 1979.

Assadourian, Carlos S. *El sistema de la economía colonial: Mercado interno, regiones y espacio económico*. Lima: Instituto de Estudios Peruanos, 1982.

Bakewell, Peter. *A History of Latin America: Empires and Sequels, 1450–1930*. Malden, Mass.: Blackwell Publishers, 1997.

———. *Miners of the Red Mountain: Indian Labor in Potosi, 1545–1650*. Albuquerque: University of New Mexico Press, 1984.

Balbi, Carmen Rosa. *Identidad clasista en el sindicalismo: Su impacto en las fábricas*. Lima: Centro de Estudios y Promoción de Desarrollo, 1989.

Bardella, Gianfranco. *Un siglo en la vida económica del Perú*. Lima: Banco de Crédito del Perú, 1989.

Basadre, Jorge. *Elecciones y centralismo en el Perú*. Lima: Centro de Investigación de la Universidad del Pacífico, 1980.

———. *Historia de la República del Perú, 1822–1933*. 10 vols. 7th ed. Lima: Editorial Universitaria, 1983.

———. *La vida y historia*. Lima: Industrial Gráfica, 1981.

Bauer, Brian. *The Development of the Inca State*. Austin: University of Texas Press, 1992.

Bauer, Brian, and David S. P. Dearborn. *Astronomy and Empire in the Ancient Andes: The Cultural Origins of Inca Sky Watching.* Austin: University of Texas Press, 1995.

Belaúnde, Víctor Andrés. *Meditaciones peruanas.* Lima: Compañía de Impresiones y Publicidad, 1932.

Boloña, Carlos. *Cambio de rumbo: El programa económico para los 90.* Lima: Instituto de Economía de Libre Mercado, 1993.

————. *Políticas arancelarias en el Perú, 1880–1980.* Lima: Instituto de Economía de Libre Mercado, 1994.

Bonfiglio, Giovanni. *La presencia europea en el Perú.* Lima: Fondo Editorial del Congreso del Perú, 2001.

Bonilla, Heraclio. *Gran Bretaña y el Perú, 1826–1919. Informes de los cónsules británicos.* 4 vols. Lima: Instituto de Estudios Peruanos, Fondo del Libro del Banco Industrial del Perú, 1977.

————. *Guano y burguesía en el Perú.* Lima: Instituto de Estudios Peruanos, 1974.

Bonilla, Heraclio, and Karen Spalding. *La independencia en el Perú: Las palabras y los hechos.* Lima: Instituto de Estudios Peruanos, 1980.

Bourricaud, François. *Poder y sociedad en el Perú.* Lima: Instituto de Estudios Peruanos, Instituto Francés de Estudios Andinos, 1989.

Bowser, Frederick. *The African Slave Trade in Colonial Peru, 1524–1650.* Stanford, Calif.: Stanford University Press, 1974.

Boyd-Bowman, Peter. *Patterns of Spanish Emigration to the New World (1493–1580).* Buffalo: Council of International Studies, State University of New York at Buffalo, 1973.

Brading, David A. *Miners and Merchants in Bourbon Mexico: 1736–1810.* Cambridge, U.K.: Cambridge University Press, 1971.

Bromley, Juan and José Barbagecata. *Evolución urbana de Lima.* Lima: Talleres gráficos de la editorial Lumen, 1945.

Bronner, Fred. "Peruvian Encomenderos in 1630: Elite Circulation and Consolidation." *Hispanic American Historical Review* 57, no. 4 (1977): 633–659.

Burga, Manuel. *De la encomienda a la hacienda capitalista: El valle de Jequetepeque del siglo XVI al XX.* Lima: Instituto de Estudios Peruanos, 1976.

Burga, Manuel, and Alberto Flores Galindo. *Apogeo y crisis de la república aristocrática.* Lima: Editorial Rikchay, 1979.

Burga, Manuel, and Wilson Reátegui. *Lanas y capital mercantil en el sur: La Casa Ricketts, 1895–1935.* Lima: Instituto de Estudios Peruanos, 1981.

Burkholder, Mark. *Politics of a Colonial Career: José Baquíjano and the Audiencias of Lima.* Wilmington, Del.: SR Book, 1990.

Burkholder, Mark, and D. S. Chandler. *From Impotence to Authority: The Spanish Crown and the American Audiencias, 1787–1808*. Columbia: University of Missouri Press, 1977.

Burkholder, Mark, and Lyman L. Johnson. *Colonial Latin America*. 3d ed. Oxford, U.K.: Oxford University Press, 1998.

Bushnell, David, ed. *The Liberator, Simón Bolívar: Man and Image*. New York: Knopf, 1970.

Caballero, Víctor. *Imperialismo y campesinado en la sierra central*. Huancayo, Peru: Instituto de Estudios Andinos, 1981.

Cahill, David. "Crown, Clergy, and Revolution in Bourbon Peru Diocese of Cuzco 1780–1814." Ph.D. thesis, University of Liverpool, Liverpool, 1984.

Cameron, Maxwell, and Phillip Mauceri, eds. *The Peruvian Labyrinth: Polity, Society, Economy*. University Park: Pennsylvania State University Press, 1997.

Caravedo, Baltazar. *Burguesía e industria en el Perú, 1933–1945*. Lima: Instituto de Estudios Peruanos, 1976.

———. *Desarrollo desigual y lucha política en el Perú*. Lima: Instituto de Estudios Peruanos, 1978.

Celestino, Olinda, and Albert Meyers. *Las cofradías en el Perú: Región central*. Frankfurt/Main, Germany: Verlag Klaus Dieter Vervuert, 1981.

Chandler, Dewitt S. *Social Assistance and Bureaucratic Politics: The Montepios of Colonial Mexico, 1767–1821*. Albuquerque: University of New Mexico Press, 1991.

Ciccarelli, Orazio. "Fascism and Politics During the Benavides Regime, 1933–1939: The Italian Perspective." *Hispanic American Historical Review* 70, no. 3 (1990): 405–432.

Cieza de León, Pedro. *The Chronicle of Pedro Cieza de León*. Ed. and trans. Alexandra Parma Cook and Noble David Cook. Durham N.C.: Duke University Press, 1998.

Clayton, Lawrence A. *Peru and the United States: The Condor and the Eagle*. Athens: Georgia University Press, 1999.

Cobo, Father Bernabé. *Inca Religion and Customs*. Trans. and ed. Roland Hamilton. Austin: University of Texas Press, 1993.

Conrad, Geoffrey W., and Arthur A. Demarest. *Religion and Empire: The Dynamics of Aztec and Inca Expansionism*. Cambridge, U.K.: Cambridge University Press, 1984.

Contreras, Carlos. *La ciudad del mercurio: Huancavelica, 1570–1700*. Lima: Instituto de Estudios Peruanos, 1982.

————. *Mineros y campesinos en los Andes: Mercado laboral y economía campesina en la sierra central, siglo XIX*. Lima: Instituto de Estudios Peruanos, 1987.

Contreras, Carlos, and Marcos Cueto. *Historia contemporánea del Perú*. Lima: Instituto de Estudios Peruanos, 2000.

Cook, Noble D. *Demographic Collapse: Indian Peru, 1520–1620*. New York: Cambridge University Press, 1981.

Cook, Alexandra P., and Noble D. Cook. *The Chronicle of Pedro Cieza de León*. Durham, N.C.: Duke University Press, 1998.

Cotler, Julio. *Clases, estado y nación en el Perú*. Lima: Instituto de Estudios Peruanos, 1978.

Crabtree, John, and Jim Thomas, eds. *El Perú de Fujimori, 1990–1998*. Lima: Instituto de Estudios Peruanos, Universidad del Pacífico, 1999.

Davies, Nigel. *The Incas*. Boulder: University Press of Colorado, 1995.

Deere, Carmen D. *Familia y relaciones de clases: El campesino y los terratenientes en la sierra norte del Perú, 1900–1980*. Lima: Instituto de Estudios Peruanos, 1992.

Deere, Carmen D., and Magdalena León. *Mujer rural y desarrollo. Reforma agraria y contrareforma en el Perú: Hacia un análisis de género*. Lima: Ediciones Flora Tristán, 1998.

Degregori, Carlos Ivan. *El surgimiento de Sendero Luminoso: Ayacucho 1969–1979*. Lima: Instituto de Estudios Peruanos, 1990.

Degregori, Carlos Ivan, Cecilia Blondet, and Nicolás Lynch. *Conquistadores de un nuevo mundo: De invasores a ciudadanos en San Martín de Porres*. Lima: Instituto de Estudios Peruanos, 1986.

Degregori, Carlos Ivan, and Romeo Grompone. *Demonios y redentores en el nuevo Perú*. Lima: Instituto de Estudios Peruanos, 1991.

Derpich, Wilma. *El otro lado azul: 150 años de inmigración china al Perú*. Lima: Fondo Editorial del Congreso del Perú, 1999.

Deustua, Jose. *La minería peruana y la iniciación de la República, 1820–1840*. Lima: Instituto de Estudios Peruanos, 1986.

Dobyns, Henry E., and Paul L. Doughty. *Peru: A Cultural History*. New York: Oxford University Press, 1976.

Durand, Francisco. "Los doce apóstoles del Perú, 1986–1996." In *Incertidumbre y soledad: Reflexiones sobre los grandes empresarios de América Latina*. Lima: Fundación Friedrich Ebert, 1996.

Espinoza Soriano, Waldemar. *Enciclopedia departamental de Junín*. Huancayo: Editor Enrique Chipoco Tovar, 1973.

Favre, Henri. *La evolución de las haciendas en la región de Huancavelica, Perú*. Lima: Instituto de Estudios Peruanos, 1966.

Fisher, John R. *Gobierno y Sociedad en el Perú colonial: El régimen de las intendencias, 1784–1814.* Lima: Pontificia Universidad Católica del Perú, 1981.

———. *Minas y mineros en el Perú colonial.* Lima: Instituto de Estudios Peruanos, 1977.

Flores Galindo, Alberto. *Arequipa y el Sur Andino.* Lima: Editorial Horizonte, 1977.

———. *Aristocracia y plebe: Lima 1760–1830.* Lima: Mosca Azul, 1984.

———. *Buscando un inca. Identidad y utopía en los Andes.* Lima: Instituto de Apoyo Agrario, 1989.

———. *La agonía de Mariátegui.* Lima: Instituto de Apoyo Agrario, 1989.

———. *Los mineros de la "Cerro de Pasco," 1900–1930.* Lima: Pontificia Universidad Católica del Perú, 1974.

Flores Galindo, Alberto, ed. *Tupac Amaru 1780: Antología.* Lima: Instituto Nacional de Cultura, 1976.

Fukumoto Sato, Mary N. *Hacia un nuevo sol. Japoneses y sus descendientes en el Perú: Historia, cultura e indentidad.* Lima: Asociación Peruano-Japonesa del Perú, 1997.

García Calderón, Francisco, Sr. *Diccionario de legislación peruana.* 2d ed. Lima, Paris: Libería Laroque, 1879.

García Jordán, Pilar. *Iglesia y poder en el Perú contemporáneo, 1821–1919.* Cuzco: Centro Bartolomé de las Casas, 1992.

Giesecke, Margarita. *Masas urbanas y rebelión en la historia. Golpe de estado: Lima, 1872.* Lima: Centro de Divulgación de Historia Popular, 1978.

Gilbert, Dennis L. *La oligarquía peruana: Historia de tres familias.* Lima: Editorial Horizonte, 1982.

Glave, Luis Miguel, and Marisa Remy. *Estructura agraria y vida rural en una región andina: Ollantaytambo entre los siglos XVI y XIX.* Cuzco: Centro de Estudios Rurales Andinos Bartolomé de las Casas, 1983.

Golte, Jürgen. *La racionalidad de la organización andina.* Lima: Instituto de Estudios Peruanos, 1980.

Gonzales de Olarte, Efraín. *El neoliberalismo a la peruana: Economía política del ajuste estructural, 1990–1997.* Lima: Instituto de Estudios Peruanos, 1998.

González Prada, Manuel. *Pájinas libres.* Lima: Fondo de Cultura Popular, 1966.

Gootenberg, Paul. *Between Silver and Guano: Commercial Policy and the State in Postindependence Peru.* Princeton, N.J.: Princeton University Press, 1989.

————. *Población y etnicidad en el Perú republicano.* Lima: Instituto de Estudios Peruanos, 1995.

————. *Caudillos y comerciantes: La formación económica del estado peruano, 1820–1860.* Cuzco: Centro Bartolomé de las Casas, 1997.

Hahner, June E., ed. *Women Through Women's Eyes: Latin American Women in Nineteenth-Century Travel Accounts.* Wilmington, Del.: Scholarly Resources, 1998.

Halperin-Donghi, Tulio. *The Aftermath of Revolution in Latin America.* New York: Harper and Row, 1973.

Hamilton, Roland. Austin: University of Texas Press, 1993.

Hamnet, Brian. *Revolución y contrarevolución en México y el Perú: Liberalismo, realeza y separatismo, 1800–1824.* Mexico City: Fondo de Cultura Económica, 1978.

Hardoy, Jorge E. *Ciudades precolombinas.* Buenos Aires: Ediciones Infinito, 1964.

————. *Cartografía urbana colonial de América Latina y el Caribe.* Buenos Aires: Instituto Internacional de Medio Ambiente y Desarrollo, Grupo Editorial Latinoamericano, 1991.

Hoberman, Louisa S., and Susan M. Socolow, eds. *Cities and Society in Colonial Latin America.* Albuquerque: University of New Mexico Press, 1986.

Hunefeldt, Christine. *Mujeres, esclavitud, emociones y libertad.* Lima: Instituto de Estudios Peruanos, Documento de Trabajo 24, 1988.

Hunt, Shane. "Guano y crecimiento en el Perú del siglo XIX." *Historia Económica y Social de America Latina HISLA* no. IV (1984).

Husson, Patrick. *De la guerra a la rebelión (Huanta, siglo XIX).* Cuzco: Centro Bartolomé de las Casas, Instituto Francés de Estudios Andinos, 1992.

Jacobsen, Nils. "Ciclos y *booms* en la agricultura de exportación latinoamericana: El caso de la economía ganadera en el sur peruano, 1855–1920." *Allpanchis* vol. XVIII, no. 21. Cuzco: Instituto de Pastoral Andina, 1983.

Johnson, Julie Greer. *Women in Colonial Spanish American Literature: Literary Images.* Westport, Conn.: Greenwood Press, 1983.

Johnson, Lyman L., and Enrique Tandeter, eds. *Essays on the Price History of Eighteenth-Century Latin America.* Albuquerque: University of New Mexico Press, 1990.

Kapsoli, Wilfredo, ed. *Los movimientos campesinos en el Perú, 1879–1965.* Lima: Delva Editores, 1977.

Keith, Robert, et al. *Hacienda, comunidad y clase en el Perú.* Lima: Instituto de Estudios Peruanos, 1976.

Klaren, Peter. *La formación de las haciendas azucareras y los orígenes del APRA.* Lima: Insituto de Estudios Peruanos, 1970.

———. *Peru: Society and Nationhood in the Andes.* New York: Oxford University Press, 2000.

Konetzke, Richard. *América Latina.* 2 vols. Madrid: Siglo XXI de España Editores, 1973.

Levin, Jonathan. *The Export Economies: Their Pattern of Development in Historical Perspective.* Cambridge: Harvard University Press, 1960.

López, Sinesio. *Ciudadanos reales e imaginarios: Concepciones, desarrollo y mapas de la ciudadanía en el Perú.* Lima: Instituto de Diálogo y Propuestas, 1997.

Lowenthal, Abraham, and Cinthia McClintock, eds. *El gobierno militar: Una experiencia peruana, 1968–1980.* Lima: Instituto de Estudios Peruanos, 1985.

Lumbreras, Luis G. *Los orígenes de la civilización en el Perú.* Lima: Carlos Milla Bartres, 1983.

Lynch, John. *The Spanish-American Revolutions, 1808–1826.* 2d ed. New York: Norton, 1986.

Lynch, Nicolás. *Una tragedia sin héroes: La derrota de los partidos y el origen de los independientes. Perú, 1980–1992.* Lima: Fondo Editorial de la Universidad Nacional Mayor de San Marcos, 1999.

MacCormack, Sabina. *Religion in the Andes: Vision and Imagination in Early Colonial Peru.* Princeton, N.J.: Princeton University Press, 1991.

Macera, Pablo. "Las plantaciones azucareras andinas." In *Trabajos de Historia IV.* Pablo Macera. Lima: Instituto Nacional de Cultura, 1977.

Macera, Pablo. "Instrucciones para el manejo de las haciendas jesuitas del Perú CSS. XVII–XVIII." *Nueva Crónica,* vol. II, fascículo 2001. Lima: Universidad Nacional Mayor de San Marcos, 1966.

MacEvoy, Carmen. *La utopía republicana: Ideales y realidades en la formación de la cultura política peruana (1871–1919).* Lima: Pontificia Universidad Católica del Perú, 1997.

Mallon, Florencia. *The Defense of Community in Peru's Central Highlands: Peasant Struggle and Capitalist Transition, 1860–1940.* Princeton, N.J.: Princeton University Press, 1983.

Manrique, Nelson. *Campesinado y nación: Las guerrillas indígenas en la guerra con Chile.* Lima: Centro de Investigación y Capacitación, Editora Italiana del Perú, 1981.

————. *Colonialismo y pobreza campesina: Caylloma y el valle del Colca, siglos XVI–XX.* 2d ed. Lima: Centro de Estudios y Promoción de Desarrollo, 1986.

————. *Historia de la República.* Lima: Corporación Financiera de Desarrollo, 1995.

————. *Mercado interno y región: La sierra central, 1820–1930.* Lima: Centro de Estudios y Promoción de Desarrollo, 1987.

————. *Yawar Mayu: Sociedades terratenientes serranas 1879–1910.* Lima: Centro de Estudios y Promoción de Desarrollo, Instituto Francés de Estudios Andinos, 1988.

Markham, Clements K. *A History of Peru.* Chicago: Charles H. Sergel and Co., 1892.

Martin, Luis. *Daughters of the Conquistadores: Women of the Viceroyalty of Peru.* Albuquerque: University of New Mexico Press, 1983.

Martinez-Alier, Juan. *Los huacchilleros en la sierra central del Perú.* Lima: Instituto de Estudios Peruanos, 1974.

Marzal, Manuel. *La utopía posible: Indios y jesuitas en la América colonial (1549–1767).* Lima: Pontificia Universidad Católica del Perú, 1992.

Matos Mar, José. *Desborde popular y crisis del estado: El nuevo rostro del Perú en la década de 1980.* Lima: Instituto de Estudios Peruanos, 1984.

Matos Mar, José, and José Manuel Mejía. *La reforma agraria en el Perú.* Lima: Instituto de Estudios Peruanos, 1980.

McClintock, Cynthia. *Peasant Cooperatives and Political Change in Peru.* Princeton, N.J.: Princeton University Press, 1981.

Medina, José Toribio. *Historia del Tribunal de la Inquisición de Lima.* Santiago de Chile: Fondo Histórico y Bibliográfico J. T. Medina, 1956.

Mejía, José M. *La neoreforma agraria: cambios en la propiedad de la tierra 1980–1990.* Lima: Cambio y Desarrollo, 1990.

Méndez, Cecilia. "Los campesinos, la independencia y la iniciación de la República. El caso de los iquichanos realistas: 1825–1828." In *Poder y violencia en los Andes.* Ed. Henrique Urbano. Cuzco: Centro Bartolomé de las Casas, 1991.

Miller, Rory. "La oligarquía costera y la república aristocrática en el Perú, 1895–1919." *Revista de Indias* (1988): 182–183.

Millones, Luis. *Peru colonial: De Pizarro a Tupac Amaru II.* Lima: Fondo Editorial Cofide, 1995.

Mitchell, W. P. *Peasants on the Edge: Crop, Cult and Crisis in the Andes.* Austin: University of Texas Press, 1991.

Mörner, Magnus. *The Andean Past: Land, Societies and Conflicts*. New York: Columbia University Press, 1985.

―――. "Spanish Migration to the New World Prior to 1810: A Report of Research." In *First Images of America, ed.* Fred: Chiapell. Berkeley, Los Angeles: University of California Press, 1976.

Morse, Richard M. *Lima en 1900: Estudio crítico, antología, Joaquín Capelo*. Lima: Instituto de Estudios Peruanos, 1973.

Moseley, Michael E. *The Incas and Their Ancestors: The Archaeology of Peru*. London, New York: Thames and Hudson, 1992.

Murra, John V. *The Economic Organization of the Inka State*. Greenwich, Conn.: SAI Press, 1988.

Nash, June. *We Eat the Mines and the Mines Eat Us: Dependency and Exploitation in Bolivian Tin Mines*. New York: Columbia University Press, 1979.

Palma, Ricardo. "Anales de la Inquisición de Lima." In *Tradiciones peruanas,* tomo VI. Barcelona: E. Cappeletti, 1983.

O'Phelan, Scarlett. *Un siglo de rebeliones anticoloniales: Perú y Bolivia, 1700–1783*. Cuzco: Centro de Estudios Rurales Bartolomé de las Casas, 1988.

Paredes, C. E., and J. Sachs, eds. *Peru's Path to Recovery: A Plan for Economic Stabilization and Growth*. Washington, D.C.: Brookings Institution, 1991.

Pareja, Piedad. *Aprismo y sindicalismo en el Perú*. Lima: Editorial Rikchay, 1980.

Pease, Franklin. *Breve historia contemporánea del Perú*. Mexico City: Fondo de Cultura Económica, 1995.

―――. *Del Tahuantinsuyu a la historia del Perú*. Lima: Pontificia Universidad Católica del Perú, 1989.

―――. *Los incas: Una introducción*. Lima: Pontificia Universidad Católica del Perú, 1991.

Pease, Henry. *El ocaso del poder oligárquico: Lucha política en la escena oficial, 1968–1975*. Lima: Centro de Estudios y Promoción de Desarrollo, 1977.

―――. *Los años de la langosta: La escena política del fujimorismo*. Lima: La Voz Editores, 1994.

Peralta, Victor. *En pos del tributo: Burocracia estatal, élite regional y comunidades indígenas en el Cusco rural (1826–1854)*. Cuzco: Centro Bartolomé de las Casas, 1991.

Pietschman, Horst. *Lateinamerika: Die staatliche Organisation des kolonialen Iberoamerika*. Stuttgart, Germany: Klett-Cotta, 1980.

Pike, Frederick. *The Modern History of Peru.* New York: Frederick A. Praeger Publishers, 1967.

Poole, Deborah. *Vision, Race, and Modernity: A Visual Economy of the Andean Image World.* Princeton, N.J.: Princeton University Press, 1997.

Poole, Deborah, and Gerardo Renique. *Peru: Time of Fear.* Nottingham, U.K.: Russell Press, 1992.

Portocarrero, Felipe. *El imperio Prado: 1890–1970.* Lima: Centro de Investigación de la Universidad del Pacífico, 1995.

Portocarrero, Gonzalo. *De Bustamante a Odría: El fracaso del Frente Democrático Nacional, 1945–1950.* Lima: Editorial Horizonte, 1983.

Quijano, Anibal. *La emergencia del grupo cholo y sus implicancias en la sociedad peruana.* Lima: n.p., 1967.

Quiroz, Alfonso. *Banqueros en conflicto: Estructura financiera y economía peruana, 1884–1930.* Lima: Centro de Investigación de la Universidad del Pacífico, 1989.

———. *La deuda defraudada: Consolidación y dominio económico en el Perú.* Lima: Instituto Nacional de Cultura, 1987.

Rivera Serna, Raúl. *Las guerrillas del centro en la emancipación peruana.* Lima: Edición Talleres Gráficos Villanueva, 1965.

Rodríguez Pastor, Humberto. *Hijos del celeste imperio en el Perú, 1850–1900: Migración, agricultura, mentalidad y explotación.* Lima: Instituto de Apoyo Agrario, 1989.

Rostworowski de Diez Canseco, María. *History of the Inca Realm.* New York: Cambridge University Press, 1999.

———. *Pachacútec y la leyenda de los chancas.* Lima: Instituto de Estudios Peruanos, 1997.

Rowe, John H. "El movimiento nacional inca en el siglo XVIII." In *Tupac Amaru—1780.* Comp. A. Flores Galindo. Lima: Instituto Nacional de Cultura, 1976.

Rudolph, James D. *Peru: The Evolution of a Crisis.* Westport, Conn.: Westview Press, 1992.

Sala, Nuria. *Y se armó el tole, tole: Tributo indígena y movimientos sociales en el Virreinato del Perú, 1784–1811.* Ayacucho: Instituto de Estudios Regionales José María Arguedas, 1996.

Soler, Ricaurte. *Idea y cuestión nacional latinoamericanas de la independencia a la emergencia del imperialismo.* Mexico City: Siglo XXI Editores, 1980.

Spalding, Karen. *Huarochiri: An Andean Society under Inca and Spanish Rule.* Stanford, Calif.: Stanford University Press, 1984.

Starn, Orin, et al. *The Peru Reader: History, Culture, Politics.* Durham, N.C.: Duke University Press, 1995.

Stein, Steve. *Populism in Peru: The Emergence of the Masses and the Politics of Social Control.* Madison: University of Wisconsin Press, 1980.

Stein, Steve, and Carlos Monge. *La crisis del estado patrimonial en el Perú.* Lima: Instituto de Estudios Peruanos, 1988.

Stern, Steve J. *Peru's Indian Peoples and the Challenge of Spanish Conquest: Huamanga to 1640.* Madison: University of Wisconsin Press, 1982.

Sulmont, Denis. *El movimiento obrero peruano (1890–1980): Reseña histórica.* 3d ed. Lima: Ediciones Tarea, 1982.

Tamayo Herrera, José. *Historia del Indigenismo cusqueño, siglos XVI–XX.* Lima: Instituto Nacional de Cultura, 1980.

———. *Historia social e indigenismo en el altiplano.* Lima: Ediciones Treintaitrés, 1982.

———. *Nuevo compendio de historia del Perú.* Lima: Editorial Lumen, 1985.

Tanaka, Martín. *El espejismo de la democracia: El colapso del sistema de partidos políticos en el Perú, 1980–1995.* Lima: Instituto de Estudios Peruanos, 1998.

Tandeter, Enrique. *Coercion and Market: Silver Mining in Colonial Potosi, 1692–1826.* Albuquerque: University of New Mexico Press, 1993.

Tandeter, Enrique, Brooke Larson, and Olivia Harris. *Ethnicity, Markets, and Migration in the Andes: At the Crossroads of History and Anthropology.* Durham, N.C.: Duke University Press, 1995.

Tantaleán, Javier. *Política económico-financiera y formación del estado en el Perú, siglo XIX.* Lima: Centro de Estudios para el Desarrollo y la Participación, 1983.

Taylor, Lewis. *Estates, Freeholders, and Peasant Communities in Cajamarca, 1876–1972.* Cambridge, U.K.: Centre of Latin American Studies, 1986.

———. *Gamonales y bandoleros: Violencia social y política en Hualgayoc-Cajamarca, 1900–1930.* Cajamarca, Peru: Asociación Editora Cajamarca, 1993.

Thorp, Rosemary, and Geoffrey Bertram. *Perú, 1890–1977: Crecimiento y políticas en una economía abierta.* Lima: Mosca Azul–Fundacion Friedrich Ebert–Universidad del Pacífico, 1985.

Tibesar, Antonine. *Franciscan Beginnings in Colonial Peru.* Washington, D.C.: Academy of American Franciscan History, 1953.

Trazegnies, Fernando de. *La idea del derecho en el Perú republicano del siglo XIX.* Lima: Fondo Editorial de la Pontificia Universidad Católica del Perú, 1980.

Trelles Aréstegui, Efraín. *Lucas Martínez Vegaso: Funcionamiento de una encomienda peruana inicial.* Lima: Pontificia Universidad Católica del Perú, Fondo Editorial, 1982.

Tristán, Flora. *Peregrinaciones de una paria*. Havana: Casa de las Américas, 1984.

Urrutia, Jaime. *Huamanga: Región e Historia, 1536–1770*. Ayacucho, Peru: Universidad Nacional de San Cristóbal de Huamanga, 1985.

Varese, Stefano. *La sal de los cerros*. Lima: Retablo de Papel Ediciones, 1973.

Varón Gabai, Rafael, and Javier Flores Espinoza, eds. *Homenaje a María Rostworowski: Arqueología, antropología e historia en los Andes*. Lima: Instituto de Estudios Peruanos, 1997.

Vargas Ugarte, Rubén. *Historia de la Compañía de Jesús en el Perú*. Burgos: Imprenta de Aldecoa, 1963–65.

Wachtel, Nathan. *The Vision of the Vanquished: The Spanish Conquest of Peru Through Indian Eyes, 1530–1570*. New York: Barnes and Noble, 1977.

Wallestein, Immanuel. *The Modern World System*. N.Y.: Academic Press, 1974–90.

Watanabe, Luis K. *Culturas preincas del Perú*. Lima: Fondo Editorial de Fondo Editorial Cofide, 1995

Werlich, David. *Peru: A Short History*. Carbondale: Southern Illinois University Press, 1978.

———. *Research Tools for Latin American Historians: A Select, Annotated Bibliography*. New York: Garland Publications, 1980.

Whitaker, Arthur P. *The United States and the Independence of Latin America, 1800–1830*. Baltimore, Md.: Johns Hopkins University Press, 1941.

Wu, Celia. *Generales y diplomáticos: Gran Bretaña y el Perú 1820–1840*. Lima: Pontificia Universidad Católica del Perú, 1993.

Yépez del Castillo, Ernesto. *Perú, 1820–1920: Un siglo de desarrollo capitalista*. Lima: Instituto de Estudios Peruanos, 1972.

Zapata, Antonio, and Juan Carlos Sueiro. *Naturaleza y política: El gobierno y el fenómeno del Niño en el Perú*. Lima: Instituto de Estudios Peruanos, 1999.

Appendix 4

Suggested Reading

General Surveys of Contemporary Issues

Cameron, Maxwell A., and Philip Mauceri, eds. *The Peruvian Labyrinth: Polity, Society, Economy.* University Park: Pennsylvania State University Press, 1997.

Hudson, Rex, ed. *Peru: A Country Study.* Washington, D.C.: Department of the Army, 1993.

Sheahan, John. *Searching for a Better Society: The Peruvian Economy from 1950.* University Park: Pennsylvania State University Press, 1999.

General Surveys

Brading, David A. *The First America: The Spanish Monarchy, Creole Patriots, and the Liberal State, 1492–1867.* New York: Cambridge University Press, 1991.

Dobyns, Henry F., and Paul L. Doughty. *Peru: A Cultural History.* New York: Oxford University Press, 1976.

Gonzales de Olarte, Efraín, ed. *The Peruvian Economy and Structural Adjustment: Past, Present, and Future.* Coral Gables, Fla.: North-South Center Press, 1996.

Moerner, Magnus. *The Andean Past: Land, Societies, and Conflicts.* New York: Columbia University Press, 1985.

Palmer, Scott. *Peru: The Authoritarian Tradition.* New York: Praeger Publishers, 1980.

Werlich, David P. *Peru: A Short History.* Carbondale: Southern Illinois University Press, 1978.

On the Inca and Pre-Incan Groups

Classen, Constance. *Inca Cosmology and the Human Body.* Salt Lake City: University of Utah Press, 1993.

Malpass, Michael A. *Daily Life in the Inca Empire.* Westport, Conn.: Greenwood Press, 1996.

Morris, Craig, and Adriana von Hagen. *The Inka Empire and Its Andean Origins.* New York: Abbeville Press, 1993.

Murra, John V. *The Economic Organization of the Inka State.* Greenwich, Conn.: JAI Press, 1988.

Urton, Gary. *The History of a Myth: Pacariqtambo and the Origins of the Inkas.* Austin: University of Texas Press, 1990.

Zuidema, R. T. *Inca Civilization in Cuzco.* Austin: University of Texas Press, 1990.

Colonial Period

Andrien, Kenneth J. *Andean Worlds: Indigenous History, Culture and Consciousness under Spanish Rule, 1532–1825.* Albuquerque: University of New Mexico Press, 2001.

Andrien, Kenneth J., and Rolena Adorno, eds. *Transatlantic Encounters: Europeans and Andeans in the Sixteenth Century.* Berkeley: University of California Press, 1991.

Blanchard, Peter. *Slavery and Abolition in Early Republican Peru.* Wilmington, Del.: SR Books, 1992.

Bradley, Peter T. *Society, Economy, and Defense in Seventeenth Century Peru: The Administration of the Count of Alba de Liste (1655–1661).* Liverpool, U.K.: Institute of Latin American Studies, University of Liverpool, 1992.

Burns, Kathryn. *Colonial Habits: Convents and the Spiritual Economy of Cuzco, Peru.* Durham, N.C.: Duke University Press, 1999.

Cook, Noble D. *Demographic Collapse: Indian Peru, 1520–1620.* Cambridge, U.K.: Cambridge University Press, 1981.

Cushner, Nicolás P. *Lords of the Land: Sugar, Wine, and Jesuit Estates of Coastal Peru, 1600–1767.* Albany: State University of New York Press, 1980.

Griffith, Nicholas. *The Cross and the Serpent: Religious Repression and Resurgence in Colonial Peru.* Norman: University of Oklahoma Press, 1996.

Larson, Brooke, Olivia Harris, and Enrique Tandeter, eds. *Ethnicity, Markets, and Migration in the Andes: At the Crossroads of History and Anthropology.* Durham, N.C.: Duke University Press, 1995.

Lockhart, James. *Spanish Peru, 1532–1560: A Colonial Society.* Madison: University of Wisconsin Press, 1994.

MacCormack, Sabine. *Religion in the Andes: Vision and Imagination in Early Colonial Peru.* Princeton, N.J.: Princeton University Press, 1991.

Mills, Kenneth R. *Idolatry and Its Enemies: Colonial Andean Religion and Extirpation, 1640–1750.* Princeton, N.J.: Princeton University Press, 1997.

Pagden, Anthony. *The Fall of Natural Man: The American Indian and the Origins of Comparative Ethnology.* New York: Cambridge University Press, 1982.

Ramírez, Susan. *The World Upside Down: Cross-Cultural Contact and Conflict in Sixteenth Century Peru.* Stanford, Calif.: Stanford University Press, 1996.

Robinson, David J., ed. *Migration in Colonial Spanish America.* New York: Cambridge University Press, 1990.

Stern, Steve J. *Peru's Indian Peoples and the Challenge of Spanish Conquest: Huamanga to 1640.* Madison: University of Wisconsin Press, 1982.

Varón Gabai, Rafael. *Francisco Pizarro and His Brothers: The Illusion of Power in Sixteenth-Century Peru.* Norman: University of Oklahoma Press, 1997.

Wachtel, Nathan. *The Vision of the Vanquished: The Spanish Conquest of Peru Through Indian Eyes, 1530–1570.* New York: Barnes and Noble, 1977.

Independence

Anna, Timothy E. *The Fall of the Royal Government in Peru.* Lincoln: University of Nebraska Press, 1979.

Burkholder, Mark A. *Politics of a Colonial Career: José Baquíjano and the Audiencia of Lima.* Albuquerque: University of New Mexico Press, 1980.

Fisher, John. *Commercial Relations Between Spain and Spanish America in the Era of Free Trade, 1778–1796.* Liverpool, U.K.: Center for Latin American Studies, University of Liverpool, 1985.

Stern, Steve J., ed. *Resistance, Rebellion, and Consciousness in the Andean Peasant World: 18th to 20th Centuries.* Madison: University of Wisconsin Press, 1987.

Walker, Charles F. *Smoldering Ashes: Cuzco and the Creation of Republican Peru, 1780–1840.* Durham, N.C.: Duke University Press, 1999.

Age of Liberalism (19th Century)

Deustua, José R. *The Bewitchment of Silver: The Social Economy of Mining in Nineteenth-Century Peru.* Athens: Ohio University Press, 1999.

Gootenberg, Paul. *Between Silver and Guano: Commercial Policy and the State in Postindependence Peru.* Princeton, N.J.: Princeton University Press, 1989.

Hunefeldt, Christine. *Liberalism in the Bedroom: Quarrelling Spouses in Nineteenth-Century Lima.* University Park: Pennsylvania State University Press, 2000.

Hunt, Shane. "Growth and Guano in Nineteenth-Century Peru." Working paper. Woodrow Wilson School of Public and International Affairs, Princeton University, 1973.

Klaiber, Jeffrey. *The Catholic Church in Peru, 1821–1985: A Social History.* Washington, D.C.: Catholic University of America Press, 1992.

Mallon, Florencia. *Peasant and Nation: The Making of Postcolonial Mexico and Peru.* Berkeley: University of California Press, 1995.

Peloso, Vincent, and Barbara Tenenbaum, eds. *Liberals, Politics and Power: State Formation in Nineteenth-Century Latin America.* Athens: University of Georgia Press, 1996.

Quiroz, Alfonso W. *Domestic and Foreign Finance in Modern Peru, 1850–1950: Financing Visions of Development.* Pittsburgh, Pa.: University of Pittsburgh Press, 1993.

Salvatore, Ricardo, and Carlos Aguirre, eds. *The Birth of the Penitentiary in Latin America: Essays on Criminology, Prison Reform, and Social Control, 1840–1940.* Austin: University of Texas Press, 1996.

Stewart, Watt. *Chinese Bondage in Peru: A History of the Chinese Coolie in Peru, 1849–1874.* Westport, Conn.: Greenwood Press, 1970.

Thurner, Mark. *From Two Republics to One Divided: Contradictions of Postcolonial Nationmaking in the Andes.* Durham, N.C.: Duke University Press, 1997.

Toward Modernity (20th Century)

Becker, David G. *The Bourgeoisie and the Limits of Dependency: Mining, Class, and Power in "Revolutionary" Peru.* Princeton, N.J.: Princeton University Press, 1983.

Blanchard, Peter. *The Origins of the Peruvian Labor Movement, 1883–1919.* Pittsburgh, Pa.: University of Pittsburgh Press, 1982.

Chavarría, Jesús. *José Carlos Mariátegui and the Rise of Modern Peru, 1880–1930.* Albuquerque: University of New Mexico Press, 1979.

Collier, David. *Squatters and Oligarchs: Authoritarian Rule and Policy Change in Peru.* Baltimore, Md.: Johns Hopkins University Press, 1976.

Cueto, Marcos. *The Return of Epidemics: Health and Society in Peru During the Twentieth Century.* Burlington, Vt.: Ashgate, 2001.

Davies, Thomas M., Jr. *Indian Integration in Peru: A Half Century of Experience, 1900–1948.* Lincoln: University of Nebraska Press, 1974.

Fleet, Michael. *The Catholic Church and Democracy in Chile and Peru.* Notre Dame, Ind.: University of Notre Dame Press, 1997.

Gardiner, Harvey C. *The Japanese and Peru, 1873–1973.* Albuquerque: University of New Mexico Press, 1975.

Gonzales, Michael J. *Plantation Agriculture and Social Control in Northern Peru, 1875–1933.* Austin: University of Texas Press, 1984.

Kruijt, Dirk, and Menno Vellinga. *Labor Relations and Multinational Corporations: The Cerro de Pasco Corporation in Peru, 1902–1974.* Assen, Netherlands: Van Gorcum, 1979.

Masterson, Daniel M. *The Military and Politics in Latin America: Peru from Sánchez Cerro to Sendero Luminoso.* New York: Greenwood Press, 1991.

Nugent, David. *Modernity at the Edge of Empire: State, Individual and Nation in the Northern Peruvian Andes, 1885–1935.* Stanford, Calif.: Stanford University Press, 1997.

Orlove, Benjamin. *Alpacas, Sheep, and Men: The Wool Export Economy and Regional Society in Southern Peru.* New York: Academic Press, 1977.

Palmer, David S., ed. *Shining Path of Peru.* New York: St. Martin's Press, 1994.

Parker, David S. *The Idea of the Middle Class: White Collar Workers and Peruvian Society, 1900–1950.* University Park: Pennsylvania State University Press, 1998.

Peña, Milagros. *Theologies and Liberation in Peru: The Roles of Ideas in Social Movements.* Philadelphia: Temple University Press, 1995.

Pinelo, Adalberto J. *The Multinational Corporation as a Force in Latin American Politics: A Case Study of the International Petroleum Company in Peru.* New York: Praeger, 1973.

Romero, Raul R. *Debating the Past: Music, Memory, and Identity in the Andes.* New York: Oxford University Press, 2001.

Stanfield, Michael E. *Red Rubber, Bleeding Trees: Violence, Slavery, and Empire in Northwest Amazonia, 1850–1933.* Albuquerque: University of New Mexico Press, 1999.

St. John, Ronald B. *The Foreign Policy of Peru.* Boulder, Colo.: Rienner Publishers, 1992.

Tarazona-Sevillano, Gabriela. *Sendero Luminoso and the Threat of Narcoterrorism.* New York: Praeger, 1990.

Taylor, Lewis. *Bandits and Politics in Peru: Landlord and Peasant Violence in Hualgayoc, 1900–1930.* Cambridge, U.K.: Centre for Latin American Studies, University of Cambridge, 1983.

Weeks, John. *Limits to Capitalist Development: The Industrialization of Peru, 1950–1980.* Boulder, Colo.: Westview Press, 1985.

INDEX

Page numbers followed with the letter *f* indicate illustrations; the letter *m* indicates a map; the letter *t* indicates a table.